D0374809

THE
HISTORY OF
GERMANY

ADVISORY BOARD

THE HISTORY OF GERMANY

Eleanor L. Turk

The Greenwood Histories of the Modern Nations
Frank W. Thackeray and John E. Findling, Series Editors

Greenwood Press
Westport, Connecticut • London

Library of Congress Cataloging-in-Publication Data

Turk, Eleanor L., 1935–
    The history of Germany / Eleanor L. Turk.
        p.   cm.—(The Greenwood histories of the modern nations,
    ISSN 1096–2905)
    Includes bibliographical references and index.
    ISBN 0–313–30274–X (alk. paper)
    1. Germany—History.   2. Germany—Economic conditions—20th
century.   3. Germany—Politics and government—20th century.
    I. Title.   II. Series.
DD90.T87   1999
943—dc21   98–35258

British Library Cataloguing in Publication Data is available.

Library of Congress Catalog Card Number: 98–35258
ISBN: 0–313–30274–X
ISSN: 1096–2905

First published in 1999

Greenwood Press, 88 Post Road West, Westport, CT 06881
An imprint of Greenwood Publishing Group, Inc.
www.greenwood.com

Printed in the United States of America

The paper used in this book complies with the
Permanent Paper Standard issued by the National
Information Standards Organization (Z39.48–1984).

10 9 8 7 6 5 4 3 2 1

Copyright Acknowledgments

The author and publisher gratefully acknowledge permission for use of the following material:

Map of contemporary Germany originally published in *World Eagle*, November 1994. Copyright © 1998 World Eagle/IBA, Inc. Reprinted with permission from World Eagle, 111 King Street, Littleton, MA 01460 U.S.A. 1-800-854-8273. All rights reserved.

Map of Roman Germany and map of the German Confederation, originally published in Donald S. Detwiler, *Germany: A Short History*, 2nd ed., revised (Carbondale, IL: Southern Illinois University Press, 1989). Copyright (1989) by the Board of Trustees, Southern Illinois University, reprinted by permission.

To Hanna Knoke Donderer,
friend and teacher,
with love and thanks for pointing the way—
a gift to music

Contents

Series Foreword
by Frank W. Thackeray and John E. Findling   ix

Preface   xiii

Timeline of Historical Events   xv

1   An Introduction to Modern Germany   1

2   Germans in Antiquity and the Early Middle Ages   19

3   The German Dynasties   33

4   The Rise and Impact of Prussia   55

5   The Second German Empire, 1871–1914   75

6   The First World War and the Weimar Republic   93

7   Hitler and the Second World War   113

8   From Occupation to Sovereignty, 1945–1949   133

9   The German Federal Republic, 1949–1990   145

10   The German Democratic Republic, 1949–1990   163

11   The German Federal Republic after 1990   181

Notable People in the History of Germany   191

Annotated Bibliography   205

Index   223

Series Foreword

The Greenwood Histories of the Modern Nations series is intended to provide students and interested laypeople with up-to-date, concise, and analytical histories of many of the nations of the contemporary world. Not since the 1960s has there been a systematic attempt to publish a series of national histories, and, as series editors, we believe that this series will prove to be a valuable contribution to our understanding of other countries in our increasingly interdependent world.

Over thirty years ago, at the end of the 1960s, the Cold War was an accepted reality of global politics, the process of decolonization was still in progress, the idea of a unified Europe with a single currency was unheard of, the United States was mired in a war in Vietnam, and the economic boom of Asia was still years in the future. Richard Nixon was president of the United States, Mao Tse-tung (not yet Mao Zedong) ruled China, Leonid Brezhnev guided the Soviet Union, and Harold Wilson was prime minister of the United Kingdom. Authoritarian dictators still ruled most of Latin America, the Middle East was reeling in the wake of the Six-Day War, and Shah Reza Pahlavi was at the height of his power in Iran. Clearly, the past thirty years have been witness to a great deal of historical change, and it is to this change that this series is primarily addressed.

With the help of a distinguished advisory board, we have selected nations whose political, economic, and social affairs mark them as among the most important in the waning years of the twentieth century, and for each nation we have found an author who is recognized as a specialist in the history of that nation. These authors have worked most cooperatively with us and with Greenwood Press to produce volumes that reflect current research on their nation and that are interesting and informative to their prospective readers.

The importance of a series such as this cannot be underestimated. As a superpower whose influence is felt all over the world, the United States can claim a "special" relationship with almost every other nation. Yet many Americans know very little about the histories of the nations with which the United States relates. How did they get to be the way they are? What kind of political systems have evolved there? What kind of influence do they have in their own region? What are the dominant political, religious, and cultural forces that move their leaders? These and many other questions are answered in the volumes of this series.

The authors who have contributed to this series have written comprehensive histories of their nations, dating back to prehistoric times in some cases. Each of them, however, has devoted a significant portion of the book to events of the past thirty years, because the modern era has contributed the most to contemporary issues that have an impact on U.S. policy. Authors have made an effort to be as up-to-date as possible so that readers can benefit from the most recent scholarship and a narrative that includes very recent events.

In addition to the historical narrative, each volume in this series contains an introductory overview of the country's geography, political institutions, economic structure, and cultural attributes. This is designed to give readers a picture of the nation as it exists in the contemporary world. Each volume also contains additional chapters that add interesting and useful detail to the historical narrative. One chapter is a thorough chronology of important historical events, making it easy for readers to follow the flow of a particular nation's history. Another chapter features biographical sketches of the nation's most important figures in order to humanize some of the individuals who have contributed to the historical development of their nation. Each volume also contains a comprehensive bibliography, so that those readers whose interest has been sparked may find out more about the nation and its history. Finally, there is a carefully prepared topic and person index.

Readers of these volumes will find them fascinating to read and useful in understanding the contemporary world and thc nations that comprise it. As series editors, it is our hope that this series will contribute to a heightened sense of global understanding as we enter a new century.

Frank W. Thackeray and John E. Findling
Indiana University Southeast

Preface

After many years of teaching parts of German history in courses on Europe and western civilization, as well as writing tightly focused scholarly articles, I have found writing this national history a very satisfying experience. It gives me the opportunity to share with others my enthusiasm and appreciation for a people and culture that I have long enjoyed exploring. My own exploration of Germany began in 1953, thanks to the American Field Service, as a high school exchange student in Munich. Having grown up in the intensity of World War II anti-German propaganda, I had much to learn. This work is meant to introduce German history and to help others begin their own exploration. I hope it points the way toward their learning more about Germany in all its complexities. In addition to the narrative overview, the timeline and short biographies provide quick access to specific facts. The annotated bibliography offers opportunities to explore specific topics in more depth.

Many have helped me complete this task. I am grateful to Indiana University East for the Summer Faculty Fellowship and sabbatical leave, which supported the time required for research and writing. To Marthea Christ and Bea Herbkersman of Richmond High School, Cheryl Hinshaw of Northeastern High School, Faith Phillips of Lincoln High School, Lynn Wells of Centerville Senior High School, and Doris Ashbrook, Richmond's Morrisson-Reeves Public Library, my many thanks for their invaluable advice as I sought to identify and meet the needs of students and general readers. Jerri Libert, student, colleague, and friend, mastered the challenge of building a workable index with remarkable calm and clarity! To the series coeditors, Frank Thackeray and John Findling who invited me to join the project, I give profound thanks for extending the challenge and for their encouragement and skillful editing throughout it. Barbara Rader and Betty Pessagno of Greenwood Press expertly helped bring the work to completion. I have benefited from all their help. They bear no responsibility for any shortcomings in the final product.

Timeline of Historical Events

ANTIQUITY

1000 B.C.E.	In migration of Germanic tribes to Roman Gaul and central Europe
9 C.E.	Arminius defeated three Roman legions at Teutoberg Forest
98	Tacitus wrote *The Germania* describing Germanic culture; third-century regional alignments of Germanic tribes, continued in-migration
407	Roman troops recalled from England to combat Germans
410	Visigoth King Alaric sacked Rome
476	Last Roman Emperor, Romulus Agustulus, deposed by Odoacer
481–511	Clovis, king of the Franks; 498 converted to Christianity

MIDDLE AGES

732	Battle of Tours, defeat of Muslims in France by Charles Martel

800–911   Carolingian dynasty

800   Charlemagne crowned Emperor of the Romans by
                 Pope Leo III

843   Treaty of Verdun divided Carolingian Germany into
                 three parts

919–1002   Ottonian dynasty

1002–1125   Salian dynasty

1138–1254   Hohenstaufen dynasty

1245–1273   Foreign interregnum, rise in the power of the German
                 princes

1273–1918   Hapsburg dynasty

1338   German electors agreed to elect emperor and end his
                 coronation by the pope

1348–1350   Black Death killed one-third of German population

1356   Papal Golden Bull confirmed imperial election pro-
                 cess

EARLY MODERN
PERIOD

1453–1519   Emperor Maximilian I consolidated Flanders, Bur-
                 gundy, Spain, Hungary, and Bohemia with Hapsburg
                 German holdings

1517   Martin Luther posted 95 Theses; beginning of Prot-
                 estant Reformation

1519–1555   Charles V, Holy Roman Emperor

1521   Martin Luther outlawed by Charles V

1524–1525   Peasants' War in southern Germany

1530–1555   Sporadic Reformation wars in Germany

1555   Peace of Augsburg legalized Roman Catholicism and
                 Lutheranism in Holy Roman Empire

1556   Charles abdicated and divided the Empire, giving
                 Spain and Burgundy to his son, Philip II, and Ger-
                 many to his brother, Ferdinand

1618–1648	Thirty Years' War over religious, dynastic, and political issues
1648	Peace of Westphalia ended the war, recognized powers of the individual states, and stripped Holy Roman Emperor of political power over German states
1655–1660	First Northern War with Sweden
1667–1697	Wars with King Louis XIV of France; cession of Strassburg and Alsace
1700–1721	Great Northern War with Sweden

RISE OF PRUSSIA

1701	Founding of independent Hohenzollern kingdom in Brandenburg/Prussia
1740–1786	Reign of Frederick II, the Great
1789	Outbreak of French Revolution
1792	Prussia joined European alliance against revolutionary France
1803	Napoleon reorganized Germany through *Reichsdeputationshauptschluss*, consolidating hundreds of sovereign states into 35 states
1806	Confederation of the Rhine; end of the German Holy Roman Empire
1807	Prussia at war with Napoleon; October, Prussia defeated at Jena and Auerstaedt when Napoleon occupied Berlin; November, Napoleon issued the Berlin Decree to end British trade with the continent; Treaty of Tilsit reduced Prussia to a territorial remnant
1812	Napoleon began his retreat from Russia
1813–1814	Frederick William III rejoined Austria and Russia in the War of Liberation; October 16–19, Battle of All Nations at Leipzig began Napoleon's retreat to France; May 1814, Treaty of Paris ended war
1815	Congress of Vienna established German Confederation under Austrian presidency

GERMAN
UNIFICATION

1834	Formation of German Customs Union (*Zollverein*) by Prussia
1848	German revolutions failed to unify Germany under constitution written at the Frankfurt Parliament
1850	Prussian attempt to unify German monarchs failed; restoration of the German Confederation under Austrian leadership
1862	Otto von Bismarck appointed chancellor in Prussia to resolve budget crisis
1864	German-Danish War won by Prussia
1866	Austro-Prussian War won by Prussia
1867	Formation of the North German Confederation under Prussian leadership
1870	Franco-Prussian War won by German Confederation, which accepted surrender of Emperor Napoleon II on September 2
1871	January 18, German princes signed unification treaty and created constitution establishing the second German Empire; Treaty of Frankfurt in May, formally ended war with France
1871–1883	*Kulturkampf* in Prussia against Roman Catholics
1878–1890	Anti-Socialist Laws banned Social Democratic Party
1879	Austro-German Dual Alliance
1883–1889	Germany enacted Europe's first sickness, accident, old-age social insurance laws
1890	Resignation of Bismarck; beginning of "personal regime" of William II
1905–1906	First Morocco crisis, German diplomatic defeat in Morocco
1908	*Daily Telegraph* affair
1911	Second Morocco crisis

| 1914 | Beginning of World War I: Germany invaded France |
| 1918 | November 9, abdication of Kaiser William II; November 11, Armistice |

MODERN
GERMANY

1919	January 5–15, Spartacist revolt; January 18, convening of Paris Peace Conference to settle World War I; April–May, Soviet Republic in Bavaria; June 1, proclamation of Rhineland Republic; July 7, German government's ratification of Treaty of Versailles in which Germany was forced to accept war guilt, demilitarization, and reparations; July 31, adoption of Weimar Constitution for a German Republic
1920	March 13–17, Kapp Putsch by monarchist military faction failed
1923	Skyrocketing inflation; January 11, occupation of Rhineland by French and Belgians over reparations dispute; November 8–11, Munich Beer Hall Putsch by Hitler and followers; Hitler arrested
1924	Dawes Plan by American bankers to aid German economic recovery
1925	General Hindenburg elected president
1926	Locarno Treaties settled Germany's western boundaries; Germany admitted to the League of Nations
1932	Hindenburg reelected; asked von Papen to form cabinet; "cabinet of barons" marked end of parliamentary government system
1933	January 30, Adolf Hitler appointed German chancellor; February 27, Reichstag fire resulted in proclamation of martial law and suspension of civil rights; March 23, Enabling Act gave Hitler dictatorial powers; October, Germany withdrew from International Disarmament Conference and League of Nations
1934	Night of the Long Knives purge of Nazi party
1935	Nuremberg Laws began legal discrimination against German Jews

1936	German military force reentered the Rhineland
1938	March, annexation of Austria (*Anschluss*); September, Munich Agreement and annexation of Sudetenland of Czechoslovakia
1939	March, march into Czechoslovakia, creation of Bohemian and Moravian protectorates; September 1, invasion of Poland; beginning of World War II
1939–1945	World War II
1945	April 30, Hitler committed suicide; May, Germany surrendered to the Allies on both the Soviet and western fronts

POST–WORLD
WAR II GERMANY

1945	August, Potsdam Conference of Allies created four-power agreement on de-Nazification, demilitarization, decentralization, and democratization of occupied Germany
1945–1946	Nuremberg trials of 20 major Nazi leaders
1946	Compulsory merger of political parties into Socialist Unity Party (SED) in Soviet zone
1947	Economic merger of British and American zones (*Bizonia*); France joined in 1949; Marshall Plan for European economic recovery announced
1948	Currency reform in western zones resulted in Soviet blockade of West Berlin and Berlin Airlift; ended May 12, 1949
1949	May 23, adoption of Basic Law created German Federal Republic (FRG/BRD); Konrad Adenauer elected federal chancellor; October 7, German Democratic Republic (GDR/DDR) created; Stalin recognized Berlin as capital; Walter Pieck became president
1951	United States, Britain, France declared that Germany was no longer an enemy
1952	Stalin's overture on German reunification rejected by Adenauer; *Laender* dissolved in Democratic Republic; local government control by SED strengthened.

1953	June 17, popular uprising in East Berlin suppressed by Soviet military
1955	January, Soviet Union declared that Germany was no longer an enemy; May, repeal of occupation statute in Federal Republic; admission of Federal Republic to NATO; People's Republic joined Warsaw Pact
1956	Communist Party outlawed in Federal Republic
1957	Treaty of Rome established European Economic Community; Adenauer reelected
1958	Upper house of legislature eliminated in Democratic Republic
1960	Collectivization of agriculture in Democratic Republic
1961	July 25, Kennedy's "Ich bin ein Berliner" speech demands free access to Berlin; August 13, construction of the Berlin Wall completed
1962	September, Adenauer reelected; *Der Spiegel* affair in Federal Republic suggested repression of freedom of the press
1963	Adenauer and de Gaulle signed Elysée Treaty of Franco-German friendship; Erhard succeeded Adenauer as federal chancellor; New Economic System introduced in Democratic Republic
1966–1969	Grand Coalition of conservatives and Social Democrats in Federal Republic
1968	New constitution in Democratic Republic gave government role to SED
1969	Brandt elected federal chancellor
1970	Russia and the Federal Republic signed a treaty recognizing status quo and renouncing use of force and any territorial claims on other countries; December 7, Treaty of Warsaw confirmed Oder-Neisse border with Poland
1971	Chancellor Willi Brandt won Nobel Peace Prize; Erich Honecker succeeded Ulbricht in the Democratic Republic

1972	Basic Treaty between two Germany for normal relations and de facto recognition of each by the other
1973	Federal Republic and Czechoslovakia signed treaty nullifying 1938 Munich Agreement
1974	Schmidt succeeded Brandt as federal chancellor
1975	Federal Republic approved Helsinki Agreements
1976	Schmidt reelected as federal chancellor
1982	Helmut Kohl elected federal chancellor
1989	Honecker succeeded by Egon Krenz in Democratic Republic; Hungary opened border with Austria, providing exit for East Germans defecting to the Federal Republic; November 9, Democratic Republic permitted free travel, Berlin Wall opened
1990	March, elections in East Germany won by West German conservatives; Two Plus Four talks on German unification; May Treaty established Monetary, Economic and Social Union; Trust Agency (Treuhand) established to liquidate East German state industries October 3, Day of German Unity

POST-
UNIFICATION

1991	Maastricht Treaty established a European Economic and Monetary Union
1993	European Community Common Market began; asylum law revised
1994	Last Soviet troops withdrew from Germany; Bundestag elections held
1995	Treuhand Trust Agency dissolved; Federal Republic troops participated in UN peacekeeping forces in Bosnia
1996	January 16, Israeli President Ezer Weizman addressed the German Bundestag
1998	Gerhard Schroeder elected federal chancellor

1

An Introduction to Modern Germany

GEOGRAPHY

Modern Germany is the heart of Europe. Its geographic coordinates are 55° N and 47° 16' S; 6° W and 15° E. Bounded on the north by the North Sea, Danish peninsula, and Baltic Sea, it stretches southward some 876 kilometers to the Alps Mountains and the frontiers of Switzerland and Austria. The Netherlands, Luxembourg, and France are its western neighbors, while Poland and the Czech Republic lie some 640 kilometers away on its eastern frontier. It has a total area of 356,910 sq km, and a land boundary of 3,621 km.

Population. At the end of the twentieth century, Germany has a population of 83,536,115 (July 1996 estimate), making it one of the most densely populated European nations (an average of 229 people per square kilometer). Its population is the second largest in Europe (Russia has the largest population), although it is smaller in area than France or Spain. As might be expected in a nation that has gone through two recent major wars, German birthrates have fluctuated in the twentieth century. These two factors have affected the population structure. There was a significant decline in the birthrate during both wars. Among the elderly population aged 60 and above, there is a substantial surplus of women

GERMANY

— International boundary

— State (land) boundary

★ National capital

◎ State (land) capital

The boundaries of Germany are depicted according to the Treaty on the Final Settlement on Germany signed September 12, 1990, in Moscow by the Federal Republic of Germany, the German Democratic Republic, the United States, the United Kingdom, France, and the Soviet Union. This Treaty will not enter into force until all six states parties complete their domestic ratification proceedings. The German Parliament will decide the location of the seat of government. Names and boundary representation are not necessarily authoritative.

| 0 | 50 | 100 kilometers |
| 0 | 50 | 100 miles |

SWEDEN

DENMARK

Baltic Sea

SCHLESWIG-HOLSTEIN

◎Kiel

North Sea

MECKLENBURG-VORPOMMERN

◎Schwerin

HAMBURG

◎Hamburg

BREMEN

Bremen◎

NIEDERSACHSEN

BRANDENBURG

BERLIN ★ Berlin

Potsdam◎

NETHERLANDS

POLAND

◎Hannover

Magdeburg◎

NORDRHEIN-WESTFALEN

SACHSEN-ANHALT

◎Düsseldorf

BELGIUM

Dresden◎

SACHSEN

Erfurt◎

HESSEN

THÜRINGEN

Wiesbaden◎

RHEINLAND-PFALZ

Mainz

LUXEM-BOURG

CZECHOSLOVAKIA

SAARLAND

◎Saarbrücken

BAYERN

Stuttgart◎

BADEN-WÜRTTEMBURG

◎Munich

FRANCE

AUSTRIA

SWITZERLAND

over men. Despite the casualties of World War II, there has been a small surplus of men over women in the population since the war. Another decline in the birthrate began in 1970, and only began to recover in 1990. There are currently 10.5 births per 1,000 people, making this one of the lowest birthrates in the world. The German population is growing at a rate of 0.67 percent per year. Life expectancy in Germany is increasing, however. In 1950 the number of individuals over 65 years of age per 100 people of working age was 16.3. In 1995 that figure had reached 24.7, and by 2040 it is projected to be 56.2, if the current birthrate continues. In 1992 the Bundestag established a Commission of Inquiry on Demographic Change to study the social and economic implications of this potential shift in demographic structure.

The German population is 95.1 percent ethnic German and 2.3 percent Turkish, with Italians, Greeks, Poles, and refugees from the former Yugoslavia comprising the remainder. The post–World War II influx of some 13 million refugees and Germans expelled from other lands accounted for much of the population growth after the war. Over 7 million foreigners are included in the current population total. Some 45 percent of the population are Protestant and 37 percent are Roman Catholic; the remainder are predominantly unaffiliated. The national language is German, and literacy is estimated at 99 percent of all residents over the age of 15.

The German population is unevenly distributed, with the heaviest concentrations occurring in the Rhine-Main valleys, the industrial region of the Rhine-Neckar valleys, the industrial area around Stuttgart, and the major cities of Bremen, Cologne, Dresden, Hamburg, Leipzig, Munich, and Nuremberg. The western regions hold over 80 percent of the nation's population, while only 15.5 million live in the eastern 30 percent of the nation. Only three of the 19 cities with 300,000 or more inhabitants are in the east. Some 26 million Germans, nearly one-third of the population, live in the 84 cities with 100,000 or more residents. Yet the majority of Germans live in small towns and villages.

Physical Geography. Germany has a complex geography of plains in the north and mountains in the south, separated by terraces and hilly uplands in the central region. The sandy North German Plain has many lakes and broad expanses of moors. In the center are a number of low mountain ranges, including the Rhenish, Hessian, Weser, Leine ranges and Harz Mountains. They give rise to the Weser and Ems Rivers, which flow northward into the North Sea. On west, the Rhine River forms a north-south axis, its valley a primary route for transportation and set-

Table 1.1
Physical Geography

Rivers (within Germany):	Rhine	865 km
	Elbe	700 km
	Danube	685 km
	Main	524 km
	Weser	440 km
	Spree	382 km
	Mosel	242 km
Mountains:	Zugspitze (northern Alps)	2,962 m
	Watzmann (northern Alps)	2,713 m
	Feldberg (Black Forest)	1,493 m
	Grosser Arber (Bavarian Forest)	1,456 m
	Fichtelberg (Ore Mountains)	1,215 m
	Brocken (Harz Mountains)	1,142 m

Source: Arno Kappler, ed., *Facts about Germany* (Frankfurt am Main: Societaets-Verlag, 1996), p. 68.

tlement. Rising in Switzerland, the Rhine is joined by the westward flowing Main River at Mainz and, further downstream, by the eastward flowing Moselle River at Koblenz. The Elbe River flows northwestward out of the Czech Republic to empty into the North Sea, forming another major trade and population route. The Rhoen and Ore Mountains, as well as the Bavarian, Upper Palatinate, Franconian, and Thuringian Forests contour the area south of the Elbe. The Oder River forms the nation's eastern frontier with Poland. The Danube River rises in the Swabian-Bavarian highlands and Black Forest of southwestern Germany, then flows eastward through a region of hills and lakes. South of the Danube, the Bavarian and Berchtesgaden Alps stretch to the southern border. The highest German mountain is the Zugspitze, at 2,962 meters. There are also several islands in the North Sea, including Ruegen, Fehmarn, Sylt, and a part of Usedom, that are German possessions.

Climate. Its position close to the Atlantic Ocean moderates Germany's climate, giving it a temperate and marine classification. There are four seasons, and precipitation throughout the year. The average humidity is relatively high. The average temperature ranges slightly below 32 degrees Fahrenheit in the winter to 70 degrees in the hottest month, July. Snow is particularly heavy in the Harz Mountains as well as in the Alpine regions. There are occasional warm wind phenomena, known as the Foehn, occurring in the mountains.

GOVERNMENT

Constitution. The official name of the country is the Federal Republic of Germany, or Bundesrepublik Deutschland. It is most usually referred to as Germany or Deutschland. The national flag has three equal horizontal bars of black (top), red, and gold. The German Constitution is the Basic Law of May 23, 1949. Its first section begins with 19 articles defining the breadth of civil rights accorded to all Germans. These include basic freedoms of expression, religion, and the right to form associations and coalitions; they also define freedom of movement, of art and scholarship, of the right to choose occupation, of privacy, and of the right to conscientious objection. The Basic Law then defines the federation and the states (Section II), the Bundestag (Section III), the Bundesrat (Section IV), the federal president (Section V), the federal government (Section VI), the process of federal legislation (Section VII), the execution of federal law and the federal administration (Section VIII), the judiciary (Section IX), and finance (Section X). The concluding section deals with implementation of the constitution.

The Basic Law, as adopted in 1949, was enacted by the legislatures of the individual West German states (only the Bavarian legislature voted against it). At that time, when Germany was divided into the Federal Republic (west) and the German Democratic Republic (east), the Constitution applied only to the Federal Republic. In 1990, following the adoption of the Unification Treaty between the two Germanys, both the preamble and concluding article were amended, and the Basic Law now applies to the entire nation. The federal Constitution may be amended by a two-thirds majority in the Bundestag and in the Bundesrat.

Federal States. Germany's government, defined in the Basic Law of May 23, 1949, is that of a federal republic, now composed of 16 states, or *Laender* (singular, *Land*). Since 1990 Berlin is the designated capital. Berlin, Hamburg, and Bremen are self-governing city-states. The 16 federal states are listed in Table 1.2.

Federal President. The Basic Law has established a republican system with a federal president as chief of state and two legislative houses: the nationally elected Bundestag and the Bundesrat, consisting of members of the state governments. The federal president is elected for a five-year term by the Federal Convention, which consists of members of the Bundestag and an equal number of representatives elected by the state legislatures. The federal president may serve only two terms. The president

Table 1.2
Federal States

State	Capital	State Population
Baden-Wuerttemberg	Stuttgart	10,300,000
Bavaria	Muenchen	12,000,000
Berlin		3,472,000
Brandenburg	Potsdam	2,500,000
Bremen		680,000
Hamburg		1,700,000
Hessen	Wiesbaden	6,000,000
Mecklenburg-Vorpommern	Schwerin	1,800,000
Lower Saxony	Hanover	7,800,000
North Rhine-Westphalia	Duesseldorf	17,800,000
Rhineland-Palatinate	Mainz	4,000,000
Saarland	Saarbruecken	1,100,000
Saxony	Dresden	4,600,000
Saxony-Anhalt	Magdeburg	2,800,000
Schleswig-Holstein	Kiel	2,700,000
Thuringia	Erfurt	2,500,000

Source: Kappler, *Facts about Germany*, pp. 84–156 passim.

represents the nation in diplomatic matters and appoints and dismisses federal judges, civil servants, and military officers (commissioned and noncommissioned). He nominates the federal chancellor and appoints the government ministers. He has the responsibility for assuring that federal laws are properly enacted before they are registered in the *Federal Law Gazette*. He may also pardon convicted criminals. In July 1994, Roman Herzog was elected president by the federal council.

Federal Legislature. The members of the Bundestag are elected every four years. All German elections are conducted on the basis of general, direct, free, equal, and secret voting rights for everyone who has had German nationality for at least one year and who is aged 18 by election day. Candidates are proposed by their political parties. Voters vote both for individual candidates and for a party list. Ballots are counted on a system of proportional party representation designed to assign legislative representation to parties in proportion to the votes they obtained. The first vote identifies the legislators; the vote on the party list determines the proportional representation. If the first vote on candidates re-

Table 1.3
Party Representation, 1998 Bundestag

Party	Pct. of Votes	No. of Representatives
SPD	40.9	298
CDU	28.4	198
CSU	6.7	47
Alliance 90/The Greens	6.7	47
FDP	6.2	43
PDS	5.1	36

Source: Kappler, Facts about Germany, p. 173.

sults in a number of legislators larger than the party list would indicate, the size of the Bundestag is temporarily increased in order to reflect voter choice. As a result of the 1998 election, party representation in the 669-member Bundestag was distributed as in Table 1.3.

The Bundestag passes laws and elects the federal chancellor. Most of the work is done in legislative committees, whose responsibilities correspond to those of the government ministries. Committee membership is determined by the relative strengths of the political parties. The Bundestag president is elected from the membership of the strongest political party in the house. Bundestag representatives are paid, and receive a pension if they serve for eight years or more.

Federal Council. The Bundesrat represents the 16 federal states, whose delegations are based on the size of their population. The 68 seats are apportioned as follows: North Rhine–Westphalia, Bavaria, Baden-Wuerttemberg, and Lower Saxony have 6 seats each; Hesse, Saxony, Rhineland-Palatinate, Berlin, Saxony-Anhalt, Thuringia, Brandenburg, and Schleswig-Holstein each have four seats. Mecklenburg-Vorpommern, Hamburg, Bremen, and the Saarland each have three votes. Each state must cast its votes in a bloc, and these often reflect state rather than party interests. Bundesrat approval is required for all bills that pertain to the financial and administrative concerns of the federal states and all proposed constitutional amendments. The president of the Bundesrat is elected for a 12-month term from among the state minister presidents, with the office rotating among the states. He presides over the Bundesrat and may serve as acting federal president if the incumbent is unable to function. In 1997, the party strengths in the Bundesrat were: SPD-led states with 41 representatives, CDU-led states with 27 representatives.

Federal Government and Chancellor. The federal government consists of a cabinet headed by the federal chancellor. The chancellor presides over the cabinet and serves as head of government. He nominates the ministers, determining their number and responsibilities. Of all the government officials, he alone is elected by the legislature and responsible to it. He may lose his position if the legislature votes, through a "constructive vote of no confidence," to replace him with another leader. This has occurred only once, in 1982, when Helmut Schmidt was replaced by Helmut Kohl by an absolute majority of the Bundestag.

The federal government administers diplomacy, defense, the national budget, the monetary system, air transport, and other elements, such as taxation, in which uniformity of law is necessary on a national basis. The civil, criminal, and commercial law codes and environmental concerns are all matters of federal jurisdiction. The federal government is also responsible for the government policies on naturalization and political asylum.

Judiciary. The German Federal Republic is based on a system of mainly written laws. Since the days of Roman law, the various German states have enacted laws, which, late in the nineteenth century, were consolidated for the first time. The Civil Code and Commercial Code were the first to be consolidated. Since unification in 1990, the legal codes of the Federal Republic and the German Democratic Republic have been merged, with consideration given to some of the particular problems emerging from reconciling the two codes. The court structures have also been adjusted following unification.

There is also a Federal Constitutional Court, located in Karlsruhe, made up of two panels of eight judges each. Half of the judges are elected by the Bundestag, half by the Bundesrat. Constitutional Court judges serve for 12 years and may not be reelected. At the request of either the federal government, the state governments, at least one-third of the Bundestag members, or of lower courts, the Federal Constitutional Court reviews laws to determine whether they are in conformity with the Basic Law. Individuals may also appeal to the Federal Court if they feel their basic rights have been infringed, but only after having exhausted all appeals available at lower levels.

The German judiciary works with the system of administrative law. Judges have the responsibility for determining whether individuals may be imprisoned and the length of the sentence. These judges, once appointed, are independent and may not be dismissed or transferred against their will. There are no special tribunals; however, there is a hierarchy of civil jurisdiction from local court, through regional and higher regional courts, to the Federal Court of Justice beneath the Federal Constitutional Court. These courts deal with basic criminal and civil matters, probate, and guardianship. Similarly, there are four federal legal jurisdictions—Administrative Federal Court, Finance Federal Court, Labor Federal Court, and Social Federal Court—each with its own hierarchy beginning at the regional level. The labor courts deal with employment contracts and any disputes between labor and management. The social courts handle disputes dealing with social security. The finance courts deal with taxation. The administrative courts handle all other matters that fall under the jurisdiction of administrative law.

To administer this judicial system, there are some 2,000 professional judges, over 4,000 public prosecutors, and some 60,000 independent lawyers. All of these have to have completed a university law school program as well as a compulsory state training program and must have passed a state examination. This preparation entitles them to serve in any of the three legal positions.

Federal Capital. In 1949, when Berlin was under the administration of a four-power military commission, the Rhineland university city of Bonn was selected as the capital of the Federal Republic. The Basic Law stipulated that the capital would be moved to Berlin once free elections were possible in eastern Germany. Bonn became synonymous with the rehabilitation of Germany diplomatically, politically, and economically in the decades after World War II. Nevertheless, following German reunification in 1990, the Bundestag voted narrowly (337 to 320) to transfer the federal legislature and administration to Berlin, symbolic of national unity. The Bundesrat, however, voted in July 1991 to remain in Bonn. In addition, some of the federal ministries and other federal offices previously located throughout the Federal Republic are being centralized in Bonn. In recognition of its significance for German history, Bonn has been given the title of Federal City. As a major university site, Bonn continues to be a center for scholarship, research, and the arts.

Political Parties. In 1997, Germany had six major political parties in the Bundestag (see Table 1.4). There are also some parties represented in state legislatures that do not have representation in the Bundestag: the Republikaner, Rolf Schlierer, chair; the National Democratic Party (NPD), Ellen-Dorris Schere, chair; the Communist Party, Rolf Priemer and Heinz Stehr, cochairpersons. There have also been issue- and locality-oriented pressure groups of expellees, refugees, and veterans.

Party members pay dues, which cover only a portion of party ex-

Table 1.4
Political Parties, 1997

Party	Chair	Membership (1995)
Social Democratic Party (SPD)	Oskar La Fontaine	818,000
Christian Democratic Union (CDU)	Wolfgang Schaeuble	662,000
Christian Social Union (CSU)	Theo Waigel	180,000
Party of Democratic Socialism	Lothar Bisky	123,000
Free Democratic Party	Wolfgang Gerhardt	80,000
Alliance 90/The Greens	Gunda Roestek/Antje Radcke	46,000

Source: Kappler, Facts about Germany, p. 191.

penses. To prevent special interests from controlling parties through their financial contributions, the Parties Financing Act went into effect in January 1994. Parties will receive 1.30 deutschmarks per vote for up to 5 million votes polled in the elections to the Bundestag, European Parliament, and state parliaments. They receive 1 deutschmark for each valid vote above 5 million and 50 pfennigs for each 1 deutschmark received through dues or contributions. The law limits the public grants to all parties to a total of 230 million deutschmarks.

Since the founding of the Federal Republic, some 36 different political parties have stood for election to the Bundestag. Due to the Five Percent Clause introduced in 1953, however, only those parties that receive at least 5 percent of the national election votes or win three Bundestag constituencies may be represented in the national legislature. The purpose of this clause, strengthened in 1957, is to prevent the paralysis of the Bundestag through the emergence of multiple splinter parties.

The SPD, CDU, CSU, and FDP were formed in West Germany between 1945 and 1947. The CDU had no representation in Bavaria, where the CSU is the primary Christian party. In the Bundestag, however, the CDU and CSU collaborate. The FDP promotes a traditional liberal platform, while the SPD maintains a strongly prolabor orientation. The Greens were founded in 1979 in the Federal Republic, voicing a strong pro-ecology, antinuclear, pacifist platform. The PDS is the successor to the former Socialist Unity Party of Germany (SED) of the German Democratic Republic. It has been based in the eastern states, and won only four Bundestag seats in the 1994 national election based on its victories in Berlin.

State and Local Government. With the exception of the 12-year period of the Third Reich (1933–1945), Germany has always been divided into states. At the beginning of the nineteenth century, there were over 300 separate sovereign political entities loosely united in the Holy Roman Empire. That authority was destroyed by Napoleon, who reduced the number to 35 by consolidating many of the territories. In 1871 there were 26 sovereign states, who united by treaty to form the German Empire. In the twentieth century, through war and consolidation, the number of states was reduced further, until by the end of World War II there were 11 states in the Federal Republic of 1949 and 5 in the German Democratic Republic. With unification in 1990, these 16 states have been retained, and Berlin has been consolidated into a single city.

Each of the federal states is self-governing, with a minister president and state legislature (Landtag) and judiciary. State governments are primarily responsible for implementing federal legislation, and may only pass legislation on matters not strictly reserved to the federal government. For the most part, states deal with aspects of social welfare, such as higher education and regional planning of water and land resources, and conservation, local police, and law enforcement. However, the states exercise considerable influence on federal legislation through the Bundesrat and through their administrative bureaucracy.

There is also a strong tradition of local self-government in Germany. Local governments have especial impact on the infrastructure of local transportation, water and sewage facilities, energy facilities, regional planning, and cultural facilities. They are a primary voice in local educational and cultural concerns, and have the authority to finance their activities through local property and commercial taxes. They also receive allocations from the state and federal governments.

ECONOMY

The German monetary unit is the deutschmark (DM), which is subdivided into 100 pfennigs. The exchange rate on December 31, 1997 was $ = DM 1.799. The deutschmark is considered to be a "hard" currency, which is traded on the world market. The German Federal Bank (Deutsche Bundesbank) is responsible for managing the money supply. It is advised by a Business Cycle Council, the Financial Planning Council, and the Council of Experts on the Assessment of Economic Trends, together with councils from the trade unions and employers' groups.

Gross Domestic Product. In 1995 the German gross domestic product (GDP) was DM 3,500 billion, averaging a per capita annual income of DM 45,200 ($17,900 overall, but $21,100 in western Germany and only

Table 1.5
Gross Domestic Product, 1995

Production (%)		Consumption (%)	
Service Industries	36.1	Private Consumption	56.8
Manufacturing Industries	34.7	Gross Capital Investment	22.6
Government, Households	14.3	Government Consumption	19.6
Trade and Transport	13.8	External Contribution	1.0
Agriculture, Fisheries, Forestry	1.1	(exports less imports)	

Source: Kappler, *Facts about Germany*, p. 260.

$6,600 in the five new eastern states). This high level of productivity made Germany the world's third largest economy, after the United States and Japan. The GDP is estimated to be growing at an average annual rate of 1.8 percent per year. This growth rate is unevenly distributed, however: the government has allocated about $100 billion annually to develop the economy of the five new states incorporated after the dissolution of the socialist German Democratic Republic. Thus, in the east the average annual GDP growth rate is 6.3 percent, while the larger economy of the western states has an average annual increase of 1.5 percent. About 1.5 percent of the GDP is expended on defense. The average annual national inflation rate, based on consumer prices, is 2 percent. The 1995 GDP was generated and expended as in Table 1.5.

Employment. The German workforce is estimated at 36,750,000, of which some 28.4 million work in the western 11 states. Some 2.6 million are foreign workers, many of them registered Turks, Greeks, Italians, and other asylum seekers from the former Yugoslavian regions. Most of the foreign workers are employed in the western states. Unemployment in the western states is at a rate of 8.7 percent; in the eastern states it is 14.9 percent.

Social Market Economy. The German government has a social market economy, that is, an economy that supports and promotes private enterprise and competition while at the same time supporting public well-being. The marketplace determines the nature of goods and services produced without government planning or regulation of prices and wages. The government does, however, support a system of social security funded by the employee, the employer, and the government. Thus German citizens are supported with retirement, accident, unemployment, job retraining, and child and housing benefits. In 1994, after unification of the economically depressed states of the former German

Democratic Republic, these expenditures amounted to 33.3 percent of the GDP. In January 1996, with unemployment standing at 4.2 million, the government, the business community, and the unions joined in an Alliance for Jobs and a Competitive Germany to reduce unemployment by one-half by the end of the century.

Agriculture, Forestry, and Fishing. This sector generates slightly more than 1 percent of the GDP. Approximately 34 percent of the land is arable, with another 30 percent in forests and woodlands, and 16 percent in pastures and meadows. Most German farms are smaller than 250 acres, and agriculture (including forestry and fishing) employs only about 1.7 million workers. The primary crops are wheat, potatoes, sugar beets, and barley. The major livestock sectors are pigs, cattle, sheep, and poultry. Germany also produces significant amounts of coniferous wood and harvests tons of Atlantic fish. Agricultural products comprise 5 percent of exports and 10 percent of imports.

Industry and Technology. Germany is the world's third largest economy, and one of its most technologically advanced. Its approximately 48,000 industrial firms employ nearly 6.8 million workers. They produce iron, steel, coal, cement, chemicals, machinery, vehicles, machine tools, electronics, food, and beverages. Large firms, which employ 1,000 workers or more, comprise less that 2 percent of the total number of enterprises; over three-quarters of the enterprises employ fewer than 100 workers. The industrial production grows at a rate of 2.8 percent per year (based on production in the western states).

The ten largest German industrial firms demonstrate the strength of German industry in modern technological fields (see Table 1.6).

Industrial research and technology are promoted by the Federal Ministry for Education, Science, Research, and Technology and the Ministry for Economics. In 1995 these two ministries allocated DM 1.21 billion to support research, apply it to production processes, and promote cooperation in developing new products. German products lead the field in chemicals, pharmaceuticals, and medical and optical instruments. Germany is second only to the United States in environmental protection technology and in biotechnology.

Transportation. Since 1991, the German government has launched a number of initiatives, under a program known as German Unity, to consolidate the transportation structure and infrastructure across the 16 federal states by the year 2000. By April 1996, some DM 60 billion had been allocated to this project. In 1994 the two German state railway systems

Table 1.6
Ten Largest Firms, 1997

Firm (Location)	Product	Turnover (BnDM)	No. of Workers
Daimler/Benz (Stuttgart)	Auto/Aerospace	124,050	300,100
Volkswagen AG (Wolfsburg)	Automotive	113,245	279,900
Siemens AG (Munich)	Electronics	106,930	386,000
VEBA AG (Duesseldorf)	Energy/Chemicals	76,067	130,000
RWE AG (Essen)	Energy/Building	72,136	136,100
Bayerische Motorenwerke (Munich)	Automotive	60,137	117,200
BASF AG (Ludwigshafen)	Chemicals/Pharmaceuticals	55,780	105,000
Bayer AG (Leverkusen)	Chemicals/Pharmaceuticals	55,005	144,600
Hoechst AG (Frankfurt/a.M)	Chemicals/Pharmaceuticals	52,100	118,200
VIAG AG (Munich)	Holding	49,545	95,600

Source: Kappler, *Facts about Germany*, p. 307.

were merged into the *Deutsche Bahn AG* and privatized. Germany has an extensive transportation establishment:

Railways	43,966 km
Highways	636,282 km (531,018 paved; 105,264 unpaved)
Waterways	5,222 km, of which 70% are usable by craft of 1,000-ton capacity or higher
Pipelines	3,644 km for crude 3,946 km for petroleum products 97,564 km for natural gas
Merchant Marine	452 ships of 1,000 GRT or over
Airports	617
Heliports	55

Communications. Germany has an estimated 44 million telephones, 44.8 million televisions, and 70 million radios. There are 103 AM broadcast stations (80 in the west, 23 in the east) and 487 FM broadcast stations (470 in the west, 17 in the east). There are 246 television broadcast stations.

CULTURAL AFFAIRS

Education. Education is compulsory in Germany. Every child, from the age of 6 to 18, must attend school. The states are responsible for administering the schools and for legislating any educational changes. Attendance at public schools is free to the students, and in most cases so are the texts and instructional materials. The Basic Law provides for religious instruction to be part of the curriculum, and parents can decide whether their children under the age of 14 will take religious instruction. Students 14 or older make that decision for themselves. The Basic Law also permits the establishment of private schools, although they must be approved by the state authorities. In 1994, there were 12.2 million students, 772,600 teachers, and 52,400 schools in the Federal Republic. Gross public spending on education was DM 151.9 billion.

The school system is complex. *Kindergartens* for children under age 6 are private, and generally run by churches, charitable societies, companies or, in some cases, municipalities. All children have the legal right to attend, but attendance is not compulsory. The curriculum is designed around learning through play. About 67 percent of preschool children between the ages of 3 and 6 attended a kindergarten in 1994.

The primary school, or *Grundschule*, offers the first four years (six in Brandenburg and Berlin) for formal education for students aged 6 and above. The curriculum emphasizes the basic skills. Grades five and six are used to analyze individual student progress and to address specific areas of weakness.

Starting with the seventh grade, students may attend one of a variety of schools, each of which offers a special certificate required for additional education. About 25 percent proceed to a general secondary school (*Hauptschule*) for five or six years to prepare for vocational training in industrial and craft fields. Some 40 percent of students study at an intermediate school (*Realschule*), which offers six years of a more comprehensive curriculum as preparation for additional vocational education in a professional school (*Berufschule*) or technical school (*Fachoberschule*). The grammar school (*Gymnasium*) presents a nine-year curriculum leading toward the successful completion of the school-leaving exam (*Abitur*), which qualifies individuals for entrance into a university or advanced technical institute.

Germany has hundreds of universities and technical institutes. The oldest is the University of Heidelberg, which was founded in 1386. In the nineteenth century, Germany set the model for the great research universities, especially those in the United States. After World War II, a number of specialized technical institutes were founded to meet the changing demands of science and industry. Most of the universities and institutes are publicly financed by the states, although there are some private church-supported institutions.

There are also federal universities for the armed forces and for public administration. The higher education institutions are self-governing, with a constitution, an elected president or rector, and responsibility for managing their own affairs. Unification created a need to consolidate the differing educational structures and curricula of the two former republics. The Federal/State Commission for Educational Planning and Research Promotion works to promote educational development. One of the recent developments is the program of distance learning at the University in Hagen, which uses correspondence courses and regional centers to help some 40,000 students advance their studies.

Approximately 30 percent of students (1.85 million individuals in the 1995 winter semester) attend one of the institutions for higher education. They take courses leading to a master's degree (*Magister*) or a diploma, or to pass a state examination in a specialized field. In 1995 there were also some 142,000 foreign students enrolled. German students may receive financial aid under the Federal Training Assistance Act; they are also aided by some 65 student welfare agencies. About 60 percent of German students at the university level are employed in addition to pursuing their studies.

Because of the increasing number of student applicants and a limited number of places in higher education, placement is determined by the Central Office for Allocation of Study Places in Dortmund. Scores on the *Abitur* are a primary factor, and many applicants are placed on a waiting list.

Churches. Article 4 of the Basic Law guarantees religious freedom. There is no state church in the Federal Republic, although there are partnerships, as for kindergartens and schools provided by religious organizations. Clerics are trained in state universities, and the churches have some influence over the appointments to the faculty of theology.

The Catholic Church is organized into some 27 dioceses, with seven archdioceses. In all there are 70 bishops and archbishops who meet at the German Bishops Conference every spring and fall. The conference secretariat is located in Bonn. The Evangelical Church in Germany (EKD) has some 24 Lutheran, Reformed, and United churches throughout Germany, governed by a synod headquartered in Hanover. There are also a number of Protestant free churches, the largest of which are the Methodists and the Evangelical Community. Smaller in number are the Baptists, the Old Catholics, the Mennonite congregations, the Society of Friends (Quakers) and the Salvation Army. There are some 54,000 Jews in Germany today, with the largest communities in Berlin (10,000 members), Frankfurt am Main (6,000), and Munich (almost 5,000). The Central Council of Jews is headquartered in Bonn.

The Arts. Germans love music, and support some 121 opera houses through state subsidies and 141 professional orchestras. Berlin, for example, has three opera houses and two major symphony orchestras. More than 100 annual musical festivals, such as the Richard Wagner Festival at Beyreuth, regularly attract thousands of listeners. In 1994 there were over 1,000 public music schools, some 40,000 choral groups, and 25,000 orchestras ranging from amateur to professional and of all sizes. Music is a compulsory general education subject in Germany, and approximately 25 percent of schoolchildren participate in some applied music activity.

Approximately 160 public theaters and 190 private theaters attract audiences to performances throughout Germany. Many have ensemble casts that perform a wide repertory. Theaters benefit from financial support from the states and cities, which provide some DM 4.3 million every year. Theaters employ about 60,000 individuals across the nation to facilitate approximately 100,000 theater and concert performances annually.

There are more than 3,000 museums of all kinds in the Federal Republic, with an infinite variety of public and private sponsors. Over 100 million people visit art museums annually, and are willing to spend time in long lines in order to view special exhibitions. Among the major museums are 24 art museums, 8 museums of science and technology, 7 specializing in cultural history, and 10 specializing in ethnology.

The German Arts Council, founded in 1982, is a nongovernmental organization that works to promote communication among the arts and art education.

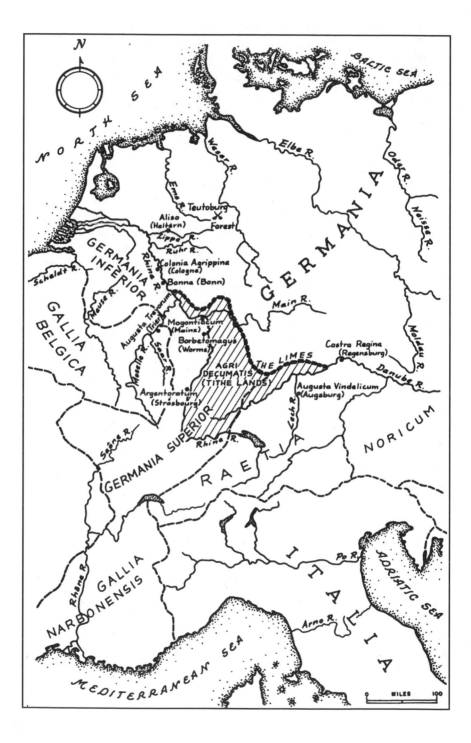

2

Germans in Antiquity and the Early Middle Ages

Tribes of migrant Germans came out of the eastern plains of the great Eurasian continent in antiquity. Led by councils of warriors, they elected their generals in time of battle. The tribes were independent, small, and linked by language and their militaristic lifestyle rather than any form of government. They had many names for themselves, based on tribal identification. Germani, the name by which they were later known, was given them by the Celts, whom they eventually displaced in western Europe.

At first the Germans slowly infiltrated the densely forested plains of northern Europe. They moved in small bands through to the eastern bank of the Rhine River and to the northern bank of the Danube River. Some, like the Cimbri, even crossed into Gaul (present-day France) and Italy, where they fought and merged with the resident Celts. Most, however, stayed on the eastern banks of the Rhine. As the Romans under Julius Caesar campaigned in northern Europe, they encountered and defeated the Celtic and Germanic tribes in Gaul (58–51 B.C.E.). Caesar's famous statement, "I came, I saw, I conquered," celebrated his victory over Gaul.

The Roman Empire. Augustus Caesar, the first Roman emperor, was worried about the security of Gaul's Rhine frontier, and sent forces across it on several campaigns to try to subdue the Germans. Some crossed the Rhine in 12 B.C.E; there was even a naval expedition from the North Sea and down the Weser River. The Germanic tribal forces alternately fought and retreated, frustrating the Roman armies. For 20 years the Romans and Germans skirmished along the Rhine and Danube frontiers. Then, in 9 C.E., three Roman legions moved into Germany to establish control. There, in the battle of the Teutoberg Forest near present-day Paderborn, the Roman Empire suffered one of its worst defeats. On a narrow way between the forest and a great marsh, the legions were ambushed by a German confederation led by Hermann (Arminius). Although a German, he was a former officer of the Roman army and knew how to thwart Roman battle strategies. Remnants of the shattered legions fled back across the Rhine, and the Germans didn't pursue them. Augustus Caesar accepted the defeat of his plan to subdue the Germans and withdrew his troops. Thereafter the Rhine became a permanent frontier between the two powerful Latin and Germanic cultures.

The early Germans were illiterate pagans, and left no permanent records of themselves in writing or in monuments. One of our first glimpses of them comes from the Roman historian Tacitus, writing *The Germania* in 98 C.E. He described the Germans as big-framed peoples, with reddish hair and fierce blue eyes. Their most prized possessions were their cattle and their weapons, which they carried with them at all times. Their warriors formed a hereditary nobility, but they elected their most valiant men to lead them in battle. The warriors swore loyalty to each other and to their leader, an oath now known by the Latin word *comitatus*. It was a disgrace for a German warrior to leave the battlefield or to survive comrades slain in battle. Their wives and children stayed at the battle-front and urged them on. Some German women even fought. Success in battle gave this warrior aristocracy the right to make decisions for the tribe and to obtain gifts of goods and land from the chiefs. While Tacitus disapproved of the warriors letting the women and children do all the farm and domestic work, he admired the loyalty of the Germans, their strong and sensible family values, their cleanliness, and their generous hospitality.

Tacitus identified over 60 German tribes testing the Roman Empire in the first century C.E. By that time the Germans were transforming from a migrant to a settled population. While the Romans preferred to live in cities with rows of stuccoed houses lining the paved streets, the Germans lived in isolated single farmsteads made of wood and covered with mud plaster. They had few roads. The center of tribal life was the great meeting house, a large crude hall, often constructed of turf and logs, where the warriors met to socialize and to carry on tribal business. Sleeping benches lined the wall, and there was a large hearth in the center for warmth and cooking. Smoke escaped through a hole in the roof. One of our best pictures of this warrior life comes from the epic poem *Beowulf.* Sitting around the fire of the great lodge, warrior after warrior boasted of his brave ancestors and his own tribe. And when daybreak came, the warriors set off in small armed groups to do great deeds in hopes of winning praise and precious gifts.

Regionally, the tribes formed loose military confederations that cooperated with each other in times of danger. By the third century C.E., these were identifiable regional alignments, the Franks along the eastern banks of the lower Rhine, the Alemanni on the upper Rhine and north of the Danube, the Frisians in present-day Netherlands, and Saxons further eastward between the Weser and the Elbe. Through their contact with the Romans and the Romanized Gauls, some Germans had accepted Christianity and established well-ordered regional centers. The cities of Augsburg, Strassburg, Worms, Speyer, Bonn, and Cologne have roots in this twilight period of the Roman Empire.

To the east, the migratory populations were again pressing. In central Europe, ranging between the Vistula and Niemann Rivers down to the Black Sea, were the fierce and nomadic eastern Goths (Ostrogoths). To their east were the Slavs in the north, the Asiatic Huns to the east, and the nomadic Alans moving out of the Persian Empire. To their north, Germanic tribes moved into the Jutland peninsula (modern-day Denmark) and up into Scandinavia. Gradually, these populations developed their own distinctive languages. Their lifestyles were based on alternating farming in the short northern growing system with long distance trade through the Baltic Sea and the European rivers that flowed into it. This diversity of peoples and cultures was a very important feature of European society from the very beginning.

The Roman Empire, huge and cumbersome, consisted of too many peoples and cultures to rule from one center. In addition to the pressures from the Germans in the north and west of Europe, the Persians were recapturing territory in the Middle East. Of necessity, the army became the driving force of the Empire, displacing the power of the civilian government. There were over 50 provinces and some 250 cities, all claiming their own rights. In 284 C.E. the emperor Diocletion came to power and split the Empire along a north-south line running from the Danube to the southern Adriatic. He also divided the military and political power with a coemperor. Each emperor chose an assistant, who was to be his successor. Diocletion's successor, Emperor Constantine, reunited the Empire briefly and moved his imperial capital to the Black Sea, founding the city of Constantinople in 326. This weakened the prestige and political power of Rome and the west. Constantine was also the first emperor who gave full equality to Christianity. In 325 he called the Council of Nicaea to establish the official church doctrine of the trinity. Although the center of Christianity moved eastward, Rome was still recognized as one of its holiest sites.

The apparent stability of the Roman Empire was interrupted in the fourth century by new and powerful waves of migration from the east. Germanic Goths, Vandals, and Burgundians swept forward from the Baltic region around the Vistula River and pressed into Gaul and through it into Spain and Italy. The Vandals surged on to found a kingdom in North Africa. The force of this new invasion even eclipsed the relatively stable settlement of the Franks in Gaul. Defensively, they moved their center from Trier in Gaul to Arles near the Mediterranean coast. Some Franks fought against the invaders in the early fifth century, but others used the invasions as an opportunity to rebel against the Romans.

The new migrations were so disruptive that the Romans were forced to bring troops back from England in 407 C.E. to deal with them. The imperial armies never returned to Britain. The Romanized natives there were left on their own to deal with the wild Picts in the north and Germanic tribes from Saxony, who came by sea and established settlements at the mouth of the Thames River. The legends of King Arthur reflect the defeat of Roman Britain by these new, less civilized Germanic invaders.

As the waves of these new Germans passed through to Spain and Italy, they established settlements of Visigoths (western Goths) in southwestern Gaul and Burgundians in the Rhone district to their east. The imperial government moved its capital from Rome to Ravenna as a defensive measure. The Visigoth king, Alaric, led the forces that destroyed Rome itself in 410 and pushed on into southern Italy, where he later died. In 412 the Visigoths moved into Gaul, deposing the rulers of the Franks and the Alemanni. By 416, when they had conquered Spain and defeated a number of the remaining smaller German confederations, the Visigoths held the upper hand throughout Europe.

In 418 C.E. their leaders agreed to exchange military service for the right to settle in the Roman Empire. Some scholars argue that the Romans gave them land in exchange for service. This placed a greatly expanded and powerful force of Germans at the borders of Italy itself. At midcentury an even more terrible foe invaded, the Huns, led by the fierce Attila. They drove rapidly from the Caspian Sea across the heart of Europe, swarming across the Rhine into Gaul and the Danube to the upper reaches of Greece. Everywhere, they laid waste to the land and demanded huge payments. They conquered the Germanic tribes, allowing only Italy and northeastern Gaul to escape their grasp. The Huns were a disaster for Europe.

The Empire turned to the Germans for help. Friendly German tribes, known as *foederati*, allied with imperial forces and pushed back the Huns in 451. Almost as rapidly as they had come, the Huns retreated. But the weakened empire was open to the Vandals, who ended Roman rule in the African provinces and sacked Rome in 455. The western Roman Emperor, Valentinian III, was assassinated by German bodyguards, and Roman superiority ended in the western part of the empire. As a result, Germanic tribes gained political power through these successful alliances with Rome. Within 20 years there were established German kingdoms and federations from the Atlantic to the Elbe River, while the western Roman Empire was a small region along the Adriatic coast across from Italy.

For the next twenty years the western emperors were actually puppets of the Germanic chiefs. In 476 C.E. the last Roman emperor, Romulus Augustulus, was deposed by a German mercenary captain, Odoacer, who agreed to rule in the west as the agent of the emperor in Constantinople. In 493, Odoacer was deposed by Theodoric, the king of the eastern Goths (Ostrogoths), and Italy was turned into a Germanic kingdom. The Vandals in Africa controlled the western Mediterranean, including the western islands of Corsica and Sardinia and the western tip of Sicily. This marked the end of the western Roman Empire and the transformation of western Europe into a region of Germanic kingdoms and confederations.

Although Roman imperial power had ended in the west, Roman Christianity remained a powerful cultural force. By the end of the fourth century, the Burgundians, Lombards, and Vandals had all adopted Christianity. Yet Christianity was full of internal dissension by the fifth century. Inevitably, Christianity was influenced by beliefs that conflicted with church doctrine, and were therefore branded as heresies. At issue was the nature of the Trinity. Many Germanic tribes believed that the divinity of God the Father was separate from that of Christ the Son. This heresy was known as Arianism, and it made great headway in Germanic

Spain, Italy, and confederations of the upper Danube region. Indeed, as they spread their power, the Arian Vandals and Goths persecuted those who stayed with the orthodox Christianity.

The Franks. In Gaul, however, Clovis, king of the Franks, used the official Catholicism as a unifying force to solidify his power and his kingdom. The Kingdom of the Franks that Clovis established was the most important early Germanic state to emerge from the period of the migrations. From its roots sprang the feudal Germanic society that dominated Europe throughout the Middle Ages.

The Romans first began to write about the Franks in the late third century. They used the term *Franci* to describe the fierce warriors they encountered along the lower Rhine and northwestern Gaul. To these Germans the word meant "free," and they proudly used it to refer to their independence of Roman rule. Later, the Franks collaborated with the Alemanni to attack Roman strongholds, expanding their territories down to the Loire River in France. The strength of their opposition to the Empire can be gauged by the fact that in poetry and eulogies, a number of Roman emperors were praised for their victories over the Franks. By the early fourth century, when Emperor Constantine briefly reunited the Empire, the Franks began cooperating with the Romans. They provided forces for the army, and there is evidence that they served loyally in Africa and the Middle East, as well as in Gaul. Some served as highly regarded officers.

Gregory, the bishop of Tours, wrote the *History of the Franks* in the sixth century. The son of the Romanized elite in Gaul, he spent most of his life on the Loire frontier centered on the old Roman crossroads city of Tours. As the burial site of St. Martin, the first Christian missionary to the Gauls, Tours was a famous and important pilgrimage center. Bishop Gregory was outraged at the way the Catholics were persecuted by the Arian Vandals, Visigoths, and Huns. It is not surprising, therefore, that he would center his *History* on the one prominent German kingdom that professed Catholicism.

The Kingdom of the Franks, who sang of their great ancestor Mero-vech, were *foederati* under the leadership of King Childeric. When he died (481), he was succeeded by his son, Clovis. The new king fought to expand his territory. At first he ruthlessly plundered all wealth in the regions he conquered, including that of the churches. But in 498, at the pleading of his Catholic wife, Chlotilda, Clovis underwent a battlefield conversion. In a battle with the Alemanni, Clovis was near defeat when he burst into tears and, raising his eyes toward heaven, shouted that if

Jesus Christ would grant him the victory, he would be baptized in the Catholic faith. According to Gregory, this so terrified the Arian Alemanni that they instantly retreated, leaving their king to be killed and their officers to surrender. Clovis was baptized at Reims and went forward to conquer other Germanic kingdoms throughout Gaul. By the time of his death in 511, Clovis had doubled the size of his kingdom and had incorporated much of Romanized Gaul into it.

With the singular success of wedding the Franks to Catholicism and to the old imperial regions, Clovis distinguished himself from those past German leaders who fought and moved on. He had established a territorial basis for a monarchical state. When word of his victory reached Constantinople, the emperor gave him the title of *Consul aut augustus*, conferring the legitimacy of imperial civil authority on this supremely military ruler. This consolidation of power also recognized the line of Merovech, called the Merovingians, and their customary tribal law, called the Salic Law. Clovis moved his capital to Paris, and is considered to have been the greatest king of the Merovingian dynasty.

Clovis built a government which blended Roman and Frankish practice. The local civil government, *civitas*, was administered by a count, or *graf*. From their fortified homestead, the counts exercised authority with the aid of other local landowners. They made the laws and were responsible for collecting local taxes. These local governments were all part of larger military administrative districts, ruled over by dukes, or duces, loyal to the king. The dukes and counts received land from the king in return for their services and loyalty. They built their great homes, called manors, and gathered followers around them as military and administrative agents. Together, they made up the political-military nobility, often called vassals of the king, characteristic of feudalism. The Catholic Church, too, benefited from this distribution of power. The kings often incorporated the educated bishops into their courts as trusted advisors and administrators. They were rewarded with funds to found monasteries or to build cathedrals. Powerful local lords also frequently allied themselves with the local clergy.

Gradually, this new aristocratic structure, based on land ownership and local control, led to the rise of strong regional warlords. The old *comitatus* remained, in the form of local armies loyal to their counts and dukes. The king often had to compete with his powerful nobility for territory, wealth, and power.

The Franks' Salic Law required that the wealth of the father be divided equally among his heirs. Thus, when Clovis died in 511, the lands he ruled were divided among his four sons, and each established a separate capital. As expansion continued, especially against the Saxons in the east and the Visigoths in Spain, the brothers feuded among themselves. Their sons did the same, until the territory once ruled by Clovis was divided into the three kingdoms of Austrasia (northeast along the Rhine River), Burgundy (southeast, centered on the Rhone River), and Neustria (northwest along the channel coast from the mouth of the Rhine to the Brittany peninsula). The sixth century thus began a period of Frankish conquest along the frontiers and feuds internally among the many heirs to the thrones.

Nevertheless, the Merovingians maintained nominal control over these kingdoms of the Franks into the eighth century. From their capitals in Metz, Paris, Orleans, and Soissons, the kings and their courtiers traveled through their realms, imposing a royal visit (and all the costs of it) on one manor or monastery after another. Because there were few roads and communication was poor, they relied on their vassal nobility to keep them informed about the affairs of the kingdom. It was a weak and ineffective form of government, but it was backed by the support of the Catholic bishops and by the prestigious association with the Roman Empire. Often, in fact, the Frankish kings found more support from the bishops than from their counts and dukes. They appointed favorites to the church and used church councils as a second source of information about the affairs of the kingdom.

The Carolingians. While the Merovingian kings were on royal tour, their affairs were entrusted to faithful courtiers in the capitol. Their chief of staff held the title of mayor, and these men often used their position to marry well and accumulate wealth and power. In 687, Pippin, the mayor of Austrasia, seized control of Neustria. With the forces at his disposal, he established his family as the new dynasty in these two regions and ruled until his death in 714. It was his illegitimate son, Charles Martel, "Charles the Hammer," who gave the new dynasty its name, however. Because of his effective defeat of Neustrian resistance, he solidified the throne and is considered the founder of the next German ruling family, the Carolingian dynasty.

By the eighth century, the Roman Empire had been eclipsed in the Mediterranean by the extraordinary crusades (*jihads*) of Islam. This newly proclaimed monotheistic religion was founded in 622, when the Prophet, Mohammed, fled persecution in the Arabian city of Mecca for the nearby city of Medina. The Muslim calendar begins with that event, known as the Hegira. With its simple creed, "There is but one God,

Allah, and Mohammed is his Prophet," Islam appealed to many who found the Christian doctrine confusing and paganism unfulfilling. The Muslim (a follower of Islam) prayed directly to God, without the intervention of a priest. Like Judaism and Christianity, Islam was a "religion of the book." The Koran, written in Arabic, was the written message of God as received by Mohammad. It offered guidance for correct living and the promise of salvation in paradise. And those Muslims who died fighting for the faith would pass instantly into paradise.

Fervent Muslim converts traveled throughout the eastern shore regions of the Mediterranean as missionaries and as warriors to establish their faith. Their conquest was extraordinarily swift and successful: by 655 they controlled Syria, the Persian Empire, and Egypt; then they turned westward and conquered northern Africa, subduing the old Vandal kingdoms and replacing Arian Christianity with Islam.

Muslim forces laid siege to Constantinople in 717-718, threatening the existence of the Byzantine Empire (the eastern successor to the Roman Empire). While they could not defeat the empire, they reduced its territory to Asia Minor (contemporary Turkey) and the Balkan peninsula. Other Muslims crossed the Straits from Africa into Spain in 711, smashed the Visigothic kingdom, and pushed across the Pyrenees Mountains into the territories of the Merovingian Franks. There, in 732, just 100 years after the death of Mohammad, they suffered another significant check. They were halted at the holy city of Tours by a determined Christian Frankish army. Its leader was Charles Martel.

Islam, which replaced both Roman and Christian influences in the Middle East, north Africa, and Spain, had changed the Mediterranean world significantly by the eighth century. Western civilization was now divided between Islam and Christendom, which was anchored by the Byzantine Empire in the east and the Kingdom of the Franks in the west. But these two halves of Christendom couldn't have been more different. Whereas Constantinople gave the Byzantine Empire a glittering urban capitol and a wealthy center of commerce and culture, the Kingdom of the Franks was economically backward and decentralized, with few large cities and only poor roads connecting them. It was surrounded by hostile Muslims in Spain, unruly Lombards in Italy, and hosts of warring Saxons, Thuringians, Bavarians, and Alemanni on the eastern banks of the Rhine. The Carolingian dynasty needed warrior-kings to sustain itself.

The foundation built by Charles Martel reached its fulfillment with his grandson, "Charles the Great," known as Charlemagne. When Charlemagne came to the throne of Frankland, in 768, the interaction of Germanic feudalism and the Roman Catholic Church had built a distinctive society in Europe. True, it lacked the long cultural history and great commercial wealth of the urbanized east: European society was centered on manors and monasteries, pilgrim sites and cathedral cities, and the royal court that constantly traveled among them. This blending of the Germanic secular society with the church, called the "medieval synthesis," was one of the most important factors in developing medieval Europe.

Feudalism. Under the control of the feudal landlords, the rural population grew in Germanic Europe. The peasants cleared the forests and opened up new agricultural lands. They developed heavier plows to break the dense soils and learned how to drain the lands of the abundant northern rainfall. Through agreement with the feudal nobility, they worked the landlord's land as sharecroppers. Known as serfs, they agreed to work the land, paying taxes in labor and in kind, in exchange for protection by the landowners. This contractual arrangement gave the countryside a stability not known before. In their villages the serfs developed communal cooperation and limited self-government. As more land came into use, they developed a two-field and, eventually, three-field pattern of crop rotation that significantly increased local productivity. They often owned draft animals communally, since no single individual could afford the purchase and maintenance costs. The landlords harnessed streams for flour mills and built communal ovens, which serfs could use for a fee. This economic cooperation between landlord and serf is called manoralism. It permitted the growth of the European economy well before there was long-distance trade.

Most serfs combined agricultural work during the growing season with some sort of village craft during the long winter season. They bartered these goods locally to help make ends meet. At best, it was a precarious life. Famines were frequent, and sometimes resulted in local incidents of cannibalism. Yet, European serfdom offered more individual rights and security than slavery, which had been the economic basis of the ancient Mediterranean economy. Some peasants even managed to own land as free men, although they were in the minority.

The monasteries also assisted in European development. Originally, the pious had retreated to the wilderness to lead a religious life. There they often improved marginal lands and developed agricultural technology that benefited the rural economy that spread out to enfold them. Monasteries served as orphanages, hospices for the ill, and inns for the travelers. The roads that connected them to the villages and manors helped open the rural districts for trade and travel.

Monasteries also served as the center for religious teaching and missionary work. The Benedictines, founded in Italy in the sixth century, rapidly spread throughout the west. They provided a model for piety and self-discipline, which enhanced their missionary work. In the eighth century, missionaries from England began to preach among the Germans. The most important of them was Boniface, later St. Boniface, whom the pope appointed bishop of Mainz in 732. There he gained the support of Charles Martel and his sons, and became an important link between the Carolingians and the papacy. Boniface founded a Benedictine monastery at Fulda that became one of the most influential religious centers in Germany. His missionary work east of the Rhine helped form the basis for the later German Catholic church. The monastery school for training priests and monks played an important role in the development of German culture. The bishops, who headed the urban churches, and the abbots, who administered the monasteries, were important political supporters of the expanding Carolingian monarchy.

The pope supported this interaction with the Franks, for the papacy needed a strong ally. When the Lombards campaigned in Italy in 750, they captured Ravenna, which was the outpost of the Byzantine church in the west. Cut off from Byzantine help, the papacy appealed to Pippin, the son of Charles Martel. To secure his help, Pope Vitalian authorized the formal anointing of Pippin as king of the Franks. In a ceremony at Soissons in 751, the aging Bishop Boniface performed the ceremony, and the Carolingian dynasty formally replaced the Merovingians. Pippin then led his forces into Italy, defeated the Lombards, and allocated a large portion of central Italy to the pope. This "Donation of Pippin" was the basis for the Papal States of Italy, which existed until the late nineteenth century. Pippin went on to expel the Muslims from the southwest of Frankland, and left a much expanded kingdom to his son and heir, Charlemagne.

Charlemagne. We are indebted to Einhard, an aristocratic monk from the monastery of Fulda, for *The Life of Charlemagne*, completed in 836. Einhard was a friend and personal advisor of the great king, whom he described as tall, strong, and well built, with a stomach that was "a trifle too heavy." Charlemagne was a rugged outdoorsman who loved to hunt, swim, and ride, especially if the activity was followed by a steam bath. Einhard says that Charlemagne actually built his capitol at Aachen in

794 because of the hot springs found there. The king was adamant about wearing the national dress of the Franks and, with the exception of his gold and silver sword belt, looked like an ordinary man on most days. On feast days, however, he wore a suit of cloth of gold and a crown of gold and precious stones. Moderate in diet, he loved to be read to during meals. He could converse in Latin and could understand Greek. He studied mathematics and mastered the techniques of public speaking but, despite great effort, never learned to write.

Charlemagne was responsible for an intellectual movement now called the Carolingian Renaissance. In his capitol in Aachen his builders and sculptors copied the elegant Byzantine styles of architecture. To cope with Frankish illiteracy, he set up a palace school at Aachen under the famous monk Alcuin of York (England). He endowed other cathedral and monastery schools throughout his realm. He enjoyed gatherings of scholars and poets, and provided for scriptoriums to copy famous books of classical and religious importance. Einhard's biography and Paul the Deacon's *History of the Lombards* came out of this tradition. The Carolingian miniscule, a form of lowercase writing, evolved to make these works more legible than traditional Latin—not only were the individual letters more readable, but the words were henceforth separated by spaces.

The number of the educated remained very small, but they were sufficiently trained and highly placed to provide for regular channels of government communication. The king appointed bishops and counts as agents, called *missi dominici*, to work in the various regions as links between the royal court and the local governments. This more centralized government meant that taxes and army recruitment were put on a regular basis. The *missi dominici* could also hear cases at law, and even had the power to overrule errant nobility. Above all, this was a Christian government. Charlemagne's laws, known as capitularies, regulated both state and church in his realm, and he even made laws affecting church doctrine.

But Charlemagne was a warrior king as well. He fought in the Aquitaine region of southwestern Frankland, and in the early 770s mounted an expedition to subdue the Lombards. In 778, withdrawing from battle with the Muslims in Spain, his rear guard was ambushed and slaughtered by Christian Basques. A young nobleman of his court, Count Roland of the Breton Marches, was slain. The incident was related in poetry by unknown authors. They took poetic license, however, converting the treacherous Basques into ferocious Muslims, and created the French national epic, *The Song of Roland.*

Charlemagne also conquered Bavaria and Ostmark (later Austria), looting their riches and sending them back to Frankland. He spent 32 years campaigning against the Saxons on his northeastern frontier, a brutal struggle in which he tried to impose Frankish rule and Christian baptism. In 782 he had 4,500 Saxons executed in one day, but the fierce tribes on the east side of the Rhine were not subdued until 804. By arms, education, religion, and administration, Charlemagne consolidated western Christendom. He ruled from the Danish peninsula south to the Adriatic, from the Brittany peninsula east to the Elbe, and from the English Channel to the Pyrenees. Thanks to his alliance with the church, he also controlled more than half of the Italian peninsula. Only England, the Danish kingdom, and southern Italy lay outside his domain. Yet, for all its expanse, Charlemagne's kingdom was still a domain of sparsely settled regions, with little economic development and only a thin veneer of government.

First German Empire. On Christmas day in the year 800, Charlemagne was at St. Peter's Cathedral in Rome. Pope Leo III used the occasion to crown him Emperor of the Romans. Einhard said that the ceremony was a surprise, but more modern historians doubt that such an act could have taken place without Charlemagne's advance knowledge. This coronation formally cemented the medieval synthesis of the Frankish state and the papacy. Each gained a certain aura of power from the event: the Franks were placed on a level of power and legitimacy with the ancient Romans; the pope appeared to have the power to create emperors. It was not, actually, a restoration of the long gone Roman Empire. It was the acknowledgment of shift in power from the Mediterranean basin to Europe, and of a new Germanic empire in Europe. Charlemagne clearly perceived that his political power took precedence over that of the pope. He always used his German title King of the Franks and the Lombards along with the Roman imperial title. And, when his son, Louis, was crowned in his lifetime, Charlemagne performed the ceremony, not the pope.

Charlemagne died in 814, after 32 years as king and 14 years as emperor. His grandson, the historian Nithard, wrote some thirty years later: "When Emperor Charles of blessed memory, rightfully called the Great by all nations, died at a ripe old age, about the third hour of the day, he left the whole of Europe flourishing."[1] His son Louis the Pious inherited the kingdom. Louis was the product of the palace school, educated and devoutly Catholic. At his own request, he was recrowned by the pope.

Louis learned that inheriting the throne was easier than exercising power. He had neither the ruthless determination nor the charismatic leadership of his father. He did have three sons, however, and from the outset they quarreled with their father and schemed among themselves to gain as much power and wealth as possible. Disappointed in his efforts to try to maintain a unified Christian kingdom, Louis tried to settle the succession by a series of agreements partitioning his holdings among his heirs. When he died, in 840, there was a brief interval of peace, followed by war among the brothers.

In 843 the Treaty of Verdun resolved the conflict and ended Carolingian unity. Lothair received the title of emperor, and with it a narrow strip of territory that ran from the North Sea coast above the Rhine River mouth south to the Rhone River valley and to Rome. To the west, his brother Charles the Bald ruled the Kingdom of the Franks, identified as Francia occidentalis. To the east, Louis the German ruled Francia orientalis, which soon became known as Germania.

In addition to their own internal conflicts, the three Carolingian rulers had to contend with turbulent waves of new invaders: Vikings from Scandinavia, who terrorized as they rampaged along the North Sea coasts and up the rivers, Hungarians, also known as Magyars, whose mounted raiding parties swept into central Europe from Asia; and piratical Muslims, called Saracens, who, like the Vikings in the north, preyed on the shipping of the Mediterranean and the rivers, pillaging and plundering. They destroyed the peace, the trade routes, and any further potential for Carolingian unity in Europe. Increasingly, each state had to deal with its own immediate crises. Germania, separated from its Roman and Frankish roots, would carve out its own history.

NOTE

1. Nithard, *Historus*, Bernhard Walter Scholg, trans. (Ann Arbor: University of Michigan Press, 1972), p. 129.

3

The German Dynasties

The Middle Ages in Europe saw the development of the constitutional elements that later characterized its major states: England, France, Spain, Germany, and Russia, in particular. At issue were the nature of the monarchy, the role and power of the nobility, the relationship of the church to the temporal (nonchurch) powers, and, in many cases, the definition of national boundaries. All of these major states evolved into strong centralized monarchies except Germany. In central Europe historical factors supported, instead, the persistence of localized power, known as particularism, loosely joined in an empire of states rather than a strong monarchy. This chapter examines the political and constitutional elements that determined the nature of the first German Empire.

The Frankish monarchy that Charlemagne founded established royal power based on military force combined with consecration by the church. Thus he had the right to appoint both the feudal and church nobility and to give them lands (fiefs). His monarchy epitomized the medieval synthesis, the interlocking of church and state. The king perceived himself as the vicar of God and equal in power to the pope. Thus he sought the acknowledgment of his vassals, but did not consider himself dependent on them for his political legitimacy.

The German feudal duchies, the military regions controlled by dukes, had been created as a part of Frankish expansion to the east. They formed in the territories of the Germanic tribes that Charlemagne subdued, such as Saxony. The dukes in these regions were given fiefs by the king and established secondary dynasties in their own right, dynasties that often sought to replace that of the monarchy. In Franconia, Bavaria, and Swabia in the south, and in Saxony and Thuringia in the north, the dukes became powerfully entrenched. They were known as the tribal (*Stamm*, in German) dukes, and established themselves as semiroyal rulers of virtually independent states.

For the monarchy to succeed, the king had to control the dukes, the church, and the territory of the state—no easy task! When crises arose, the German rulers sometimes called meetings of the combined clerical and feudal nobility, called *Diets*. These were advisory rather than legislative. Out of these elements, four dynasties tried in vain to create a viable centralized monarchy in Germany: the Ottonians (919–1002), the Salians (1002–1125), the Hohenstaufens (1138–1254), and the Hapsburgs (1273–1918).

Carolingian Legacy. The Treaty of Verdun (843 C.E.) created three separate hereditary states for the grandsons of Charlemagne. Lothair, in the center, had the imperial title and the two imperial capitols of Aachen and Rome, but they gave him no supremacy over his two brothers, Charles the Bald in Francia and Louis the German in Germania. In fact, they all competed with each other for superiority. Louis the German also had to protect his territory from the attacks of both Vikings and Huns. He just barely held his own through his death in 876.

Louis's son and heir, Charles the Fat, had less success. Between negotiating with the Vikings, guarding his western border from Charles the Bald, and traveling to Italy to defend the pope, he lost control of his nobility. In 887 he was deposed by the tribal dukes in favor of a nephew, Arnulf. After defeating Viking and Slav invaders and staving off the Hungarians, Arnulf left his kingdom, still under attack, to his son, Louis the Child, in 899. The boy king was unequal to the task, and the tribal dukes used his reign to establish their own virtually autonomous rule. The last of the eastern Carolingians, Louis died in 911.

To prevent claims from the western Carolingians, the tribal dukes selected the least threatening of their number, Conrad I, duke of Franconia, as the new king. He was too weak to control the Huns and rebellions in the duchies. After seven futile years, Conrad, on his deathbed, designated Henry, duke of Saxony, as his successor. It was a fortunate choice.

The Ottonian Dynasty from Saxony. There is a nice irony in the fact that the very Saxons Charlemagne fought so viciously to subdue formed the dynasty that reestablished the German monarchy. Sober, practical, and a determined aristocrat, Henry extended his personal holdings through advantageous marriage. He gained peace on his western border by marrying his daughter to the duke of Lorraine. He paid tribute to the marauding Huns for nine years in order to obtain peace on his eastern border. He located fortified citadels throughout his kingdom and put loyal troops in them. Then he campaigned against the Slavs along his eastern border, gaining considerable territory and forcing the Bohemians to pay tribute.

Before Henry I died in 936, he designated his second son, Otto, as his successor. Otto was duly acknowledged by the Saxon nobility and anointed king at Aachen by the archbishop of Mainz. Throughout his long reign (936–973) he struggled to realize his dream of consolidating a German state by working closely with the church. He too had to defeat warring Slavs and Hungarians. He used a typically feudal strategy: creating new and loyal nobility by giving them fiefs from land conquered from the Slavs. He also formed four new bishoprics in these territories and an archbishopric in Magdeburg. He especially liked to create bishoprics, since church lands were not passed on to individual heirs who might be of questionable loyalty. By using bishops rather than feudal vassals as agents of government, he had trustworthy administrators in the rebellious duchies and the grateful support of the church. To cement this bond, Otto generously provided funds for monasteries and other church activities.

Early in his reign Otto also gained control of Burgundy. By redistributing land among loyal followers, gradually he weaned the lesser nobility away from its mighty dukes. Yet for some 20 years Otto had to contend with vicious civil wars and the betrayal of his brothers. In 955 at Lechfeld, near Augsburg, his forces finally smashed the Huns and ended their intimidation of the upper Danube region. The fearful climate of this period may have inspired the *Niebelungenlied*, the turbulent tale of greed, lust, and betrayal that became the German national epic.

Otto prevailed in Germany. He also wanted to control Italy and the papacy, but not to incorporate them into his state. In 951 he married the widow of the Italian king and claimed the title of king of the Lombards. The Lombards proved to be as stubbornly rebellious as the Germans, however, and Otto had to return to Italy again in 961 to rescue the pope. On that occasion he had himself crowned Roman emperor and made the pope swear loyalty to him; in exchange, he guaranteed all the papal lands in Italy. In 962, when a new, less pliable pope was elected, Otto deposed him and made the church promise not to install any pope without the approval of the emperor. This agreement, of course, was against church law, and proved impossible for the German emperor to enforce. But it represented that integral bond between the papacy and the empire. To the pope it gave a powerful protector. To the new German dynasty it gave the veneer of historical legitimacy, a dynastic link with the Caesars and with Charlemagne. Otto I became known as King Otto the Great.

Otto I designated his 7-year-old son as his heir to the kingdom and had him crowned as well in 962. At his father's death in 973, when Otto II was aged 18, he assumed full power. Symbolic of his status, he married the daughter of the Byzantine emperor and received full diplomatic recognition of his imperial status from the eastern potentate.

Immediately on the succession of Otto II, the dukes in Bavaria and Bohemia rebelled. It took Otto five years to defeat them. He redistributed some of Bavaria's eastern territories below the Danube, creating the new, more loyal duchy of Carinthia and the regions of Ostmark (later Austria). No sooner had he banished the duke of Bavaria than Germany was attacked by the king of the Franks, whom it took two years to defeat. Flushed with victory, Otto II launched a naval campaign against the Saracens threatening southern Italy. The expected help from his Byzantine relations never came, however. Otto II was disastrously defeated in southern Italy and died in Rome (983) without returning to Germany.

The defeat and death of the 27-year-old emperor set off a wave of uprisings in Italy and among the Slavs of the eastern territories of the empire. His son and heir was only 3 years old, so his wife, backed by the loyal bishops, formed a regency government until Otto III took full power in 994. This bright boy, educated in the Byzantine heritage of his mother as well as the Roman traditions, was contemptuous of his Saxon heritage. Instead, he saw himself as an autocrat, a Roman, and a high priest along with the pope. He tried to impose Byzantine ritual on his court and to subordinate the Catholic Church to his state. His religious aims were opposed by the Clunaic reform movement sweeping the monasteries and by a mystical Christian movement anticipating the millennium.

Otto III thus focused his attention on Rome, eventually moving there and initiating an ambitious building plan to restore its antiquities in Byzantine style. He lost interest in the political affairs of Germany, granting his Polish territories independence and a separate archbishopric in 1000

C.E. He permitted Pope Sylvester to confer a royal crown on Stephen as the new king of Hungary and raised no objection when Bohemia gained independence. But the German nobility bitterly resented Otto's actions, as did the Italians in Rome, who had no wish to assimilate Byzantine practices. Perhaps the strongest objections came from the German churches, however. When Otto III died, unmarried, in 1002, he left an empire seething with resentment.

The unlucky successor to all this turmoil was Otto's cousin, Henry II. As pious as Otto III (he and his wife were both later canonized as saints), he realized that he had to focus on Germany rather than Rome. After years of relative independence, however, the German nobility claimed that their landholdings were hereditary. They flaunted the authority of their king. His only true allies in Germany were the high church authorities.

Henry went through the motions of being crowned king of Italy and emperor in Rome, but he soon lost control of Italy. The Italian maritime city-states were becoming wealthy and powerful. They persuaded the pope to conduct a more Italian policy. Since German forces were becoming less dependable in fighting the Greeks and Saracens, the pope sought new allies in Italy and Normandy. Henry's efforts to regain control in Poland were thwarted by the rise of a strong dynastic state there. He barely held on to the loyalty of his allies in Burgundy. He died without heir in 1024, the last of the Ottonian kings.

This remarkable dynasty had shaped the German state by reviving the concept of empire and by empowering the German church. Through land distribution, a network of loyal, if independent, vassals and bishops provided competent administration and relative internal security. Over 200 new market towns grew up around fortified citadels and monasteries, evidence of economic development. These cities maintained their own internal order (*Burgfrieden*, in German), protecting new commercial interests and paying for the privilege in taxes. As educators and intellectuals, the clergy were vital influences on law, literature, art, and general culture.

The Salian Dynasty from Franconia. When Henry II died, a power struggle ensued among his cousins, and in the end Conrad II of Franconia was elected by his peers in 1024. The new Franconian, or Salian, dynasty that he founded brought Germany to the peak of its powers in the Middle Ages. Unlike his Saxon predecessors, Conrad had no real interest in promoting the church; he preferred to use statesmanship to build up the power of the monarchy.

First, he promoted a group of lesser nobles to administrative positions, called *Ministeriales*. To cement their loyalty, he gave them special privileges, made their fiefs hereditary, and let them communicate with him directly rather than through the tribal dukes or the counts. He often appointed these men to fill positions vacated by the clergy. Similarly, as former royal landholdings became available, he reclaimed them for his personal domain. He gave such lands to his relatives, then often appointed them to the clergy so the land would eventually revert to the crown. Often he demanded tribute from these clergy, a form of kickback known as simony. Using this strategy, he was able to gain control of all the tribal dukedoms but Saxony and Lorraine, and to moderate the influence of the German church.

His weakness lay in his relationship to Italy. He had to go to Rome to be anointed as emperor, and that meant that he had to maintain power over the Italian cities and nobility as well. But by the eleventh century the Italian cities of Pisa and Genoa in the north were growing wealthy, powerful, and restive, and they were tired of German domination. At one point they even offered the crown of Italy to the kings of France and Acquitaine (southwestern France). Conrad responded with a familiar strategy: he created lesser Italian nobles (*valvassores*) similar to his ministeriales to pry their loyalty away from the great Italian lords (*capitanei*). Wisely, he did not try to weaken the clergy in Italy. With the support of the *valvassores* and the bishops, he asserted control over the northern portion of the peninsula. In 1027 he staged a brilliant coronation pageant in Rome, which was attended by Canute the Great, king of Denmark, Norway, and England, and the king of Burgundy.

By the eleventh century, a new, more structured Europe was coming into its own. The Muslim Umayyad Caliphate in Spain was disintegrating. Monarchies were consolidating England and France. The new stability led to population growth and the development of new towns. Markets and fairs, often sponsored by the kings and great lords, expanded internal and long-distance trade along the great rivers. The Vikings had opened trade routes in the Baltic and down the Russian rivers to the Black Sea. Venice, perched on a lagoon at the head of the Adriatic, pushed European maritime trade down the Balkan coast to Constantinople and even to the Middle East. Constantinople traded actively through the Black Sea and the Mediterranean. In the Middle East, Aleppo and Baghdad were the western terminals of the arduous Silk Road to China, and eager to trade their goods with Europe.

The beneficiary of the new economic and social prosperity was Henry

III (1039–1056). He was the first German emperor to take power without a rebellion. Thanks to his father's land policies, he inherited the southern duchies and Burgundy. Henry reformed the court and church, and even proclaimed a Day of Indulgence to forgive all his enemies. Maintaining a firm hand, he continued to use the *Ministeriales* as administrators and the bishops as advisors. He subdued Poland, Hungary, and Bohemia, making them pay homage. In 1046 he called a number of church synods in order to gain control of the papal election. Claiming the right, as emperor, to nominate the pope, he had sufficient power to depose three elected popes in order to make his own selection. Under the guidance of his choice, Pope Leo IX, the college of cardinals was reformed and the political power of the papacy was extended into southern Italy.

The security of the German imperial state required internal peace, collaboration with the pope, and peace with the neighboring states. Henry III attained all these, and was, without doubt, the strongest of the German medieval rulers. But his very strength created a backlash. At his death in 1056, he was succeeded by his 6-year-old son, and all the emperor's enemies took advantage of that weakness.

Henry IV's long reign (1056–1106) was incredibly turbulent. In 1062 he was kidnapped by Anno, the archbishop of Cologne, who proclaimed himself regent. Anno then divided up the monasterial lands between himself and the archbishop of Bremen. At the Diet of Tribur in 1066, the other clergy and nobility finally forced an end to Anno's control, and Henry began to rule in his own right. The 16-year-old monarch was intelligent and headstrong, but possessed courage and political cunning. He began his reign by draining the churches of their revenues and requiring payments in exchange for appointments. The clergy appealed to Rome to intervene.

Henry next alienated the nobility by trying to extend the land and population directly under monarchical control. He used internal colonization—founding towns and giving privileges to the people who settled there in exchange for the right of taxation—to build the revenues of royal lands. He even planted royal colonies in the duchies, erecting castles in strategic areas and conscripting local workers and freemen. Then he garrisoned the castles with loyal troops who forced the countryside to provision them. This was a threat to the traditional manorial economy and disquieted the peasants as well as their overlords.

This astute strategy was being used to good advantage by the Capetian dynasty in France, but in Germany it created a constitutional crisis. Henry was trying to build central power by establishing himself as a landowner on a par with the great dukes and counts. The dukes would have none of it. In 1073 they rebelled and plotted to elect a counter king. Confronted by hostile forces, Henry boldly promised he would stop these policies if the nobles destroyed their castles. Then he made a direct appeal for popular support, granting the merchants of Worms exemption from tolls. It was the first time a German emperor had given a charter directly to the people without going through a bishop or feudal lord. The upshot was a dreadful civil war that Henry won, in 1075, over an exhausted and divided Saxony.

But Pope Gregory VII (1073–1085) had his own agenda for establishing the papacy as a form of universal Christian monarchy. He declared the infallibility of the church and asserted the right of the pope, exclusively, to control the appointment of bishops and synods (church meetings) and the right to depose the emperor. Gregory wanted to cooperate with the emperor, but not at the expense of his own religious principles. Henry, locked in war with his nobility, promised reforms. Once he overcame his enemies, however, he reneged. Fearing for their positions, the German bishops rejected Gregory's proposals and held their own synod at Worms in 1076. They declared the pope deposed. Henry joined in by sending an insulting letter to Rome demanding Gregory's resignation. Gregory responded by excommunicating Henry IV and all the bishops who supported him. The pope then demanded that all of Henry's subjects, for the sake of their immortal souls, end their allegiance to the monarch.

This papal counterattack created chaos in Germany, sparking a Saxon rebellion, uniting the feudal magnates and splitting the clergy. The powerful feudal nobles wanted to try Henry, and called for Pope Gregory to preside. Some nobles elected an anti-king to replace Henry IV. At issue, formally, was the right of the king to create bishoprics without prior approval by the pope, a practice called lay investiture. The conflict struck at the very nature of the imperial office as defined by the Carolingian kings—the divine right of the anointed ruler, the coequality of emperor and pope, and the integration of church and state. But there were constitutional issues at stake, as well. The nobility were willing to ally with the pope if it helped prevent the emperor from encroaching on their own territories and building the authority to control them.

Henry IV met the challenge dramatically. In one of the most famous scenes of German history, he dashed off to Italy to confront the pope. In the deep cold of January, 1077, he appeared for three days at the pope's castle of Canossa. Barefoot and contrite, dressed in sackcloth and ashes, he stood as a penitent before Pope Gregory. He begged the pope to forgive him as a Christian sinner. It was pure theater, and Gregory knew it, yet he ultimately relented and lifted the ban of excommunication. Henry returned home, dealt summarily with the rebellious nobles, and continued to appoint his own bishops. By 1085 he controlled virtually every bishop in his kingdom. When Pope Gregory again excommuni- cated Henry in 1080, the German bishops supported the emperor and declared the pope deposed. Henry then took an army to Italy and drove the pope into exile. Gregory died in Sicily that same year.

Pope Gregory's tough new stand had reinvigorated the church, how- ever. His successor, Pope Urban II (1088–1099) began his reign by issuing the Dictatus Papae. This formal declaration stipulated that the pope alone had the right to appoint bishops; that his legates (diplomatic rep- resentatives) were superior to the bishops in council; and that no church meeting or actions were legitimate without his approval. Urban also claimed important temporal powers: the sole right to use the insignia of the empire and the right to depose emperors, to annul their decrees, and to release subjects from their allegiance to "wicked rulers." As pope, he declared, he could be judged by no one.

Urban's proclamation capped several decades of church reform, which had seen a formal break between the Roman Catholic and the Orthodox Byzantine church (1054) and the establishment of the College of Cardinals (1059) to formalize the process of papal election. The move- ment, begun in the Benedictine monastery at Cluny, to strengthen the religious discipline in the monasteries had resulted in a renewal of in- terest in the cloistered life. New orders were founded, including the Car- thusian (1084) and Cistercian (1094). The image of the Christian knight, the warrior of God against the pagans and infidels, began to form the concept of chivalry.

In 1095 Pope Urban issued an exhilarating challenge to the knights of western Europe to crusade to save Jerusalem from the Persians and Mus- lims who occupied it. His words were electrifying: the "alien race . . . has destroyed the churches of God . . . destroy[ed] altars after having defiled them. . . . When they wish to torture people by a base death, they per- forate their navels, and, dragging forth their intestines, bind them to a stake; then with whipping they force the victim to walk until the viscera runs forth and the Christian dies."[1] For those who would take up the call "God wills it," he promised remission of their sins and a place in heaven. He launched a holy war.

Urban delivered his call during a meeting at Clermont, in France. The response to the call for a crusade was unprecedented. Between 25,000 and 30,000 knights and warriors, mainly from France, Normandy, and Sicily, left for Constantinople. They drove southward through Syria and, after three years, captured Jerusalem itself (1099). Showing no Christian mercy, they viciously slaughtered all Muslims and Jews they found there. An eyewitness reported that the streets ran ankle deep in blood. For those who stayed in the Holy Land, there were feudal land grants from the four new Roman Catholic crusader states.

Notably, there was little appreciable participation by German knights in the First Crusade. In 1093, backed by the pope, Henry's sons rebelled against him in both Germany and Italy. The conflicts absorbed the knights throughout the realm. During the remaining years of his reign, Henry IV had to contend with this betrayal. In the end, he was imprisoned by his sons and forced to abdicate. He died in 1106.

His son and successor, Henry V, has been dubbed the "least likable of all German rulers." Inheriting the throne of a land ravaged by years of almost continual warfare, he imposed new taxes to support his unsuccessful campaigns against Poland and Hungary. Seeking the support of the feudal aristocracy, he began delegating considerable civil authority to his favorites. This group were henceforth known as the German princes (from the Latin term *princeps*). They could administer justice, finances, and military affairs within their jurisdictions, which were hereditary. In essence, the princes combined some of the military authority of the tribal dukes with civil powers of the counts and *Ministeriales*. They claimed superiority over the other nobility and fought to establish it. In the end, rather than strengthening the monarchy through the support of this powerful new nobility, Henry V created another layer of opposition to the powers of the king.

Henry V continued the practice of lay investiture, thus alienating the papacy. Therefore, he led a military campaign into Italy in 1110 to claim his coronation as emperor, imprisoning the pope and cardinals to force them to pay homage to him. In 1122 Henry and the pope negotiated an end to the conflict over lay investiture. The Concordat of Worms recognized that in Germany the bishops had both a civil and a clerical role. It instituted a process of double investiture, the emperor conferring the territory and the administrative office, the pope designating the spiritual and clerical authority. In Germany it left the clergy and its property under the thumb of the emperor. It did not end the rivalry between the emperor and the pope; it served mainly as a truce.

Henry V was the last of the Salian kings. He died in 1125 without an heir. The conflict over the succession exposed the new balance of power in the German kingdom. In their quest for a centralized monarchy, the Salian kings had broken the back of the old tribal duchies. But through the creation of the *Ministeriales* and princes, they had created a new form of aristocracy far more wedded to territory and administration than the old military potentates. These were the nobility who had opposed Henry IV and elected the anti-king. They now sided with the bishops of the reformed German church and demanded the right to elect the new king. Ignoring the tradition of hereditary succession, they passed over Frederick Hohenstaufen of Swabia for Lothair of Saxony. Lothair was an old man with no sons. Therefore, the next succession would strengthen the Germanic principle of electing the king.

In the interregnum period between the dynasties, Lothair II (1125–1137) ruled. He was a realist who was aware of his political debts. He abandoned the Salian policy of trying to centralize the power of the monarchy, preserving the rights of the nobility to rule in their jurisdictions. He acknowledged papal supremacy by asking the pope to sanction his election. These policies broke the principle of the hereditary monarchy. However, he married his daughter to the Bavarian duke Henry the Proud in the hope of establishing a dynasty of his own. This alignment of the pope, the Saxon royal house, and the Bavarian duke became a faction known as the Welfs (sometimes written in the Italian form, *Guelph*), after Duke Henry's family. Opposition to it coalesced around Frederick Hohenstaufen of Swabia, whose hereditary rights had been ignored, and his brother Conrad. That faction became known as Waiblinger (*Ghibellines*, in Italian), after the Hohenstaufens' main town. Throughout Germany and Italy, the nobility divided their loyalties in a civil war that lasted until 1135.

Hohenstaufen Dynasty. Lothair had hoped that his son-in-law, Henry the Proud, would succeed him. But Henry was deemed far too powerful by the nobility. Asserting their electoral prerogative, they selected the Hohenstaufen candidate, Conrad III (1138–1152). The Welfs were outraged and continued the civil war. Conrad counterattacked by the old feudal policy of dividing and claiming the lands of his enemies. But he also added a new constitutional element, a decree that prevented ducal families from having holdings in more than one duchy. When Henry the Proud refused to choose between Bavaria and Saxony, he was deposed. His son, Henry the Lion, continued the fight.

Conrad III did not seek coronation by the Welf pope. He did, however, follow St. Bernard on the futile Second Crusade (1147–1148) to recover

Christian lands lost to the Muslims in the Holy Land. Henry the Lion, meanwhile, sought to add to his own power by launching a crusade against the Slavs along the eastern borders. He colonized conquered holdings east of the Elbe in Brandenburg and Pomerania. The civil war continued through Conrad's reign. When he died, the electors selected his nephew, Frederick Barbarossa (red beard), a charismatic warrior and true knight, as his successor.

Frederick I (1152–1190) holds the place in German history that King Arthur holds in English tradition. Through charismatic but decisive leadership, he calmed the civil war by awarding lands to his Welf adversaries. Henry the Lion kept Bavaria, Saxony, and his new territories east of the Elbe, Austria became an independent duchy. In 1155 Frederick obtained the imperial title from the pope and began calling his realm the Holy Roman Empire. At the Diet of Regensburg in 1156 he acknowledged the role of the princes as electors, thus confirming their constitutional role in the state.

Frederick consolidated his holdings in Franconia and Swabia. He swapped or bought land and rights from the nobility and the clergy. As the crown accumulated administrative rights, it organized a bureaucracy based on districts—individuals given the rights of office but not a fief. New titles appeared: *Burggraf*, the administrator of a town and the surrounding district, *Schultheiss*, the representative for the town; *Landgericht* for the regional court, and so forth. With the new administrative structure, Frederick pursued a course of internal colonization and economic development of towns and cities. This increased the number of "free peasants" subject to the local government rather than to the feudal ties of serfdom. Significantly, the Hohenstaufens gained most of their crown income from direct taxation of town districts.

In 1184, in a brilliant medieval pageant, Frederick conferred knighthood on his two sons, Henry and Philip. Two years later, Henry was married to the daughter of the King of Sicily, and proclaimed as his heir and caesar. Then Frederick, as a true knight of Christendom, joined King Richard the Lion Heart of England and Philip Augustus, King of France, to lead the Third Crusade (1189–1193). He drowned in 1190 without ever having reached the Holy Land. Thus he became legend: Germans denied his death, saying that he was only sleeping in the Kyffhaeuser Mountain, and would awake some day to lead Germany to greatness.

The reign of Henry VI (1190–1197) renewed the struggle between the Welf and the Waiblinger. For the next fifteen years there were two contenders for the crown, and civil war throughout Germany and Italy. At last Henry's son, Frederick II (1212–1250) gained the crown. An arrogant but charming scholar, raised in Sicily with little German tradition, he immediately promised the pope to keep his Italian and German crowns separate and to relinquish the appointment of bishops. Then, allied with Philip II of France, he helped defeat the Welf forces (allied with King John of England) at the 1214 Battle of Bouvines. King John's defeat was one of the blows that led the English barons to demand the Magna Carta the following year.

Brilliant in law and science, Frederick II was called *Stupor Mundi*, "the wonder of the world." But he spent only a few months of his long reign in Germany. He devoted most of his efforts to the weakening the pope and to building Sicily. His son, Henry, managed Germany. Frederick appeased the Germans by granting new levels of judicial and economic authority to the princes. He also increased colonization of new lands in the east, often using the Teutonic Knights to do so. The 1231 Privilege of Worms decree gave the nobility virtually sovereign power. When his son, Henry, led a rebellion of the German towns, Frederick defeated him in 1235. Henry was imprisoned and eventually committed suicide. Frederick II then left Germany, never to return. As a result of his efforts to control the Italian papacy, the popes branded him an anti-Christ, excommunicating him, fomenting assassination plots, and calling for his subjects to rebel.

At Frederick's death in 1250, Pope Innocent III declared a crusade against the Hohenstaufens. Conrad IV lasted only four years (1250–1254), and another period of civil war ensued. Conrad's son Conradin, the last of the Hohenstaufen dynasty, was captured and executed in Naples when he tried to claim possession of Sicily. With him died the possibility of a centralized German monarchy. Neither the pope nor the German princes wanted a strong ruler. If Germany was not to fragment entirely, it needed a monarch weak enough to agree to accept the privileges of the princes and papal control of the church. There was neither an heir nor a great dynastic house directly in line for the throne. The electoral process thus took primacy. The princes turned to foreign candidates, but they could not agree on one. Richard of Cornwall, brother of the English king, and Alphonso X of Castile both reigned from 1257 to 1272. Neither was crowned emperor by the pope, however. In 1272 the monarchy was vacant, and the only way to fill it was by election. The princes had control of the empire.

Indeed, it was the pope who began to press for the election of a German prince. With the Mongols invading from Asia, it was important to have a coherent state in central Europe. At his urging, the electors met in Frankfurt. They selected a Swiss prince, a marshall in the Bohemian court with a reputation as a fine Christian knight: Rudolf Hapsburg. He founded a dynasty that remained in power until 1806 in Germany and until 1918 in Austria.

Hapsburg Dynasty. Rudolf was an astute politician. Recognizing the weakness of the monarchy, he used it not to expand territory but instead to strengthen the position of his family. He made concessions of land in Italy and Sicily to the pope in order to obtain his recognition in 1275; he married three of his six daughters to imperial electors and the other three almost as advantageously. He used his position and his armies to organize lands and power in south Germany and Austria for his sons. Yet despite his ambition, Rudolf had never taken time for an official coronation. His death in 1291 left the empire, once again, in the hands of the electors.

The electors had no wish to increase the strength of the Hapsburgs. Denying the succession to Rudolf's son Albert, they elected Adolf of Nassau (1292–1298). But Adolf immediately lost control of the Swiss Forest cantons, which rebelled and formed an independent confederation in 1291. He also allied Germany with England in its conflict with France. In 1298 the electors deposed him and turned, at last, to Albert Hapsburg. During his brief reign (1298–1308), he aligned himself with France, attacked the power of the clergy, and took over the crown of Bohemia. The electors turned next to Henry of Luxumbourg (1308–1313), and then to Ludwig Wittelsbach of Bavaria. As Ludwig IV (1314–1347), he sought to strengthen the empire. He was opposed by France and the papacy (since 1309 moved to Avignon in France). In 1338, at Rense, the electors agreed that the imperial election no longer required papal sanction. The Diet concurred. But the papacy refused to acknowledge Ludwig IV, and in 1346 he was deposed.

The fourteenth century was an era of tumult and trouble in western Europe. France had forced the papacy to leave Italy (the Babylonian Captivity in Avignon, 1309–1376), and the papacy was further troubled by the claims of conflicting popes (the Great Schism, 1378–1417); England and France fought over English feudal holdings in France (Hundred Years' War, 1337–1453), the Black Death (bubonic plague) swept up from Italy to claim from one-third to one-half of the population; and the Muslims finally overwhelmed the Christian Byzantine capital at Constantinople.

Internally fragmented, further divided by electoral and religious conflicts, Germany was unable either to consolidate or to take advantage of the weaknesses of its neighbors. Even the pope's Golden Bull (1356), setting the imperial election procedures and fixing the seven electors (bishops of Mainz, Trier, and Cologne; the count of the Rhineland Palatinate, margrave of Brandenburg, duke of Saxony, and king of Bohemia to be hereditary), did not significantly strengthen the monarchy. Rent by private wars among the nobility and the imperial towns, Germany approached a state of anarchy. The Hapsburgs were returned by the election of Albert II in 1438, who had a number of reform ideas. In 1439 he and the pope agreed to leave the German church under imperial control, but his early death halted the reform movement. His successor, Frederick III (1440–1493), was the last emperor crowned by the pope in the imperial city. Little else distinguished his reign.

Maximilian I, who succeeded his father in 1493, began an effort to revitalize the structure of the Holy Roman Empire. In addition to his control of traditional Hapsburg lands in Austria, Maximilian had gained Burgundy, with its wealthy Flemish cities, by marriage. His son Philip married the Spanish heiress. This wealth gave power to his title, and it was he who enacted Albert's proposed reforms. At the Diet of Worms (1495) his Proclamation of Peace and the establishment of the Imperial Chamber (*Reichskammergericht*) put an end to private wars and created a legal chamber to resolve disputes between states as well as individuals. The Aulic Council he established (1501) functioned like a royal court of appeals. Through the Diet of Cologne, 1512, the empire was divided into ten Circles (*Landfriedenskreise*) for more efficient administration: (1) Austria, (2) Bavaria, (3) Franconia, (4) Swabia, (5) Upper Rhine, (6) Lower Rhine, (7) Burgundy, (8) Upper Saxony, (9) Lower Saxony, and (10) Westphalia. These circles had both military and civilian organization, and each paid a tax assessment to fund the imperial army. The Diets themselves functioned more effectively through three colleges, the first consisting of the seven electors, the second representing the secular and clerical princes, and the third consisting of the imperial towns. Maximilian's many successes were marred only by the loss of Switzerland, to which he was forced to concede independence in 1499. Maximilian died in 1519. He was succeeded by his 17-year-old grandson Charles, who had already become King of Spain in 1516. The youth became Emperor Charles V of Germany.

The Reformation. Charles V inherited the vast empire of Spain (Spain, Naples, America) and Burgundy (the Netherlands and southeastern France) as well as the Hapsburg holdings in southern Germany and Austria. As he sought electoral approval for the German title, however, he had also to contend with the religious movement started in 1517 by Martin Luther. Luther, a priest and professor in Wittenberg, sought reforms in the Catholic church. He stated his protests in the 95 Theses, which he nailed to the door of the church at Wittenberg. Luther refused to relent, despite orders by the bishop of Augsburg to do so; he appealed, instead, to the pope. In 1519 the pope issued a bull condemning 41 of Luther's points. It was at this point that Charles was elected Holy Roman Emperor. Loans from the powerful Fugger family, Bavarian bankers and merchants, had helped him buy electoral favor over competing claims from Francis I of France and Henry VIII of England.

In 1520, when the pope excommunicated Luther, Charles went to Germany. He was earnest and devout, and held the dream of uniting Europe in a unified Roman Catholic empire. At the Diet of Worms (1521) he heard Luther out, then pronounced him outlaw in the Empire for his disobedient demands. The Edict of Worms also outlawed all new religious doctrines. But the Duke of Saxony gave Luther sanctuary at the Wartburg Castle at Erfurt. There Luther completed his translation of the Bible into German and began to elaborate the tenets of Lutheranism, including justification by faith alone and elimination of the priesthood. His movement began to spread in north Germany, especially in imperial towns and in Prussia, Brandenburg, Schleswig, and Braunschweig. In Switzerland, Ulrich Zwingli led a similar Protestant movement.

Much of Charles's long reign (1519–1555) was disturbed by conflict that frustrated his great plan. From 1521 to 1526 he fought with Francis I of France over lands he claimed in Burgundy and Italy, defeating the French king at the Battle of Pavia. In southern Germany the Peasants' War blazed from 1524 to 1525 as peasants followed Luther's model. They demanded the right to elect their priests and raised protest against the abuses of feudalism. They were branded "mad dogs" by Luther, however, and brutally suppressed. From 1526 to 1532 the Empire staved off the Turks. In 1527 war with France resumed, fought mainly in Italy, where Charles's unruly forces took and ransacked Rome, angering the pope. The conflict was settled by the Peace of Cambrai (1529), by which Francis paid an indemnity and renounced his claims to Italy. Indeed, Charles was so preoccupied by war that he postponed his imperial coronation until 1530. It took place in Bologna, and was the last imperial coronation by the pope.

In Germany, however, the religious dissension had bred political rebellion. Following the Diet of Sepia in 1529, demanding strict enforcement of the Edict of Worms, the Lutheran princes objected, earning the brand Protestants. In their name, Philip Malanchthon presented the Augsburg Confession to a Diet at Augsburg in an abortive attempt at reconciliation with the Catholic Church. In 1531 Protestants formed the Schmalkaldic League of Protestant princes and imperial cities and prepared to take up arms. Because the Turks had just renewed their attacks on the empire, Charles relented in the hope of unity, and allowed religious freedom until another council could be held. In 1536 Charles led another campaign against Francis, who, in pursuit of claims in northern Italy, allied with Sulieman, the Turkish ruler. Pressed on two fronts, Charles accepted the Truce of Nice (1538). After a four-year respite, Francis again allied with Sulieman, and war between the Empire and France resumed. Charles gained support from Henry VIII of England, and the two forces fought to a standstill. By the Treaty of Crespy (1544) each renounced claims on the other's territory. Francis died three years later.

Charles turned to the religious dissidents in the Empire. Further elaboration of Lutheran doctrine had given responsibility for church affairs to the local ruler, not the emperor. Charles was determined to eliminate these heretics. The Schmalkaldic War broke out (1546–1547), and he defeated them at the Battle of Muehlberg (1547). But Protestant uprisings continued. Exhausted, Charles finally agreed to the interim Peace of Augsburg in 1552, recognizing the Protestants as well as their acquisitions of formerly Catholic lands and property. This was reaffirmed by the Peace of Augsburg, 1555, which legalized both Catholicism and Lutheranism (but only those denominations) in the Empire on the basis of *cuius regio, eius religio* (whoever rules in the territory determines which religion it shall have). Thus the religious settlement reinforced the preexisting political fragmentation of the German states, and even accentuated it. The local rulers gained power over church affairs, and were not required to afford toleration of individuals of other faiths within their realms. This left them free to persecute other sects, such as Calvinists and Anabaptists, which began to emerge after 1530.

Charles was a medieval rather than a modern ruler. He looked back to the Roman imperial model to integrate the Catholic Church and the state in one mighty unit. He yearned for the medieval synthesis. But he sought this goal just as the forces of religious reform and political modernization were taking hold in Europe, challenging the power of the church and defining the monarchical nation-state. Thus the non-German lands escaped his grasp, and within Germany, the princes modeled their own ambitions on the achievements of the British, Spanish, and French monarchs. Rather than draw together, the German Empire threatened to fall apart. It certainly fell behind in political change.

Even the Catholic Church modernized more effectively than Germany. The church initiatives identified as the Counter-Reformation began with the establishment of a reform commission in 1536, the Universal Inquisition in 1542, and the convening of the Council of Trent in 1545. The Jesuit order, founded by Ignatius Loyola of Spain in 1534, complemented papal action by providing highly educated militant missionaries to contest the heretical beliefs in debate and to spread the Catholic faith. Reforming popes, such as Paul III (1534–1549) and Paul IV (1555–1559), laid the foundations for a more modern, more effective papacy. Sixtus V (1585–1590) updated church finances, reformed the College of Cardinals, and authorized a new edition of the Vulgate Bible. While the church did not substantially change the doctrines to which the Protestants objected, it strengthened itself internally and among the faithful, and adjusted its relationships to the new national states.

The German Empire did not fare so well. In 1556, exhausted, Charles divided, then abdicated, his many offices. He relinquished the Spanish crown and holdings in Spain, Italy, and America to his son, Philip. The imperial crown went to his brother, Ferdinand. The Hapsburg holdings were thus permanently separated. German affairs were thereafter handled by the Austrian branch of the dynasty, working with the Imperial Diet. Ferdinand I (1558–1564) and Maximilian II (1564–1576) were preoccupied by wars on the Austrian borders with the Turks, and softpedaled their relations with the northern states. Rudolf II (1576–1612), however, was a rigid and militant defender of Catholic prerogatives, and religious tensions began to mount. A Protestant League, led by the Palatine elector, and a Catholic League, led by the duke of Bavaria, began to define the opposing sides. Disputes between them, such as the War of Succession in Juelich-Cleves (1609–1614) had the effect of expanding tensions rather than resolving them. The brief reign of Emperor Matthias (1612–1619) avoided major conflict, but his cousin and successor, Ferdinand II (1619–1637), had been educated by the Jesuits and was determined to assert Catholic authority in the Empire. When he became king (and elector) of Protestant Bohemia in 1617, he started demanding conformity.

Thirty Years' War. The conflict known as the Thirty Years' War (1618–1648) may be seen as the last struggle between the centralizing forces of the emperor and Catholic Church against the decentralizing forces of the German princes and the Protestants. It started in Prague, Bohemia, when two of Ferdinand's Catholic envoys were tossed out the palace window (the "defenestration" of Prague) by the Protestant governors. They appealed to other Protestant princes for support, and the Protestants defeated the imperial armies in two battles in 1618. Ferdinand marched on Vienna, and narrowly avoiding capture, continued to Frankfurt, where he was elected emperor. The Bohemians deposed him as king, electing Frederick of the Palatinate to replace him. Known as the "Winter King," Frederick, like the Duke of Prussia, had become a Calvinist, a Protestant denomination not permitted by the Peace of Augsburg. Ferdinand had support from Bavaria, Spain, and Poland. His Catholic League, led by the formidable General Tilly, resoundingly defeated the Protestants at the Battle of White Mountain (1620) in Bohemia, and spread the conflict to the German Palatinate. The Protestant Union had to disband, and through the early 1620s, the Catholics gained the upper hand.

The conflict widened as Christian IV, the Danish king and a Protestant, took up the cause in 1625. Tilly and the imperial commander Wallenstein, who had defeated the Hungarian Protestants, defeated Christian IV in 1626 and pushed into the Danish peninsula and Pomerania. The Treaty of Luebeck (1629) returned Danish lands to Christian on his promise not to intervene in German affairs. On the strength of these victories, Ferdinand issued the Edict of Restitution in 1629, claiming back from Protestant hands a number of bishoprics and territories that they had secularized since 1522. This was not just a religious act; it was highly political, in that the emperor proclaimed law without consulting the Diet. Even some Catholic princes were angered by this usurpation of power. The nature of the conflict shifted from Protestant versus Catholic to princes versus the emperor.

The conflict widened again as Gustavus II Adolphus of Sweden, supported by France, entered the war on the Protestant side in 1630. Gustavus hoped to expand his holdings in the mainland Baltic regions to include Pomerania and Prussia. His forces pushed forward from Pomerania, defeated Tilly at Leipzig the following year, and pushed toward the Rhine. Tilly was killed in 1632, and Wallenstein had to hold back the Swedes. Late in 1632 Gustavus was killed at the Battle of Luetzen, near Leipzig. His chancellor, Axel Oxenstierna, continued the struggle. But the Swedes were badly defeated by the Spanish army in 1635. By now the conflict had become an international one, in addition to the civil war in Germany. When the German princes signed the Peace of Prague with the emperor in 1635, Catholic France, in support of the Protestants, declared war on Spain! During the final thirteen years, Holland, France, and Sweden fought the Holy Roman Emperor and Spain on German soil. The German states swung back and forth, making their own alliances and agreements in defiance of the emperor. Peace negotiations going on in the background took five years to finalize.

The Treaty of Westphalia (1648) that ended this conflict also ended Hapsburg hopes of wedding the German states into a centralized monarchical state. What emerged was a surprisingly modern, secular agreement. The religious balance of 1618 was still almost intact, protected once again by the principle of *cuius regio, eius religio*; however, Calvinism was accepted along with Lutheranism and Catholicism. But the major principle established by this treaty was that of the sovereign state—government control of both territory and people. More than three hundred territorial rulers attended the proceedings, so many, in fact, that the actual signing had to take place in two cities: Osnabrueck and Muenster. Each of the states was recognized as a sovereign entity, equal to the others irrespective of size, with the right to control its relations with other states, including foreign states. The Germans were prohibited only from making alliances against the Empire and the emperor. Although the participants in Westphalia recognized the continuation of the Empire, they demanded that all imperial legislation require the approval of the Diet. That meant that the emperor would have to work hard to gain German support for levying taxes, raising troops, or concluding diplomatic agreements. The emperor retained his feudal rights to collect fees for awarding feudal land and privileges to the aristocracy, but his power came from his role in Austria, not from the imperial office.

The Treaty of Westphalia ended, for the time being, the efforts of the old German dynasties to unify and centralize the Holy Roman Empire. It froze the German constitution at the level of medieval anarchy, making central Europe one of the weakest areas of the continent, wide open to ambitious neighbors such as Louis XIV of France. While the English Civil War and Glorious Revolution (1642–1688) and the French Revolution (1789–1799) helped define the national character and constitutions of those countries, Germany remained fragmented. Political experimentation could take place only at the individual state level, with little or no effect on Germany as a whole. If anything, Germany was even more divided than it had been during the era of the tribal dukes, when the dynastic struggle began. There seemed no possibility of forming a nation out of this complex mosaic.

NOTE

1. "Pope Urban's Speech at Clermont Concerning the Crusades against the Moslems." In Paul L. Hughes and Robert F. Fries, *European Civilization: Basic Historical Documents* (Totowa, NJ: Littlefield, Adams & Co., 1972), p. 27.

4

The Rise and Impact of Prussia

Although the Holy Roman Empire was ineffective in controlling the German states, it was still indispensable to them. Participation in the Imperial Diet gave even the smallest of the approximately 300 states a voice and sources of potential support. It placed politics above religion and established the basis for princely despotism. This gave rise to local courts, little armies and new taxing opportunities. If not powerful, the hundreds of German petty princes were certainly busy centralizing their authority in the seventeenth century. This generally occurred at the expense of the rural peasantry and townsmen, who had virtually no voice at court. It was the Age of Absolutism. King Louis XIV of France is perhaps its greatest symbol. It resulted in brilliant cultural advances as the states competed with each other for prominence, but perpetuated the territorial and political fragmentation of the German people. In Germany the Age of Absolutism began the contest between Prussia and Austria for control of central Europe.

As the largest German territorial state and the seat of the emperor, Austria and its capital city, Vienna, retained their importance. The German Catholic states of the south and the Rhineland looked to Catholic Austria as their protector. The Spanish Hapsburgs, who controlled the Netherlands (Belgium), Luxembourg, and France Comté in the western Empire, supported the emperor. By arranging for an electoral seat for Bavaria, Austria had assured a Catholic majority (with the three bishoprics) among the electors. Indeed, until the demise of the Holy Roman Empire in 1806, this majority virtually assured that the imperial dignity would remain in Hapsburg hands.

The medium-sized electoral states also benefited from the decisions at Westphalia. The Catholic Wittelsbach dynasty in Bavaria created a glittering southern capital at Munich. Protestant Dresden, on the Elbe, flourished as the Baroque jewel of the Wettin dynasty of Saxony. The elector of Saxony also ruled Poland as Augustus II (1697–1733). In the northeast, the Hohenzollern elector of Prussia held Brandenburg and Pomerania on the sandy north German plain. He also ruled Prussian territories east and outside of the Empire, lands once colonized by the Teutonic knights along the Baltic coast between the Vistula and Memel Rivers. The Hohenzollern capital, Berlin, was undistinguished by comparison with the others, but held the seeds of Germany's most powerful state.

Absolutism in Prussia. Frederick William, "the Great Elector" (1640–1688), organized absolutism in Brandenburg. He gave the landed nobility, called Junkers, rights within their own holdings to enserf their peasantry, sit as judges, and appoint local clergy. In return they granted him funds, mainly by taxing the towns, to build an army. Frederick William built a strong officer corps and administrative bureaucracy without constant appeal to the Estates (the nobles' assembly) for funds. He kept Junker loyalty by appointing nobility to elite posts in both establishments. Thus, while the peasantry and townsmen paid the price, Frederick William and the Junkers developed the apparatus of a centralized government.

Frederick William used his strength well. Sweden's King Charles X invaded Poland in an attempt to expand his holdings on the continent. Siding first with Sweden, then with Poland, the elector maneuvered for advantage during the Northern War (1655–1660). When Charles X died in 1660, the Treaty of Oliva gave Elector William full sovereignty in Prussia. His army had gained a favorable reputation as well. In 1675, when the Swedes once again invaded Brandenburg, the Prussians defeated them handily at Fehrbellin, and won strategic points in Swedish Pomerania. Though still too weak diplomatically to retain those territories, Brandenburg-Prussia was clearly a rising military power.

Frederick William's son, Elector Frederick III (1688–1713), took few concrete measures to build government power. He much preferred the elegant cultural life of a Baroque ruler. Yet his support for the emperor during the dynastic war between Louis XIV of France and Emperor Leopold I (War of the Spanish Succession 1701–1714) earned him the title of king in Prussia from his grateful ally. Because Prussia lay outside the Empire, it cost Leopold little. Frederick celebrated the rise in status by crowning himself King Frederick I on January 18, 1701, in Koenigsberg.

The main goal of his son and successor, Frederick William I (1713–1740), was to increase Brandenburg-Prussia's limited powers. He restructured the administration under the General Directory and declared his lands indivisible. He reorganized finances and doubled the size of his army to over 80,000 men by the time of his death in 1740. It was one of the largest armies in Europe, although Prussia's population was less than three million. The majority of his budget was spent on the military, and Prussia was sometimes laughingly called an army with a country. The king even had men over six feet tall kidnapped to fill his brigades! Yet his reign was, for the times, remarkably peaceful. While Austria battled with the Turks and was embroiled with Russia against France, Spain, and Sardinia over Polish succession, Frederick William I kept his troops at home, preferring them to represent power rather than exert it.

War of the Austrian Succession (1740–1748). Meanwhile, it was becoming clear that Emperor Charles VI (1711–1740) would have no male heir, which threatened the Austrian Hapsburg succession. In 1718–1719 the Empire, France, Britain, and Holland concluded a Quadruple Alliance to maintain peace following the War of the Spanish Succession. Charles persuaded his diplomatic partners also to endorse the Pragmatic Sanction, a three-point plan to preserve the Austrian Hapsburg line. The signatories agreed to preserve the Hapsburgs' Austrian holdings; that Charles's daughter, Maria Theresa, could succeed him; and that her son, Joseph, would inherit the crown through the right of primogeniture (sole inheritance by the oldest son). Charles asked other rulers to accept it. Frederick William I endorsed it in 1728. Charles VI died in 1740.

Frederick William I died the same year. His son, Frederick II (1740–1786), seemed an unlikely heir to the "Soldier-King." He preferred music and intellectual pursuits to military routine, and Europe expected him to adopt the cultured, luxuriant court style of his grandfather. Frederick did introduce many of the ideas of the Enlightenment spreading across Europe: religious toleration, elimination of torture and similar penalties from the judicial system, and relaxation of censorship. But he also added seven regiments to the Prussian army, and on December 16, 1740, used them to march southeast into Austrian Silesia. He violated the Pragmatic Sanction to make a "rendezvous with glory."

Whereas Frederick William I had avoided conflict, Frederick II had selected it as the way to make Prussia a great power. Indeed, his social, civil, and economic reforms were designed to increase Prussia's military strength. The War of the Austrian Succession (1740–1748) announced this strategy. Frederick II used diplomacy as well, building an alliance with France, Saxony, and Bavaria, whose Elector Charles Albert claimed the Hapsburg throne, to challenge the Pragmatic Sanction. The War of the Austrian Succession was fought from the Rhine to Bohemia. Maria Theresa based herself in Hungary, crowning herself Queen of Hungary in exchange for concessions to the Hungarian nobility (Magyars). Finally, she ceded Silesia to Prussia by treaty. Frederick then withdrew from the war, much to the resentment of his Saxon and Bavarian allies. But he resumed fighting in 1744 to protect his acquisition. The conflict expanded, bringing in Spain, the Netherlands, and even England. By the 1748 Treaty of Aix-la-Chapelle (Aachen), Prussia retained Silesia and Maria Theresa retained the throne. But it was clear that Prussia had joined the ranks of the European great powers and threatened Austrian leadership within the Empire.

The war nearly bankrupted Prussia. To disguise this weakness, Frederick commissioned a beautiful baroque residential palace in Potsdam, outside Berlin. In spirit, if not in size, it emulated Louis XIV's Versailles complex. Frederick even gave asylum to French Protestants (Huguenots), master craftsmen and merchants, to develop the palace and town. He named his new residence San Souci (Without a Care).

Seven Years' War (1756–1763). Maria Theresa schemed to recover Silesia. Reorganization of finances in Austria and Bohemia gave her sufficient funds to improve her army. The estates were forced to make long-term funding allocations; government representatives replaced the landlords as tax collectors and founded new district administrative offices. Central administration was reorganized as well, into the House, Court, and State Chancellery, with the judiciary separated from the administrative branch.

Maria Theresa used diplomacy to weave an alliance with Saxony, Russia, and England. (England's reigning family had come from Hanover in 1714 and still held land there.) In 1756, the French and Indian War (1756–1763) broke out in America, and England signed a defensive alliance with Prussia to protect Hanover. France joined the Austrian alliance, and thereby completed the Diplomatic Revolution, which reversed the alliance systems of 1740. Frederick, feeling surrounded, invaded Saxony and launched the European counterpart of the conflict, the Seven Years' War

(1756–1763). England, fighting the French in America and India, gave Prussia only financial assistance. Nevertheless, Frederick's armies were able to hold off the combined Austrian, French, Russian, and Saxon forces until the death of Russia's Czarina Elizabeth in 1762. Her successor, Peter III, admired Frederick II and withdrew Russia from the war. The Austrian alliance then fell apart and the conflict ended with the Treaty of Hubertusburg (1763). Frederick retained Silesia, but promised to support the succession of Joseph I in Austria. He had, however, proven that even the Austrian alliance system could not oust Prussia from the ranks of the great powers.

Frederick II, the Great. Thereafter, Frederick focused on domestic affairs. He expanded the General Directory by adding a Department of Commerce and a cabinet style of government of departmental ministers and bureaucratic officials. He unified the law codes and centralized the court system. He reorganized the treasury accounts into a complex administration to collect and handle taxes. His mercantilist economic policy was designed to accumulate wealth for the state by producing goods inexpensively at home and selling them abroad at a profit. He recruited skilled laborers for the wool and linen trades and mining. He supported the foundation of state enterprises in banking and trade, and a state porcelain factory. He promoted literacy and moral instruction, if not comprehensive education.

Frederick II traveled widely throughout his realm to gain firsthand knowledge of affairs. Above all, he confirmed the privileged status of the Junkers. He perceived the commoners mainly as fit for the military and for carrying out his extensive colonization schemes east of the Oder River. To assist economic expansion, he also expanded the transportation system, dredging rivers and building canals. Berlin, especially, benefited from the canals that linked it to the Elbe and the Baltic.

In 1772, when Czarina Catherine the Great (1762–1796) of Russia tried to take over Poland, Frederick successfully used diplomatic pressure to assure that Prussia and Austria gained territory as well. Through the first "partition" of Poland, Prussia gained most of West Prussia, Austria acquired Galicia, and Russia added Byelorussia to its empire. Poland, weakened by the collapse of self-government, lost almost half of its population and nearly as much territory.

Prussia and Austria squared off again in a dispute over the succession in Bavaria. The ruling family had died out and the crown was claimed by a related line. Austria demanded territory in Bavaria and the Palatinate in exchange for its support. Prussia and Saxony objected to that, and both sides amassed troops on the frontiers of Silesia and Bohemia. In the War of the Bavarian Succession (1778–1779), there was little actual fighting; the issues were resolved diplomatically. The Bavarian claimant was upheld, while Prussia and Austria each gained a little territory at the expense of weaker neighbors. Saxony got a monetary award. The incident demonstrated Prussia's continuing challenge to Austrian leadership. When Frederick died in 1786, he was a hero at home and a legend abroad.

Joseph II of Austria. In 1780 Maria Theresa died. Filled with Enlightenment fervor, Joseph II (1780–1790) set out to reform and modernize Austria. The result was a curious and inconsistent mixture of absolutism and radical change, most of which did not outlive him. For example, the Edict of Toleration (1781) granted equality to non-Catholics and freedom of religion. At the same time, Joseph II brought the Catholic Church under direct control, prohibiting direction from Rome in order to achieve religious uniformity. But his goal of blending Catholicism and Protestantism into a unified ethical Christianity was not realized. The Catholic Church in Rome, as well as in France and Spain, objected strenuously. Joseph freed the serfs in 1781, and made each a fully qualified royal subject. Since neither economic nor land reform accompanied this civil change, the peasantry became a layer of landless tenants and tax-paying farmers. The landlords and nobility were outraged at the government interference with their serfs, however. These examples illustrate why Joseph II was called an "enlightened despot." When Joseph II died, his brother, Leopold II (1790–1792), succeeded him. The realm was in turmoil, as peasants rioted, pushing for even greater rights, and the nobility fought against the reforms. Leopold repealed almost all of Joseph's measures, even restoring the feudal obligations of the peasantry. By the time the reactionary Emperor Francis II (1792–1806) succeeded to the Austrian throne, little remained of Joseph's experiments.

Development in the smaller German states of the Empire depended on the ability of the local prince. Frederick II, Landgrave of Hesse-Kassel, built up his state treasuries by providing mercenary soldiers for others' wars. But most princes ruled over backward agrarian economies. Education remained the province of an elite few. Enlightenment concepts and reforms were made at the pleasure of the local rulers, who often invited artists and intellectuals to grace their courts. But, with the exception of the composers Johann Sebastian Bach, Wolfgang Mozart, and Joseph Hayden, the philosopher Gottfried Leibniz, and the great author Johann Wolfgang von Goethe, German names are scarce in the annals of the Enlightenment.

French Revolution (1789–1799). Meanwhile, France was suffering the consequences of two centuries of royal extravagance, financial mismanagement, and corruption. Louis XVI inherited a monarchy deeply in debt. Nevertheless, he subsidized the American rebels in their War of Independence against the British (1775–1783). His decrees designed to increase tax revenue were rejected by the nobility, and the king was forced to call the Estates General in 1789. French monarchs had long ignored this body, a feudal assembly representing the clergy (First Estate), the nobility (Second Estate), and the common people (Third Estate). It had last been convened in 1614. But only the Estates General had the right to create new taxes. When Louis called for the election of representatives for the Estates General, it raised expectations that political and social issues could be addressed as well as economic problems. But there were competing expectations. The nobility wanted to increase its power through a constitutional monarchy; the peasantry wanted to end their feudal obligations and the privileges enjoyed by the nobles and clergy; the urban middle class (bourgeoisie) wanted greater freedom of trade and a representative legislature.

All of these demands spelled an erosion of the old monarchical absolutism, known as the ancien régime (old regime). European monarchs watched anxiously, especially in Austria. Marie Antoinette, the wife of Louis XVI, was the sister of Emperor Joseph II (1780–1790) and his successor, Leopold II (1790–1792). Any reduction in French monarchical power might threaten the security of other monarchies in general, and the dignity of the Hapsburgs in particular.

Over the summer of 1789, the events in France led to the conversion of the Estates General into a National Assembly charged with writing a constitution. As urban mobs and the rural peasantry rioted, some of the most conservative French nobility began to flee the country. The National Assembly produced a constitution (enacted 1791) that retained the monarchy with considerably reduced power and drastically revised the internal administration of France. The privileges of the nobility were abolished, and the church became a department of state. Louis accepted the constitution in July 1790, then changed heart and fled with his family to the northeastern frontier in June 1791. Caught and returned to Paris, Louis reluctantly reaffirmed the constitution. But the demand for a republic mounted among the increasingly vocal political clubs of the cities and the bourgeoisie.

Leopold II of Austria considered intervening. A number of the German bishops demanded that the emperor intervene to reverse the secularization of the clergy in France. French emigrés, now resident in German states, also called for action. In 1791 Leopold met with the Prussian king, Frederick William II (1786–1797). In the Declaration of Pillnitz (August 1791), they agreed not to act until other monarchs contributed forces to help restore Louis to his full powers. Receiving no such support, the two monarchs concluded a defensive alliance in February 1792. By this time Francis II had succeeded his father, Leopold II, as the Holy Roman Emperor. At his coronation in July, Francis II and Frederick William II tried to convince the other German princes to mount a campaign to assist the French monarchy. On news of this, the French Legislative Assembly declared a defensive war on Austria and invaded its holdings in the Netherlands (Belgium). The Revolution spilled over the French borders to confront the old order in Europe.

War of the First Coalition (1792–1797). England, Spain, Holland, Portugal, Naples, and Sardinia joined forces with the Germans and pushed back the French armies, along the eastern frontiers of France. A wave of panic hit France. Louis XVI was tried and executed for treason in January 1793. The Reign of Terror (1793–1794) sent monarchists and those who opposed the war to the guillotine. Marie Antoinette herself went to the scaffold in October 1793. A massive volunteer army was raised, which, with patriotic fervor, attacked along the Rhine and Mosel frontiers. Prussia and Spain made peace and withdrew in 1795; the British and Austrians fought on. The German states, especially the Catholic states in the south, denounced Prussia's defection and never quite forgave it. The French drove into southern Germany, forcing Baden and Wuerttemberg to accept a truce in 1796. During the turmoil in the west, Prussia, Russia, and Austria completed the second (1793) and third (1795) partitions of Poland, which disappeared entirely from the map. The French wanted to divide Austrian forces in Germany by sending an expedition, under Napoleon Bonaparte, to Italy to distract them. Disregarding his orders, Napoleon resoundingly defeated the Austrian forces and independently negotiated the Treaty of Campo Formio. In it Austria agreed to give up its Netherlands (Belgium) to France and to give independence to northern Italy, which became a French puppet state (the Cisalpine Republic). Secretly, both agreed to let France take the western bank of the Rhine from Switzerland to Mainz, so long as the river remained open for navigation. In return Austria obtained Venice and the French promise to help Austria wrest Salzburg and its territories from Bavaria. Both agreed that Prussia would get no benefit from the war.

War of the Second Coalition (1798–1801). The next year the Russians constructed another alliance against France. Two former enemies—Austria and the Ottoman Empire—joined Naples and Portugal in this pact. The war began badly for France. Financial problems and defeats in Germany weakened the French government, the conservative Directory (1795–1797) that had succeeded the Reign of Terror. In November 1799, Napoleon overthrew the Directory, imposing a new constitution introducing the government known as the Consulate (1799–1804). Uniting France and its armies as its leader, he invaded first Italy, then Bavaria, decisively defeating the Austrians on both fronts. Once again Austria and the coalition had to make peace.

The Reorganization of the German Empire. The Treaty of Luneville (1801) humiliated the German Empire. Austria reaffirmed its losses at Campo Formio. The emperor ceded the left bank of the Rhine, including the Netherlands, to France, and compensated the displaced German nobility from lands within the Empire. The Empire lost over three million inhabitants and more than 25,000 square miles. And after two years of wrangling, the German princes and church leaders agreed to a drastic reorganization within Germany, known as the Final Recess, or *Reichsdeputationshauptschluss*. The German church lost all but four of its independent states and the electoral roles for Trier and Cologne. Of the 48 imperial free cities, only 6 remained. Over 100 of the smallest states were eliminated, although their nobility retained their status and titles. Four new electorates were created: in Baden, Hesse-Kassel, Wuerttemberg, and Salzburg. This caused massive land swapping and border changes within the Empire. Bavaria and Baden traded territories; Wuerttemberg, Oldenburg, Hanover, Hesse, Nassau, and Nassau-Orange grew through the incorporation of the secularized territories. Prussia benefited from important gains in Westphalia and in the regions of the Harz Mountains.

The reorganization of the Empire eliminated many of the small states that had supported the emperor. Bavaria, Baden, and Wuerttemberg now looked to France, rather than either Prussia or Austria, to protect their interests. Emperor Francis II recognized the bitter reality. On 11 August 1804, Francis declared himself the hereditary emperor of Austria, a new title. He assured Germany that Austria retained its traditional ties there, but he could not mask the obvious. The Holy Roman Empire was all but dead.

War of the Third Coalition (1805–1807). England fought on, and in 1805 constructed another alliance. The War of the Third Coalition ranged England, Russia, Sweden, and a reluctant Austria against France. Napoleon offered Frederick William III Hanover as an incentive to join France. The Prussian king preferred to remain neutral. Baden, Bavaria, and Wuerttemberg supported France. Napoleon overrode the Austrian forces, pushing into Vienna in November 1805. Fearfully, Prussia signed a defensive alliance with France. On December 2, 1805 Napoleon achieved one of his greatest victories, destroying the Russian and Austrian forces at Austerlitz.

The Confederation of the Rhine. The humiliating Peace of Pressburg that followed cost Austria almost all of its Italian possessions and more of its remaining lands within Germany. Napoleon gave these territories to his three south German allies and elevated each of their rulers: the elector of Baden became a grand duke, the electors of Wuerttemberg and Bavaria each became kings. Then Napoleon imposed even more reorganization on Germany. On July 12, 1806, Baden, Bavaria, and Wuerttemberg joined 13 other states in the formation of the Confederation of the Rhine (*Rheinbund*), with a capital at Frankfurt. Prussia, Hesse, Braunschweig, and Austria declined to join. On August 1, the Confederation withdrew from the Holy Roman Empire; five days later, Emperor Francis II of Austria set aside his crown as the German emperor. The title was now so meaningless that Napoleon, who had made himself king of Italy and placed his relatives on thrones of states he created in Belgium and Italy, didn't even bother to claim it. After 800 years of tumult and glory, the Holy Roman Empire had finally expired. England and Russia fought on.

While Napoleon restructured France and expanded his empire, Frederick William III also began to effect changes in Prussia. Hardly an "enlightened" monarch, he was, nevertheless, a practical and reforming one. He and his beloved queen, Louise, lived in modest style. He preferred his own advisors to the self-important aristocratic government ministers. His most significant act was to free the peasants on crown lands by converting feudal labor obligations into rents. He gave these peasants the rights to the lands they worked, creating over 50,000 new independent farms. He encouraged the Junkers to do the same but was hesitant to force them. Similarly, he was too timid to impose reform on the Prussian army, which was top-heavy with aristocratic officers who commanded mercenaries of uncertain loyalty.

Humiliation of Prussia. Yet angry and threatened by Napoleon's gains in Germany, Frederick William declared war on Napoleon on October 9, 1807. It was a dreadful mistake. One week later Napoleon defeated the Prussians at Jena and Auerstaedt. The surrender of other Prussian generals and fortresses compounded the catastrophe. Napoleon entered Berlin on October 27. From there he issued the famous Berlin Decree closing

KINGDOMS of
- Bavaria
- Hanover
- Prussia
- Saxony
- Württemberg

GRAND DUCHIES of
- Baden
- Luxemburg

Austrian Empire

Borderline of the German Confederation

the continent to British trade. He elevated the elector of Saxony to the rank of king. Ignoring Prussia's request to negotiate, Napoleon dealt it even greater humiliation. He forced Prussia to break all alliances with other German states, to give up all its lands west of the Elbe, and to deny access to Russian forces that were continuing the war. Outraged, Frederick William III defied Napoleon by moving his court east to Memel on the Baltic, and contacted the Russians. They formed an alliance in January 1807, and planned how to restore the old order in Europe once they defeated Napoleon.

But the new allies could not defeat Napoleon. At the battle of Friedland (June 1807) he defeated the Russians. Czar Alexander I (1801–1825) sued for peace (the Treaty of Tilsit, 1807) without consulting Prussia. Napoleon took away Prussia's Polish territories to form the Grand Duchy of Warsaw, and Prussian land west of the Elbe, much of which went to the new Kingdom of Westphalia for Napoleon's brother, Jerome. Prussia lost other territory to Saxony. Napoleon also demanded the expulsion of Prince Karl Hardenberg, the Prussian chancellor who had designed the Russo-Prussian alliance. Prussia had no part in these deliberations, and was given 48 hours to sign the treaty. Some say the czar asked Napoleon to let the utterly indefensible rump state exist; others say that the charm of Queen Louise relented his anger. Hemmed in between Napoleon's puppet states—the German Confederation and the Grand Duchy of Warsaw—Prussia survived as a weakened, wishbone-shaped remnant that stretched along the Baltic coast and hugged the Elbe south through Silesia to the Austrian border.

Napoleon sent his armies to Spain and Portugal in 1807. In 1808 he placed his brother, Joseph, on the Spanish throne. The Spanish rebelled against him, and England opportunistically sent armies to Spain under the command of the Duke of Wellington to aid them. This started the Peninsular War (1807–1814), which Napoleon never could win. He called it the "running sore" of his empire. Encouraged by this second front, Austria reentered the conflict by invading Bavaria in 1809. Napoleon again defeated the Austrians at the Battle of Wagram (1809) and reoccupied Vienna. He imposed the Treaty of Schoenbrunn on the Austrian Empire, which lost Salzburg, its Polish territories to the Grand Duchy of Warsaw, and its Adriatic coast to French control. By 1810, only England, Portugal, Sardinia, and Sicily remained in opposition to Napoleon. Napoleon staked his claim to found a dynasty by marrying the archduchess Marie Louise, daughter of Emperor Francis II of Austria, in April 1810.

Napoleon paid the expenses of his massive empire by taking the assets of the lands he conquered. But these were running out. England's blockade of the continental ports stopped long-distance trade. Thus war and the trade restrictions severely crippled the economy of the continent. When Czar Alexander I of Russia defied the trading ban, Napoleon retaliated by launching a massive invasion of Russia in 1812. The French Grand Army totaled 600,000 men, most of whom came from the conquered lands. The Russian strategy was to keep retreating before them, stretching French supply lines. Then, while they harassed the French rear guard, they burned the crops and withdrew the supplies that Napoleon needed to feed his vast force. The Grand Army advanced rapidly over hundreds of miles without major battles until September, when it reached Borodino, close to Moscow. Both sides fought valiantly; neither could claim victory. Napoleon pushed eastward toward Moscow. When he entered it in mid-September 1812, it was abandoned and ablaze. The French army rested there for five weeks, but the czar would not sue for peace. With the Russian winter coming on and no supplies to sustain his troops through it, Napoleon was forced to retreat without victory.

War of Liberation (1813–1814). The czar again sought to build an alliance to defeat Napoleon. Overriding the objections of his king, Prussian General Ludwig von Yorck broke Prussia's alliance with the French. In the Convention of Tauroggen (December 1812), he promised Russia that Prussian forces would, for the time, remain neutral. The Prussian generals urged King Frederick William III to take stronger action. Finally, in February, Prussia and Russia signed the Treaty of Kalisch. Russia pledged to help Prussia recover its 1806 losses. Frederick William, timid no more, called for volunteers for the new national guard (*Landwehr*) "with God for King and Fatherland." Napoleon's allies in the German Confederation and the king of Saxony marshaled their forces with the French. The War of Liberation began.

The initial victory of Gross-Goerschen (Luetzen) in May went to Napoleon, but he took heavy losses. Yet the tide was turning. In June, England agreed to subsidize the allies (Treaty of Reichenbach), and Austria declared war on France, again, in August. Napoleon's victory at Dresden, late in August, was his last victory within Germany. With the Treaty of Teplitz (September 1813) Prussia, Russia, and Austria agreed both to supply and join forces for the war. They guaranteed each other's territorial integrity and pledged not to conclude a separate peace with Napoleon. A secret section promised the restoration of Prussian and Austrian territories to their 1805 holdings. Bavaria was coaxed away from the Confederation by the Treaty of Reid (October).

At the three-day bloodbath of the Battle of All Nations outside Leipzig in mid-October, Napoleon lost over 30,000 men; his ally, the King of Saxony was taken as a prisoner of war. As the French retreated, Napoleon's brother, Jerome, fled from the Kingdom of the Rhine. The king of Wuerttemberg and the grand duke of Baden joined the allies. The Confederation of the Rhine collapsed as former rulers resumed control in Kassel, Hanover, Oldenburg, and Braunschweig.

Peace of Paris, 1814. In November, Napoleon and his remnant army crossed the Rhine into France. Defiantly, he rejected allied offers of peace. In December, therefore, the allies crossed the Rhine into France. Although he won individual engagements by brilliant generalship, Napoleon lost the war. In March 1814 the allies entered Paris; they took Napoleon's unconditional abdication on April 11. The allies were surprisingly lenient with him, letting him retain the imperial title, with the island of Elba to rule, and a large subsidy. The Treaty of Paris (May 1814), which ended the war, was also generous. The allies pledged not to claim indemnities for their war losses and reestablished the French monarchy with the Bourbon King Louis XVIII and France's 1792 borders (actually larger than those in 1789). France relinquished all claims to Germany, Italy, and Switzerland, but retained a number of its island territories in the Caribbean.

The Congress of Vienna (1814–1815). The generation of continental revolution and warfare had left Europe exhausted and disordered. To the Austrian chancellor, Prince Klemens von Metternich, goes the credit for the conception and execution of the peace. His goal was to restore Europe to the conservative order that had existed before the French Revolution, and in a way that would prevent future revolution. Metternich, a Rhineland Imperial Knight whose holdings had been taken by the *Reichsdeputationshauptschluss*, was conservative, but eminently practical; he knew that for the plan to succeed, France had to accept it. Thus France joined the allied kings and councilors for the Congress of Vienna.

Thanks to Metternich, the congress was a triumph for the Germans. Austria regained its lost territories, including those in Poland, and additional holdings in Italy and along the eastern Adriatic coast. It also took Salzburg and the Tyrol from Bavaria. And what Frederick William III had lost through timidity, Prussia regained through skillful diplomacy. Its lands were restored, and enhanced by the award of new territories along the Rhine and from Saxony. Additional land in Pomerania and from the Grand Duchy of Poland widened its corridor to East Prussia. Although no such link existed with its Rhineland territories, these were expanded and consolidated, and thus became much more defensible than before the war. The trade and industries in this region gave Prussia important new economic strength as well. No attempt was made to reverse the Napoleonic reorganization of western Germany. Instead, its 39 existing states were placed in a German Confederation under the presidency of Austria.

Elsewhere on the continent, rulers were restored to power on the basis of legitimacy, that is, the rulers or their heirs who were legally in power prior to the Revolution were reinstated. This conservative restoration of Europe was reinforced by the Holy Alliance (September 1815) of three Christian majesties—Czar Alexander I, Emperor Francis I, and King Frederick William III—who were to rule guided by Christian principles. The Quadruple Alliance (November 1815), among the three nations those monarchs headed and Britain, had even more teeth, agreeing to take military action wherever revolution threatened the restoration. Napoleon's Hundred Days (March through June 1815), the attempt to rally popular support for his reinstatement, inspired this agreement. The four powers, together with most of the other European states, combined armies to halt his campaign and bring about his final defeat at Waterloo. The Quadruple Alliance continued this cooperation. The whole network of diplomatic and military agreements became known as the Metternich System, and it prevailed until 1848.

German Confederation. The restoration of the European state political systems was thus in the hands of often vengeful aristocrats determined not to let the popular masses get out of hand again. The monarch, not the people, had power. In the German Confederation, the rulers of Nassau, Saxe-Weimar, Bavaria, and Baden issued limited constitutions. The Bavarian constitution stipulated that its assembly would be "summoned in order to increase in public convocations the wisdom of deliberation without weakening the power and influence of the Government."[1] Baden permitted tax-paying males aged 25 or older to vote for the lower house of the legislature, but paired it with an upper house that included the royal family, the former imperial nobility, local nobility with holdings worth at least 200,000 marks, church officials, university deputies, representatives of the Chambers of Agriculture, Commerce, and Labor, four mayors, and any other six deputies the grand duke chose to appoint. These constitutions were handed down by the monarch, not developed by a constitutional assembly. Many of the rulers, most notably in Prussia, resumed power without providing a constitution.

Public agitation and political liberalism were suppressed by local governments and by the Confederation Diet. When German university students began to demand liberal reforms, the Diet enacted the Karlsbad Decrees (1819) to dissolve student organizations, exert controls over the universities, impose press censorship, and establish a permanent commission at Mainz to investigate secret political organizations. By containing liberalism in these ways, the German rulers used the restoration period to their own advantage. Some important reforms of the revolutionary period, such as freeing serfs and promoting urban self-government, were retained. These formed the beginnings of a class-based society.

All these actions strengthened monarchical government and increased the particularism that had always characterized Germany. There was no effort to use the Confederation Diet as a political vehicle for German unification. On the other hand, Prussia took the lead in reducing the tariff and trade barriers that existed among the German states. It began, in 1819, to sign treaties with other individual states for mutual and uniform rates. What emerged was a Customs Union (*Zollverein*) that, by the 1840s, included almost all of the German states and gave Prussia enormous economic advantage and political influence over them. Through this cooperation, the regional economy gradually recovered from the ravages of the war years.

German Revolutions. Unexpectedly, another wave of revolution rolled out across Europe from France. Popular unrest over economic problems toppled King Charles X. The tide spread into Germany, raising political as well as economic issues. Defensively, some monarchs issued constitutions. At the Hambach Festival of 1832, nearly 30,000 people assembled and demanded a unified German republic. They vowed to use armed revolt if more peaceful means were unsuccessful. The Confederation Diet acted quickly to pass the Six Articles (1832). These required every ruler to reject any petitions that weakened his sovereignty, ordered local diets to support state budgets, banned all public meetings, and increased the controls on political groups. The popular movement died quickly, and the reaction set in.

In Austria, Emperor Francis II reigned until 1835, when he was succeeded by his son, Ferdinand I. Both men, but especially the inept Ferdinand, gave Metternich wide latitude. The powerful chancellor carried out his conservative mission, keeping policies and political structures basically as they were at reconstruction (the status quo) in Germanic Austria. In Hungary, however, there was a growing movement among radicals and elite alike for self-rule.

In 1840 Frederick William IV succeeded to the throne of Prussia. He envisioned a restoration of the Holy Roman Empire in which the ruler and the aristocracy would act as benevolent protectors of the commoners. Although he invited the provincial diets in 1842 and again in 1847, as the United Landtag, to design a constitution, he rejected their proposals. His deputy in the Confederation Diet worked to build diplomatic support for a more unified German state by consent of the monarchies.

Revolution of 1848. In February 1848, another violent revolution broke out in Paris. King Louis Philippe abdicated, and a republic was proclaimed and a constituent assembly elected in April. Across Europe popular uprisings, the March Days, echoed the revolutionary movement. Prince Metternich fled to England, and the 18-year-old Francis Joseph I replaced his uncle as emperor of Austria; King Ludwig I of Bavaria was deposed, and rulers across Germany were granted freedom of assembly. In Prussia, Frederick William IV pinned the revolutionary colors to his lapel and rode out to the militant crowds, promising reform.

Frankfurt Parliament. At the end of March, a self-appointed group of 53 liberals met in Frankfurt as a preparliament (*Vorparliament*). They called for a general election, based on direct male vote, for representatives to convene in Frankfurt to write a constitution for a unified German monarchy. The terrified rulers acceded to this demand, and in May, 830 delegates began their discussions. Their first act was to suspend the Diet of the German Confederation, appointing a provisional governor (*Reichsverweser*) to represent it. The Frankfurt Parliament met for almost a year, designing a constitutional monarchy with a national bicameral (two-house) legislature, an executive responsible for the national economy, the army, and foreign policy, and an emperor. But there was sharp disagreement on whether or not Austria, with its non-German regions of Hungary and Bohemia, should be included. Those who wanted all of Austria were known as the Big German (*grossdeutsch*) faction; those in favor of excluding Austria were the Small German (*kleindeutsch*) faction. Although the parliament was able successfully to mediate between Prussia and Denmark in a conflict over Schleswig-Holstein, it could not resolve its own major dispute.

Meanwhile, the German monarchs used opportunities to recover their powers. Vienna was retaken from the radicals; Frederick William IV sent the Prussian constituent assembly packing. In the spring of 1849, Frederick William rejected the Frankfurt Parliament's offer of the German imperial throne and proclaimed his divine right to rule. The Frankfurt Parliament crumbled as the disheartened representatives were withdrawn and a rump parliament in Stuttgart was broken up by force. Historians have called this midcentury attempt to unify Germany the "turning point that failed to turn." Clearly, popular initiative could not overcome the entrenched powers of the local rulers. But Frederick William's Prussian Union plan (1850) to do just that was rejected by the majority of his fellow monarchs. Smugly, Austria reconvened the Diet of the German Confederation and forced Prussia to accept its authority.

The competition between Austria and Prussia peaked during the decade of the 1860s. Austria was struggling with its non-German ethnic groups. The nationalism that the Hungarians voiced in 1848 had affected the Slavic peoples in Bohemia and Polish Galicia. The Crimean War (1854–1856) against Russia stirred up the Balkan principalities as well. By the end of the decade, a popular revolution in Italy unified the peninsula (except the Papal States) in a constitutional monarchy. Austria was stretched thin.

Prussia, by contrast, was reaping both economic and political benefits from extending its Customs Union to all the German states but Austria. In 1850 King Frederick William IV issued a constitution that established a two-house legislature (Landtag). The nobility controlled the upper house, and the voting rights of the lower house were so restricted that wealthy conservatives controlled debate. On the surface, at least, Prussia was modernizing peacefully, and was therefore less threatening to the other German states.

Otto von Bismarck and the Unification of Germany. In 1858 Frederick William IV was declared insane, and his brother was made regent until he assumed the throne in his own right as King William I (1861–1888). In 1862 he reached an impasse with the legislature, which refused to approve his military budget. The king was ready to abdicate rather than concede, but then appointed an experienced diplomat, Prince Otto von Bismarck, to make the government's case. As minister president, Bismarck announced that the government would simply assume that the budget continued at the last funded level until the Landtag voted to increase it. That confused the legislators, but delighted the king, who thereafter left much of the policy and decision making up to his chief minister.

Danish War (1864) and the Seven Weeks' War (1866). Austria tried to use its presidency of the German Confederation to contain its rival. Bismarck knew how to manipulate the issues, however. His first success was over succession in Schleswig-Holstein. Its ruler was also the king of Denmark, and he annexed the German state to Denmark in 1863. The

Diet ordered the Confederation armies to retake both provinces, so Austria and Prussia allied and defeated the Danes in 1864. For the time being, they occupied the territories jointly in the name of the Confederation. Then Bismarck began a round of diplomatic meetings to gain support from France, Russia, and the new Italian kingdom. By 1866 he was ready to act.

Bismarck accused Austria of violating their agreement over the Danish occupation and demanded the dissolution of the German Confederation. By June the countries were at war. Prussia defeated Austria's allies in north Germany and defeated the main Austrian force in Bohemia. King William wanted to press on all the way to Vienna, but Bismarck held him back, cautioning him that Austrian friendship would be vital in the future. Instead, he negotiated the Treaty of Prague, by which Austria agreed to let Prussia annex Schleswig and Holstein and several north German states, including Hanover. The treaty also dissolved the German Confederation, and Austria lost its presence in central Europe. The defeat left the Austrian Germans a minority in their own empire, and forced them to deal with the other ethnic groups on a more equitable basis. By the Compromise (Ausgleich) of 1867 the emperor granted an autonomous government to the Hungarians and changed the nation's name to the Austro-Hungarian Empire.

North German Confederation (1867 1871). In Germany, Bismarck produced a treaty that, signed by the rulers of the German states north of the Rhine in 1867, became the constitution of the North German Confederation. The princes elected King William I of Prussia as the German emperor. The government consisted of a legislature (Reichstag) elected, surprisingly, by direct, universal and secret male ballot. An imperial council (Bundesrat) made up of deputies appointed by state governments and a federal chancellor completed the main features. Bismarck held the chancellorship together with the Prussian minister presidency. There was no question about who was in control of this Confederation! Bismarck did not pressure the south German states to join the Confederation. Rather, in the name of German solidarity, he asked them each to sign a defensive alliance to help defend the Confederation if it was attacked. Baden, Bavaria, and Wuerttemberg complied.

Franco-Prussian War (1870–1871). After that, it was only necessary to engineer such an attack. In 1868 Bismarck began by proposing a candidate from the Hohenzollern dynasty for the vacant throne of Spain. France, now ruled by Emperor Louis Napoleon (Napoleon Bonaparte's nephew), objected strenuously. William I withdrew the name of his relative, but France would not let the issue rest. It asked William for a formal guarantee. The tone was insulting, and Bismarck edited William's reply to make it even more insulting to the French. Louis Napoleon declared war on Prussia in July 1870. True to their treaties, the south German states joined the Confederation armies at the front. On September 2, Louis Napoleon and his army surrendered to the Germans. While peace negotiations dragged on, the French government escaped from besieged Paris in a hot air balloon. Bismarck did not wait for the final negotiations, however. On January 18, 1871 (the 171st anniversary of the Prussian monarchy), the rulers in the North German Confederation and the south German princes signed a revised treaty to create the second German Empire. Peace with France finally came with the Treaty of Frankfurt in May 1871.

NOTE

1. Edwin H. Zeydel, *Constitutions of the German Empire and German States* (Washington, DC: U.S. Government Printing Office, 1919), p. 5.

5

The Second German Empire, 1871–1914

The second German Empire was constructed by its princes, not by its people. That important fact distinguished Germany from nations like England, France, and the United States, where the constitutions were designed "with the consent of the governed." The German Empire was a federation of sovereign states, its constitution created by a treaty among the hereditary rulers of those states. The "wars of unification" were not revolutionary popular movements; they were narrowly focused international conflicts designed by Bismarck to help Prussia eliminate Austrian power within Germany and to create a new Prussian-led German nation within Europe. The princes agreed among themselves to accept the king of Prussia as the hereditary German emperor and to let the imperial government control the army, foreign affairs, and some taxation at the national level. The emperor alone appointed the chancellor and the government ministers. Those officials were responsible only to him, not to the Reichstag (national legislature). Within their own states, each ruler retained similar authority over his government and subjects.

The German people accepted this form of unification enthusiastically in 1871. It was a fulfillment of the destiny claimed by the unfortunate Frankfurt Parliament of 1848, which the princes had at that time rejected. The new Empire satisfied German nationalism by giving Germany equal footing with the other European great powers. The new state incorporated numbers of non-German minorities. The largest groups were the Poles in Prussia (east), the Danes in Schleswig-Holstein (north), and the French in the provinces of Alsace-Lorraine (west), gained by the Treaty of Frankfurt (May 1871) after the Franco-Prussian War. There was every confidence that they could be "Germanized."

There were two central problems for the second German Empire. The first was that unification was not accompanied by political modernization. The second was that the speed and strength with which the new nation was created roused fear among its sister states. In this chapter we examine both of these problems. The first led to social and economic crisis within the Empire as the people pressed the princes for modernizing reforms. The second led, tragically, to the First World War.

Bismarck's Domestic Politics. With its hereditary state rulers and nobility, the German Empire contained serious impediments to the political modernization that occurred in the elected governments elsewhere in western Europe. For example, the Reichstag, the new national legislature, was elected by Europe's first law permitting universal male suffrage. It looked surprisingly modern, but its deputies were unpaid and its powers were actually quite limited. All federal legislation had to have the approval of the Bundesrat (federal council of states' deputies), the chancellor, and the emperor (kaiser). Very few measures initiated by the Reichstag ever made it through that route. In fact, its greatest strengths were in its power to expose issues to public debate and to deny support to government measures, especially the budget. Usually, the political factions in the Reichstag courted the chancellor for support, rather than the other way around. Indeed, the most successful national legislation originated in the Prussian cabinet.

The Primacy of Prussia. Imperial government activity depended heavily on the decisions of the Prussian monarchy. The king of Prussia, Germany's largest state, also wore the imperial crown, and the Prussian minister president was also the imperial chancellor. This constitutional duality was based on the close personal and working relationship between Bismarck and His Royal and Imperial Majesty, William I. The king usually deferred to Bismarck on political issues. Bismarck's constitution similarly assured that Prussian domination extended into both the Reichstag and the Bundesrat. As the largest state in the Empire, Prussia controlled 26 of the 56 deputies appointed to the Bundesrat. That was enough to block, if it wished, the two-thirds majority required for approval of any measure. Moreover, Prussia was allotted 236 of the original 382 Reichstag election districts, where a simple majority was required for approval. During the 47-year history of the Empire, the original federal electoral districts were never redrawn to reflect the population shift to the industrial cities on the Rhine and in Silesia. Thus even when the Junkers' eastern agricultural districts lost population, they retained their seats in the Reichstag. Within Prussia, the lower house of the state legislature (Landtag) was elected by a complex three-class voting system based on the amount of taxes an individual paid. That put the wealthiest, most conservative representatives in charge of legislation there, as well. Members of the upper house were appointed for life by the king, and their seat could be passed on to their heirs. With the aristocracy firmly in control of Prussia, there seemed no potential for any popular political action at the national level to erode their power.

The Political Parties. What Bismarck had not foreseen, however, was the rise and impact of political parties in the Empire and, eventually, even in Prussia itself. Their origins lay in the groups of like-minded representatives to the Frankfurt Parliament of 1848, especially its opposing conservative and liberal factions. During the period of reaction after the failed revolution, the states and German Confederation Diet passed laws that virtually prohibited political organizations and meetings. It is not surprising that Bismarck underestimated the potential of political parties.

Before unification the first party to form was the National Association, in 1859; it envisioned German unification without Austria. Middle-class liberals organized the German Progressive Party (1861) to call for a constitutional state under Prussian leadership. The more conservative Reform Association (1862) took up the opposition, defending the Confederation and Austria's leadership. In the absence of a legislature or a convention to write a constitution, these organizations had little influence on affairs.

After unification, a galaxy of parties appeared, but six parties dominated the Reichstag of the North German Confederation and of the Empire. On the right were the Conservatives, mainly Prussian Junkers and their supporters in the eastern agricultural districts of Prussia. They were particularly anxious to promote their great commercial grain farms (*Latifundia*), to keep labor costs down, and to protect their crops with high tariffs against American grain imports. As a Prussian regional party, the Conservatives never gained the national constituency necessary to command a majority of the Reichstag seats. There they sought coalition with other parties, usually the Free Conservatives and National Liberals, in order to exercise their influence.

The Free Conservatives (*Reichspartei*) consisted of a small group of businessmen and industrialists, based mainly in the Rhine and Ruhr areas of western Prussia. They were conservative on most issues, but opposed high tariffs in order to promote the free trade of their manufactures. They were particularly opposed to the workers' unions and political activities.

In the middle of the political spectrum were the National Liberals, staunch supporters of the constitutional monarchy, but with a middle-class moderate platform that won voters across the nation. They promoted political reform to make the government more responsive to the legislature. In the early days of the Empire, they attracted over 30 percent of the voters and had the largest Reichstag faction. By the 1880s, however, nationalism had lost some of its appeal, and their numbers fell.

Another moderate party was the Center (Zentrum). It formed in the southern states and in the Catholic Rhineland after Austria was expelled from central Europe. Its focal point was protection of the Catholic religion in a nation dominated by Protestant Prussia. Fully supportive of the monarchy and the constitution, the Center often provided the swing vote on many issues, deciding which way to go on the basis of a measure's impact on the Catholic Church. It had the largest delegation in the Reichstag from 1890 until the election of 1912.

On the left was a cluster of liberals, who constantly split and regrouped throughout the period of the Empire. They opposed conservatism in general and Bismarck in particular, and some even favored a constitutional republic. Their major factions were known variously as Progressive Liberals (*Deutsch Freisinnige*) and the Progressive Union (*Freisinnige Vereinigung*). In 1910 they came together to form the Progressive People's Party (*Fortschrittliche Volkspartei*).

On the far left were the Social Democrats, who represented the industrial working class. Most of its voters were lower-class, propertyless wage earners. Their advantages were their great number, their economic importance, and their tradition of organizing into labor unions. The early socialists held democratic principles. Later, under the Marxist leadership of August Bebel and Wilhelm Liebknecht, some Social Democrats began to favor the Marxist concept of an international workers' movement to gain political rights and economic power for the working class. The party's 1875 Gotha Program pledged to seek "with every legal means for a free state and a socialist society." Social Democrat voters were clustered in the industrial centers that grew up in the Rhine and Ruhr valleys and in Silesia. Many were unskilled workers who had left the farms in the east for better-paying work in the cities. In the Reichstag election of 1890, the Social Democrats received the largest number of votes. But because federal election districts were never reallocated to reflect population changes, it took the party until the election of 1912 to become the largest party in the Reichstag. They won no seats at all in Prussia until 1908.

In addition to these six parties, there were also a number of smaller and regional parties that contested both national and state elections. Each party also had a number of newspapers either directly allied or closely aligned with it. By 1890 there were over 300 of these party newspapers. If anything, the second Empire had too much competition in domestic politics. The political press served mainly to reinforce their divisions. Bismarck played these factions off against each other to achieve his goal of setting an agenda that was acceptable to Prussian conservatives.

The *Kulturkampf*. Bismarck perceived real dangers to the Empire from political Catholicism. In 1870, Pope Pius IX proclaimed the doctrine of Papal Infallibility, declaring himself supreme in matters of faith and secular morals. When German bishops and priests eagerly supported this concept, Bismarck questioned their loyalty to the state. He therefore took steps to control the Catholic Church in Germany. Branded the "great cultural struggle" (*Kulturkampf*), this campaign took various forms. Bismarck abolished Catholic offices in the Prussian government in 1871, and pushed through an imperial law expelling the Jesuit order from Germany (1872). In Prussia, the May Laws (1873) put the education and discipline of the clergy into state hands, forbade religious punishment for nonreligious actions, and made it easier for members to leave the Catholic Church. In 1875 Prussia introduced obligatory civil marriage and ended financial aid to any clergy who disobeyed state law. Finally, all but nursing religious orders were dissolved in Prussia.

This conflict spurred the formation of the Center Party and considerable Catholic resentment. German Catholic clergymen emigrated, and many were in prison by the time negotiations with the papacy got under way in 1878. Pope Pius had died, and his successor, Leo XIII, was more conciliatory. Bismarck refused to rescind the May Laws outright, but, realizing that he needed more support for some of his political agenda, he gradually let them lapse.

The **Anti-Socialist Law**. Bismarck also kept his eye on the Social Democrats. They had opposed his unification strategy on two major points: they wanted Austria in the Empire, and as pacifists, they had opposed the war with France in 1870. They won only 2 seats in the first Reichstag and increased that number to only 12 in the 1877 elections. But their voices were loud, critical, and constant. When two assassination attempts were made on the emperor's life in 1878, Bismarck blamed them on the Social Democrats, whom he branded enemies of the Reich (*Reichsfeinde*). He persuaded the Reichstag to pass the Anti-Socialist Law. This exceptional law stripped Social Democrats of their rights to hold meetings, form organizations, collect money, or publish any materials that promoted the overthrow of the "existing order of state or society." Subsequent Reichstags renewed this legislation until 1890. The party formally dissolved, although its Reichstag delegates retained the right to stand for national election and to speak with immunity in the legislature. Despite the strict laws and their conscientious enforcement, the Social Democrats continued to attract voter support. By the time the ban was lifted in 1890, they had the largest constituency of any of the political parties.

Economic Growth. Much of the domestic political discussion focused on economic issues. Initially, investment was spurred by the currency reform that accompanied unification and by the one billion dollar indemnity that France was forced to pay for starting the war in 1870. Combined with the National Liberals' policy of free trade, German commerce and production grew. But in 1873 the boom of the founding years (*Gruenderjahre*) gave way to a financial crisis that led to an economic depression. Both the Junkers and the industrialists demanded higher tariffs to shield them from competition from foreign producers. With the support of the two conservative parties and the Center Party, a new high tariff was introduced in 1879.

Protectionism led to rapid growth in German productivity, despite a long worldwide depression in the last quarter of the century. A few basic statistics illustrate the magnitude of this growth (see Table 5.1). In addition, innovative industrial sectors, such as chemicals, electrical equipment, and optics, put Germany on the cutting edge of important new technology.

Agriculture, too, participated in this economic expansion. The production of rye grains rose by 50 percent in the last quarter of the century, and other grain production by about one-third. Germany led the world in harvesting potatoes. Its sugar beet productivity made it a strong competitor in the world sugar market. But with many German workers moving to the more lucrative factory jobs in the cities, the commercial farmers

Table 5.1
Growth in Productivity, 1871–1890

	1871	1890	Pct. Increase
Population	41,000,000	49,500,000	19
Pig Iron (metric tons)	1,548,000 (1875)	3,164,000	49
Coal Production (metric tons)	29,400,000	70,000,000	138
Railroad Track (Kilometers)	19,500	43,000	120

Source: J. H. Clapham, Economic Development of France & Germany 1815–1914, 4th ed. (Cambridge: Cambridge University Press, 1966), pp. 278, 281, 285, 339.

had increasingly to rely on seasonal migrant workers from Poland. The Junkers required cheap labor to be competitive.

As a result of this rapid economic expansion, German foreign trade doubled between 1872 and 1900. In Europe, only England had a greater volume of trade. Germany was, however, dependent on imports for many raw materials and for food.

The rapid and diverse economic growth caused significant changes within the society, most notably a 64 percent increase in the industrial workforce and nearly a 50 percent increase in urbanization. These changes created social issues that the middle and left parties, especially the Social Democrats, began to use against the government. In response, Bismarck's government acted defensively in order to undercut their appeal. Between 1883 and 1889, Germany enacted Europe's first comprehensive workers' welfare program. Its components were: 1883, sickness insurance (financed two-thirds by workers, one-third by employers); 1884, accident insurance (financed by employers); 1889, old-age and accident insurance (financed by workers, employers, and the state). Such extraordinary state socialism made the German wage earners more secure than any others in Europe, but it did not silence leftist critics of the monarchy. The continuing ban on the Social Democrat Party contradicted the paternalistic state help for the working class.

Bismarck's Foreign Policy. The rapid consolidation of a major state in the center of Europe significantly altered the European power situation. Throughout his tenure in office, Bismarck based his diplomacy on one principle: maintaining German security. He pursued this by trying to isolate France and by assuring Europe that united Germany was a stable, peaceful nation with no further territorial ambitions.

German security depended upon peace with its neighbors and partnership where possible. The most dangerous neighbor was France, resentful of its loss of national pride and of Alsace-Lorraine through the Franco-Prussian War (1870). To keep France diplomatically isolated in Europe, Bismarck encouraged reconciliation between Emperor William I and Austria's Emperor Franz Joseph. In 1872 these two emperors met in Berlin with Czar Alexander II of Russia. By 1873 they formed the Three Emperors' League on the bases of bilateral agreements, Germany with Russia and Austria with Russia, to come to each other's aid if any were attacked by another European power. Bismarck underscored the importance of this monarchical solidarity by characterizing France as an unstable and revolutionary republic. In 1875, the saber-rattling statements of one of the French presidential candidates for election created a war scare in Germany. When France appealed to Britain and Russia for help, they cautioned Bismarck not to take any action. Bismarck assured them that Germany would not mobilize, but realized that German security required stronger links than just the friendship of the three emperors.

In 1875 rebellion against the Turkish Empire broke out in the Slavic-populated province of Bosnia-Herzegovina in the Balkans. The Serbs and Russians supported this movement out of feelings of Slavic solidarity, known as Pan-Slavism. Russia also hoped to force Turkey out of the Balkans and open the Turkish straits (from the Black Sea into the Mediterranean) to the Russian navy. Diplomatic negotiations failed to calm the crisis, and the rebellion spread to Turkish Bulgaria. In 1876, Serbia and then Russia (1877) declared war on Turkey. Britain and Austria sent objections, and England even sent its navy into the region. Throughout early 1878, in secret negotiations, the nations schemed to carve up the Balkans as Turkey began to lose its control over the region.

Bismarck saw his chance. Claiming that Germany was an "honest broker" with no interest in gain, he convened the Congress of Berlin in June 1878 to mediate a settlement. This ended the crisis for the moment. Austria occupied Bosnia and Herzegovina; Serbia, Rumania, and Montenegro were granted independence; Russia received some Turkish territories along the Black Sea. In the manner of nineteenth-century imperialism, France and England also each received "compensations." England gained the island of Cyprus, France the right to occupy Tunis. Pointedly, Germany took no reward. But Bismarck realized that this settlement raised the potential for future conflict between Austria and Russia in the Balkans. He thought diplomacy could prevent it.

In 1879 the Dual Alliance between Austria and Germany laid the cornerstone of Bismarck's grand scheme. This was a defensive contract designed to reassure Austria and restrain it from acting aggressively. If

Russia attacked either Austria or Germany, the two nations would aid each other, if some other country attacked either one, the other would remain neutral. Italy, competing with France for expansion in North Africa, joined and made it a Triple Alliance in 1882. The new terms stipulated that the partners would aid any member attacked by two or more great powers and remain neutral if a member were attacked by one of the other powers. Renewed at regular intervals, this alliance remained in effect through World War I. Fearful of a negative reaction from Russia, Bismarck kept the Dual Alliance secret until 1888.

The German Colonial Empire. By the 1880s, Portugal, Belgium, France, and England had established colonial footholds in Africa. Bismarck resisted as much as he could the insistent demands of the German Colonial Society to acquire a German overseas empire. He did not want competition in far-flung regions to disturb the image he was projecting of Germany as a "satisfied country." But when German explorers and private companies began making treaties with African leaders near Lake Tanganyika and the island of Zanzibar during 1884, the German government agreed to establish a protectorate over these regions. This put Germany in the way of Britain's grand scheme to build and control a "Cape (of Good Hope) to Cairo" railroad from south to north on the eastern side of the continent. Taking up its mantle as the "honest broker," the German government convened the Berlin conference on African affairs from November 1884 to February 1885. The final agreement, signed by 14 nations including the United States, proclaimed the end to the slave trade, and freedom of commerce and navigation on the Niger and Congo Rivers. The signatories also accepted the claim by Belgium's King Leopold for much of the Congo River basin. This set off the "scramble for Africa" through which, until 1900, the European powers divided the continent into colonial possessions. Germany added South-West Africa (Namibia), the Cameroon, and Togoland from western Africa to its east African holdings. It also claimed the northeastern shore of the Pacific island of New Guinea and a cluster of island chains close to it—the Solomons, the Bismarck Archipelago, the Carolines, and the Marshalls. Germany established its whole colonial empire in less than three years.

Having diverted international interest to Africa, Bismarck's next diplomatic concern was to secure friendly relations with Russia. The Three Emperors' League broke down in 1887 due to tensions between Russia and Austria over Balkan affairs. To keep German influence on Russia, Bismarck designed the 1887 Reinsurance Treaty. Germany and Russia each agreed to remain neutral if the other were involved in a war unless

Russia attacked Austria or Germany attacked France. While this agreement remained secret until 1890, Bismarck did announce the dual/triple alliance, in hope of discouraging the European powers from trying to break the solidarity of Europe's three empires. Germans and some historians have argued that the Reinsurance Treaty was a contradiction to the Dual Alliance and a betrayal of Austria. That is not technically true, since the Dual Alliance only required Germany to assist Austria if it were attacked by Russia.

Three-Emperor Year, 1888. In March 1888, King and Emperor William I died at the age of 91. He was succeeded by his son, Frederick III, who was terminally ill of throat cancer. Frederick's wife, Victoria, was the daughter of Queen Victoria of England. Her classical liberal political views had influenced Frederick and placed her bitterly at odds with Bismarck. Many in Germany hoped that, as ruler, Frederick would introduce reforms in Prussia and the Empire that would modernize the German constitution and make it more responsive to the working classes. Weak and unable to speak at the time of his accession to the throne, Frederick died after only 100 days. In June his headstrong and difficult son, William II, received the double crowns and, at the age of 29, took over the reins of the Empire.

William (Wilhelm) II was a bright, extroverted young man who had the intelligence to dream great dreams without the practical sense to assess their potential impact. Born with a withered left arm and neurological damage that affected his sense of balance, William compensated by developing an exaggerated military bearing. He filled his court with officers and designed and wore many different uniforms each day. He revered his grandfather, the late emperor, and despised his widowed mother for her liberal views. While confident of his own abilities, he bitterly resented criticism, especially from Bismarck. In an age of constitutional monarchies, this young man believed he ruled by divine right. Above all, he wanted to establish a "personal regime" in which he, not his chancellor, set the nation's course. In contrast to the purposeful stability of Bismarck's era, the Wilhelmian era (1890–1918) was chaotic with political change, diplomatic adventurism, and, ultimately, world war.

The "Personal Regime." William II wanted the love and appreciation that his grandfather, William I, had enjoyed. He began by courting the working class, promising them assistance and reform. Thus he favored ending the Anti-Socialist Laws, and that brought him into conflict with Bismarck. The emperor and chancellor had a difficult relationship at best, complicated by competing egos and a significant generation gap. In

March 1890, Bismarck objected to ending the ban on socialism. As he had often done before to control William I, he offered his resignation. William II shocked Bismarck, the Germans, and Europeans alike by accepting it.

During his "personal regime," which followed, William II went through five chancellors and a variety of policies, variously characterized as the New Course, the Newest Course, the Zig-Zag Course, and others. William II perceived of the chancellor as an agent to carry out his commands. He appointed the politically inexperienced General Leo von Caprivi (1890–1894) to succeed Bismarck as chancellor and Prussian minister president. Although capable, Caprivi had a knack for creating political enemies. He put through a group of commercial treaties lowering tariffs. These benefited the industrial sector but outraged the Junkers. His agreement with England (1890) to exchange rights to Zanzibar for the North Sea island base of Helgoland delighted the military but infuriated the colonial interests. The army was unhappy with his legislation reducing the service time of enlisted men. William responded first, by giving the Prussian minister presidency to another cabinet minister (1892–1894). But without that authority, the office of chancellor had no influence in the Reichstag. William's solution was to reunite the two offices in a much more docile person, the 75-year-old Prince Chlodwig zu Hohenlohe-Schillingsfuerst (1894–1900).

Hohenlohe was a relative (William often called him "Uncle") but not a Prussian. He was a Bavarian, a Catholic, a National Liberal, and a skilled diplomat. As governor of the provinces of Alsace-Lorraine, he had kept the peace between their French and German residents. He needed all that skill as chancellor to manage the headstrong emperor. The Hohenlohe chancellorship has been characterized as "government by procrastination" or delay. By 1894, William was reacting to the strident criticisms of the Social Democrats, whom he had not won over by ending the Anti-Socialist Law. The angry emperor wanted to introduce strong restrictions on all political activity, which Hohenlohe knew would be political disaster. So the wily old chancellor simply stalled and stalled, letting public resistance to each measure grow. Thus the Anti-Revolution bill of 1894 (*Umsturzvorlage*) died in the Reichstag, as did the even more drastic Prussian Association Law of 1897 and the imperial Anti-Strike bill of 1898. In fact, Hohenlohe brought the new Imperial Civil Code through the Reichstag in 1898 by persuading the emperor to end Prussian restrictions that prevented political parties from forming national organizations.

William's Diplomacy. William II was less manageable in other ways. As the grandson of England's Queen Victoria (1841–1901), he had exaggerated confidence in the dynastic connection, but little sensitivity about the diplomatic relations between their two countries. For example, in 1896, when an English raiding party was defeated in the Boer Republic of South Africa, William sent a telegram to South Africa's President Paul Kreuger on his nation's victory. The English were outraged. William's campaign to build a mighty German navy started an arms race between them. Germany planned fewer and smaller ships, but they would use the new diesel engines and could steam further than the British coal-fired fleet. In 1898, when the first naval bill was passed, William opened the Kiel Canal across the base of the Danish peninsula. This route gave the German navy direct access to the North Atlantic from its home port in Kiel. Britain countered with the new dreadnought class of battleship (1907), which had huge naval guns. When William visited England in 1899, there was talk of an Anglo-German agreement. But the British people, by then at war with the South African Boers, would not hear of it. German plans to help Turkey build a Berlin-to-Baghdad railroad seemed, to the British, an unwarranted encroachment into the Middle East, which Britain had always regarded as its own sphere of influence. Although British imperial policy was just as heavy-handed as the German, William discounted the growing hostility between the two nations because of their dynastic relationship.

William was equally brash and patronizing toward his cousin, Czar Nicholas II of Russia (1894–1917). In regular summer vacations together on his yacht and through the "Willi-Nicki letters," he presumed to advise his cousin on how to rule. At the same time, he refused to renew the Reinsurance Treaty in 1890, which alarmed the Russians. This blundering gave France the opportunity to escape diplomatic isolation and establish positive contact with Russia. The two nations signed an agreement in August 1892 to consult and coordinate their actions, should either be threatened by a third power. This agreement was renewed, solidified, and expanded in 1894, becoming the basis for the military coalition that opposed Germany in World War I. Bismarck's basic principle for protecting German security was shattered.

Entente Cordiale. In 1900 Chancellor Hohenlohe resigned from exhaustion. His successor, Prince Bernhard von Buelow (1900–1909), was an aristocratic career diplomat unwilling to dispute the emperor's wishes. William's "world plan" (*Weltpolitik*) to give Germany its "place in the sun" continued at an even faster pace. Germany passed another navy construction bill and imposed new protective tariffs. Again, France seized the opportunity and made diplomatic overtures this time to Britain. In 1904 the two signed the Entente Cordiale (Friendly Agreement), resolving some of their long-standing colonial disputes and agreeing to consult on diplomatic concerns.

Triple Entente (1907). In 1905 France began to take over Morocco in North Africa. Germany protested, but found itself diplomatically isolated. William tested the Entente's resolve by personally visiting Tangiers and calling for Moroccan independence. His diplomats called for an international meeting to resolve the dispute. Russia, though at war with Japan, supported its French ally. So did Britain. The Morocco crisis, and the Conference of Algeciras, Spain, in 1906 confirmed that only Austria backed the German position. France got its way. Then France, Russia, and England continued diplomatic talks. Russia and England resolved their colonial conflicts over Afghanistan and Persia, and signed their Entente in 1907. With these agreements, Europe was divided between the Triple Entente and the Triple Alliance. Germany was not only isolated but encircled by the new, unfriendly Entente. And the Morocco crisis had shown that Germany's alliance system was the weaker of the two. Yet William provoked a second Morocco crisis in 1911 by sending the warship *Panther* to protect German interests in the French protectorate. Again Germany was isolated, except for Austria. England even prepared to mobilize its troops. Diplomatic agreement confirmed French rights in Morocco. In compensation, France gave Germany a small strip of territory attached to the German Cameroons. It was hardly a victory.

Germany at the Turn of the Century. Germany entered the twentieth century vastly changed from the Empire that Bismarck had constructed. Its population was growing rapidly, reaching almost 68 million in 1914. Each new generation expanded the workforce and made it more urban. Workers packed the city tenements and pushed labor union membership from under one million in 1900 to 2.5 million by 1912. Business strengthened as well, building trade associations and cartels to control trade agreements. Across Germany special interest groups formed to support their favorite projects. Some, like the Landlords' League (Bund der Landwirte) of the Junkers, the Navy League, the Industrial League, and the Colonial Society, supported Buelow's efforts to raise tariffs and to pass expansion budgets for the army and navy.

The working class was not forgotten: the social insurance codes were consolidated and expanded in 1911, and work rules were passed to protect child and women laborers. In fact, things had so improved for the working class that a split developed within the Social Democrats. Eduard Bernstein led a reform faction that recognized the gains under the existing system and muted the socialists' traditional demands for the elimination of capitalism. This lessened the political pressure on Buelow, who tried, whenever possible, to avoid conflict with the Reichstag. In 1907 he put together a Reichstag coalition of Conservatives, National Liberals, and the old Progressives, known as the Buelow Bloc. It almost seemed as if the government was becoming more parliamentary in nature. That, however, was because of Buelow's leadership style, not because there had been an actual transformation of the Empire. In fact, many working-class Germans had decided that they had better opportunities elsewhere. Almost 4.5 million Germans had emigrated to the United States by 1900.

Other problems were coming to light, however. One of them was unrest among the ethnic minorities, particularly the Poles. The Prussian government allocated funds to help Germans buy up property in the Polish regions to Germanize them; it only antagonized the Poles further. The French in Alsace-Lorraine and the Danes in north Germany had never reconciled themselves to becoming German after 1870. They formed political parties, and often received support from the mainstream opposition parties. When the imperial government passed its Association Law in 1908, these minorities were required to speak German at their political meetings so that government agents could monitor them.

Despite the rapid industrial growth, the national economy could not absorb the rising costs of the new German navy and of army expansion. The national debt increased because neither the states nor the Reichstag would vote new taxes. The Conservatives shattered the Buelow Bloc by their opposition to inheritance taxes in 1908, and Buelow resigned the following year.

Moreover, after two decades as king and emperor, William had become overconfident. On October 28, 1908, the British newspaper *Daily Telegraph* published an interview with William II. In a tactless and patronizing manner, William had boasted that he had given the British generals their strategy for winning the Boer War. While the British public laughed and ridiculed the comments, the German public was embarrassed and outraged. A storm of protest in the Reichstag swelled to a vehement criticism of the "personal regime." Buelow chose not to defend the emperor; indeed, he even promised to caution William to be more prudent in the future. William was truly shaken by the public storm and seemed more subdued thereafter. But he deeply resented Buelow for leaving him so exposed, and happily received his resignation in 1909.

He appointed Theobald von Bethmann-Hollweg (1909–1917), a Prussian bureaucrat, to succeed Buelow.

Balkan Crises and Conflicts. The two European alliance systems were designed to prevent the great powers from provoking each other. There were no such restraints on the small states, especially the recently created states in the Balkans. This ungainly peninsula, lying between the Adriatic and Black Seas north of Greece, had a long, complex, and troubled history. It was a land of competing cultures—the Slavic Croats, Slovenes, Serbs, Bulgarians, and Macedonians, as well as Albanians—that had variant languages, religions, and even alphabets. In antiquity it had formed the border between the Roman Catholic and Byzantine Orthodox empires. By the eighteenth century, much of it had been under the Islamic rule of the Ottoman Empire of Turkey. Filled with the nationalistic fervor of Pan-Slavism, these peoples sought to create their own independent states. Indeed, Rumania, Bulgaria, Serbia, and Montenegro had emerged as states in the southern Balkans. But that was not enough.

Since Austria had been expelled from Germany in 1867, it had become preoccupied with its restive Slavic populations and their links to the Slavic states in the Balkans. Particularly troublesome was the Turkish province of Bosnia-Herzegovina, which Austria had occupied since the settlement of the Russo-Turkish War (1878). The Austrians wanted to annex these territories rather than let their independence movement stir up the Slavs within the Austrian Empire. Because of Russia's patronage of the Balkan Slavs, the two powers would have to agree on any action taken. Therefore, the Austrian foreign minister, Alois von Aehrenthal, contacted his Russian counterpart, Alexander Izvolsky, in September 1908 to see if an agreement could be reached. Secretly, Russia agreed to accept Austria's annexation of the provinces, and Austria agreed to help Russia gain the right to send its navy through the Turkish straits to the Mediterranean. The Russians presumed that these actions would occur at the same time, but Austria moved immediately, in October. Russia protested the betrayal, and the Serbs, who had their own designs on the provinces, were outraged. Austria stood firm, and Germany supported its ally. Russia and Serbia were forced to back down.

After Italy had easily taken Libya from the Turks in 1912, Greece, Serbia, Bulgaria, and Montenegro allied in a Balkan League to expel the Turks from Europe. The First Balkan War (1912–1913) stripped Turkey of all but Istanbul and a small region on the northern shore of the Black Sea straits. The great powers managed the final settlement. The Treaty of London (1913) created a new Balkan state, Albania, as Austria had wished. But this denied landlocked Serbia the outlet it sought to the Adriatic Sea.

Secure in Russia's patronage, Serbia then demanded a coastal link through Macedonia (north of Greece). Bulgaria also wanted more territory in Macedonia. The Second Balkan War (1913) ranged Serbia, Montenegro, Greece, Rumania, and Turkey all against Bulgaria. The outcome was inevitable. By the Treaty of Bucharest (1913), Serbia and Greece divided Macedonia and Bulgaria lost land to Rumania. The crises and conflicts in southeastern Europe had intensified Slavic nationalism and set the two alliance systems on edge.

The tensions in the Balkans provided the immediate trigger for the Great War (1914–1918). On June 28, 1914, a Bosnian nationalist named Gavrilo Princip assassinated the heir-designate to the Austrian Empire. Archduke Franz Ferdinand, the emperor's nephew, had been named after the suicide of Franz Joseph's son in 1889. Franz Ferdinand and his wife were on tour in Bosnia, and both were killed by the terrorist. Princip belonged to a secret Serbian political group, Union or Death, otherwise known as the Black Hand. The Serbian government officially denied any knowledge of the plot, although it was later established that it was aware of it and did not intervene.

Causes of World War I. All of Europe was shocked by the incident and sympathetic to Austria. Compensation of some sort was expected; no one anticipated that this would lead to a general war. To understand why that occurred, historians look at both long- and short-range causes. The long-range causes have been described: the disturbance of the European power balance by the unification of Germany; the discarding of Bismarck's quiet diplomacy of security in favor of a provocative *Weltpolitik*, the astute diplomacy of France, which capitalized on German error; the polarization of Europe into two antagonistic alliance systems; and the growing Anglo-German hostility and arms race. The short-range cause was Austria's response to the assassination, which converted yet another Balkan incident to a fatal confrontation of the two European alliance systems.

Since being expelled from central Europe by the unification of Germany, Austria had been turned eastward. It had sought compensation in the Balkans, annexing Bosnia-Herzegovina in 1908. Both Russia and Serbia resented this encroachment. Russia was restrained by its alliances. The Serbs, however, had pursued a successful expansionist policy in the Balkan Wars and had their sights set on Bosnia-Herzegovina. That is why Austria decided to use the Sarajevo incident to teach the Serbs a lesson.

First, Austria turned to Germany for assurance of its support. On July 5, 1914, after discussion of the circumstances with an Austrian representative, William II and Bethmann-Hollweg gave Austria their backing, although no strategy had yet been described. This "blank check" emboldened Austria. Over the next two weeks, the Austrian government debated whether to take military or diplomatic action. Meanwhile, the French president and premier visited Russia, where the two powers agreed to urge a diplomatic settlement. On July 23, Austria issued an ultimatum to the Serbs, demanding immediate government suppression of any Serbian organization, publication, or officials engaged in agitation against Austria; an explanation of Serbia's relations with the assassins, and an apology.

On July 24, Russia sent a message of support to Serbia and warned Austria not to attack it. This alarmed Turkey, which concluded an alliance with Germany in the event that Russia declared war. Despite Austrian assurances, Russia decided on July 25 that it would declare war on Austria if it attacked Serbia. France assured Russia of support, another (albeit, less publicized) "blank check." The mechanisms of the two great power alliance systems were thus unlocked. Serbia responded to Austria on July 25. It agreed to the first demands but refused to apologize. It had, in fact, mobilized for war. When the Entente powers proposed a diplomatic conference on the crisis, Austria and Germany declined.

On July 28, Austria declared war on Serbia. Belatedly, on July 29, the Germans tried to restrain Austria and promised not to take military action if Britain remained neutral. Smugly secure in their Entente, the British refused the German request for neutrality, and the Russians mobilized their army. On July 31, Germany warned Russia of the danger of war and demanded that it stop all mobilization on the German frontier. On August 1, France issued the order to mobilize its army. Five minutes later, the German mobilization orders were issued. That evening, not having heard from the Russians, Germany declared war on Russia. On August 2, the Germans and the Turks signed their alliance. The following day, Germany declared war on France. World War I had begun.

6

The First World War and the
Weimar Republic

Europe stumbled into war so rapidly in 1914 that none of the countries was really prepared for it. In fact, the war was almost over before the major powers could even define their war aims. Yet they all felt that it was a just and honorable war, a war to defend principles and national pride. In press photographs of the street crowds hearing of the declaration of war, the faces are happy and gestures show cheering and excitement. It was the same in every country. It was going to be the war to end all wars.

War Plans. Of course, the European powers all had military plans for an eventual conflict. The French army had trained with the object of constant attack. Indeed, their faith in a furious offensive took on almost mystical proportions. In addition to a war of forward movement, they were going to use their 75-millimeter artillery guns, reputed to be the finest in use. The French war plan called for their armies to invade central Germany through the province of Lorraine, while the Russians invaded Germany from the rear. A two-front war should spell victory for the French-led Entente.

The Germans had long been aware of the probability of a two-front war. They also knew that Russia, lacking modern roads and railroads, would take much longer to mobilize its forces than France. Russia would also send some of its forces against Austria. So, in the early 1890s, the German General Staff, led by General Alfred von Schlieffen, developed a plan to knock France out of the war in a swift, intensive campaign, then turn to face Russia. The Schlieffen Plan called for the invading German armies to cross Luxembourg and Belgium to attack France from the north. This strategy required Germany to violate the neutrality of Belgium, guaranteed by diplomatic agreement among the great powers since 1837, but that did not deter the German military planners. Similarly, Austria planned to attack Serbia, then invade Russia through Galicia. Once the war began, Germany and Austria-Hungary were often called the Central Powers because both had to fight a two-front war. The Russians planned to attack Germany and strike through the Austrian province of Galicia on the way to helping Serbia.

When the war actually began, Italy refused to assist its Triple Alliance partners, on the grounds that they had launched the offensives. It declared its neutrality on August 3, 1914. England assembled its fleet, including twenty of the new dreadnoughts, to confront the mobile German navy on the high seas.

The vast buildup of the military forces since the late nineteenth century made each of the Alliance and Entente powers confident of victory. For example, the Germans had 1.5 million men with which to invade France, France had 800,000 men available. Even Britain, which relied on sea power, had an army of 150,000 men. The Russian army enrolled 15.5 million men. These vast armies were intended to sweep down on the enemy forces, to overwhelm them quickly. Most believed it would be a short war, that victory would be glorious, and that the troops would be back home again by Christmas.

Two-Front War. Warfare proved all those forecasters wrong. When the seven German armies marched toward France on August 4, they met stiff resistance in Belgium. Their momentum slowed but not stopped, the Germans pressed forward. With the bulk of their army on the eastern frontier with Germany, the French government fled the capital for safer quarters at Bordeaux. But the French held. From September 5 to 12, at the Battle of the Marne in northern France, the opposing armies dug in. The French stopped the Germans, but could not push them back. True to their doctrine of vigorous offense, the French tried counterattacking the Germans. As a result, they lost almost half of their total war casualties in the first 16 months of the war. They changed their strategy and went on the defensive. Instead of action there was a stalemate. For the next four years the deadly war on the western front devastated northern

France. Even Germany's control of Belgian resources could not help it break through the stout Entente lines. But then, the French couldn't break through either.

On Germany's eastern front, the direction of the war was determined by two major battles in East Prussia. Germany's General Paul von Hindenburg and his chief of staff, General Erich Ludendorff, forged smashing victories. The Russian defeat at the Battle of Tannenberg (August 26–30, 1914) was so decisive that the Russian commander shot himself and left over 100,000 soldiers to the Germans as prisoners of war. One week later, the Battle of the Masurian Lakes (September 5–15) repeated the debacle, and the Germans took an additional 125,000 prisoners. But after that the eastern front bogged down. The Russian armies never moved west of Tannenberg into Germany or south of the Carpathian Mountains into Austria. The Germans advanced through Russia's Polish provinces, but never got much beyond them into the heartland of the massive empire to threaten such cities as Minsk or Smolensk. The front between the Russians and Austrians seesawed through the Polish provinces during August and sagged down toward Hungary. The Austrians fared better against the Serbians, who were forced to retreat beyond Belgrade by the end of the year. But action on those fronts stalled as well.

New War Technology. When the war of motion ended, the battle front became a tangled killing zone of trenches and shell holes. Machine guns, developed in the American Civil War, mowed down infantrymen caught fast in the barbed wire (also from American technology) that was strewn across the battle field. Wave after human wave went out from both sides to storm the enemy trenches, only to be pinned down in the cross fire or to choke in clouds of another new weapon from Germany, poison gas. Overhead, fragile spotter airplanes guided the artillery fire to enemy trenches. In 1916 the British introduced the first tanks into the Battle of the Somme. All of these technologies were lethal to infantrymen.

From the fastness of their posts, the commanding officers sought to prove that their army had the winning spirit—élan, the French called it—by sending men to their death in this manner. One of the most futile and foolish examples of this was the Battle of Verdun, which lasted from February through June 1916. The French stubbornly held their position in a small pocket that pushed into the German lines. The Germans bombarded them with 1,400 artillery guns, yet the French held and counterattacked; neither side was willing to yield. By the end of June, the casualties in this symbolic yet senseless battle totaled almost 500,000. In the Battle of the Somme, which followed (July to November 1916), the

British and French took nearly 600,000 casualties and the Germans nearly 500,000 in a campaign that pushed the Germans back only seven miles.

Britain controlled the high seas. For the most part the splendid new German fleet, which had led to the arms race with Britain, remained safely tied up in its base at Kiel. The one Anglo-German naval encounter off the Danish coast (Battle of Jutland, May 1916) was inconclusive. Germany deployed its new submarines against Atlantic shipping in the hope of stopping supplies to the Entente powers. But these raiders mainly destroyed civilian merchant shipping, raising storms of diplomatic protest and animosity. As the war dragged on, the Entente used that protest to its advantage.

Total War. Unlike the Napoleonic wars, World War I was fought on only a small portion of European territory. The way in which it was fought made it enormously costly and raised strong emotions in both camps. The masses of civilians drafted for the front required a total reorganization of the society and economy. As the men went to the trenches, the women, youth, and elderly had to replace them in the factories and on the farms. As food and strategic materials went to the front, shortages, rationing, and price changes shocked the home front. To keep the civilians from being demoralized, governments imposed censorship on bad news and loosed an unrelenting barrage of patriotic propaganda. They assured the civilians at home that this was a just and defensive war against vicious and evil attackers, that principles of honor and justice were at stake. The horrifying, almost unbelievable number of front-line casualties seemed to prove the propaganda right. The hatreds generated by World War I lasted throughout the century. In Germany, even the Social Democrats broke with their long tradition of pacifism and voted for the government's military budget to conduct the war. Erich Maria Remarque's *All Quiet on the Western Front* gives a penetrating view of both the war zone and the home front.

War Diplomacy. When war broke out, both sides began to recruit allies to support their cause. Japan, already allied with Britain, declared war on Germany and Austria-Hungary in August 1914. Then both sides tried to woo Italy out of its neutrality. In secret diplomatic strategy they promised yet-to-be-conquered enemy lands in exchange for a wartime alliance. There was no discussion of the high principles proclaimed in the home front propaganda. When Austria resisted giving Italy territory in the Balkans, the Entente won Italy's agreement to the secret Treaty of London (April 1915): Italy could gain territory it wanted in the Balkans as well as additional Turkish territories in Africa. In May 1915, Italy renounced the Triple Alliance and declared war on Austria-Hungary.

Next, attention turned to the Balkans. In 1915 the Russians promised Rumania the Hungarian province of Transylvania as well as Turkish territory, and gained its support. The Bulgarians wanted Turkey's Macedonia and some Rumanian territory in order to sign. The Germans persuaded Turkey to agree and brought Bulgaria into the alliance.

Peace Negotiations. The United States began trying to mediate the war in 1916 on terms that favored the Entente. It called for evacuation and restoration of Serbia and Belgium, and the transferrals of Germany's Alsace-Lorraine to France, Turkey's Constantinople to Russia, and all of Italian-speaking Austria to Italy. In addition, the scattered Polish provinces were to be united into a new independent nation. Despite these decidedly pro-Entente conditions, in December 1916 Germany indicated its willingness to negotiate a peace settlement. In January 1917 Germany named its terms: retention of Alsace, an independent Poland and acquisition of lands in Russia and some new colonial territory. Germany offered to restore its battlefront conquests to France and to remove obstacles to free trade.

Meanwhile, both sides were desperate about the high war costs and losses they were enduring. Britain stepped up its diplomacy with the United States. When the British navy blockaded German ports, Germany decided to use unrestricted submarine warfare to knock Britain out of the war. Like the Schlieffen Plan, this decision defied diplomatic logic. It was bound to bring the United States, whose merchant ships would be prime targets, into the war against Germany. The only hope was to force Britain to sue for peace before the United States could mobilize. The German government issued a formal warning to the United States on January 31, 1917, that unrestricted submarine warfare would begin the next day.

United States Enters the War. The turning point was the entry of the United States into the war in April 1917. The cause was the attack on American merchant shipping by German submarines on the high seas. The United States broke relations with Germany on February 3 and called upon other nations in the Western Hemisphere to do the same. On April 6, after American ships had been sunk by the Germans, the United States declared war on Germany. By the end of the year, most of the South American countries had severed relations and entered the war against Germany. Although the Americans still had to mobilize for war, their potential to send men and military supplies clearly tipped the balance in favor of the Entente. Within Germany, war exhaustion, a devastated economy, and the continued pressure of the Entente forces created panic. In July 1917, Chancellor Bethmann-Hollweg retired. His successor, George Michaelis, was little more than a figurehead for a government run by the German military high command.

German Victory in the East. The horrendous casualties and costs had spelled disaster for the Russians. By early 1917 the Germans controlled Russian Poland and had created a Polish puppet state. The Russian home front had collapsed as workers went out on strike and rioted, joined by deserters streaming back from the war zones. Other troops mutinied against their officers. The legislature (Duma) defied the czar and created the provisional government. On March 15, 1917, the czar abdicated. The provisional government was itself overturned in November by the Bolshevik (Communist) Revolution headed by Lenin. The Bolsheviks came to power with the slogan "Land, peace, and bread." Lenin challenged the warring states to make peace without annexations or indemnities. Germany agreed to negotiate, but the Entente powers would not deal with the Communists. Therefore, on March 3, 1918, Germany and Russia signed the Treaty of Brest-Litovsk. To gain peace and a chance to build his revolution, Lenin ceded Poland, the Baltic provinces, and Finland, as well as the Black Sea regions of Ukraine and Transcaucasia to the Germans. By this agreement, Russia left the war, and Germany began to occupy eastern Europe. Rumania, the ally of czarist Russia, signed a peace treaty with Germany in May. The Entente allies condemned Germany for exacting such a drastic price for peace.

Collapse of the Eastern Front. German victories were offset by the defeat of Bulgaria and Turkey in the fall of 1918. And within Austria, the many ethnic minorities, sensing that their moment had come, rebelled against the Hapsburg monarchy. Czechs and the southern Slavs held popular assemblies to declare their independence. They received encouragement from the American government, pressed by the many Slavs that had emigrated to the United States after 1890. Thus the Turks and British signed an armistice on October 30, 1918, and Austria-Hungary agreed to one on November 3.

War Ends in the West. Thanks to American intervention, victory was in sight for the Entente on the western front by 1918. The Entente powers at last began to state their war goals. The British wanted to restore all the territories taken by the Central Powers and to help the ethnic minorities in Turkey, Austria-Hungary, and Germany to form their own nations. Woodrow Wilson's famous Fourteen Points, presented to the United States Congress on January 18, 1918, contained many of the same goals. He introduced these specific terms, however, with a statement of five principles to gain the support of the isolationist Americans: open diplomacy, freedom of the seas, free trade, disarmament, and resolution of colonial issues allowing self-determination for the people in those territories. Wilson also called for an international organization to maintain the independence and territorial integrity of the new states that would emerge at the end of the war and to assure the implementation of the peace settlement.

Germany launched a major western offensive in March 1918. But it was too late. By May American troops had landed, and the Entente powers consolidated their forces. By late summer, the German generals knew that Germany could not win. They recommended a negotiated peace. Many resigned rather than be held accountable for the defeat. On October 4, a liberal aristocrat, Prince Max von Baden, was appointed German chancellor and foreign minister, and authorized to negotiate. On October 5, both Germany and Austria informed the Americans that they would accept peace based on the Fourteen Points. Wilson, however, refused to negotiate with the imperial government. He said that the Allies would deal only with democratic governments, and the war continued.

The End of Empires. The credibility of the German government sank as the war effort failed. The navy mutinied in Kiel Harbor, and a rebellion in Bavaria forced its king to abdicate. On November 9, 1918, under pressure from the generals, Prince Max, and his advisors, William II abdicated as German emperor and fled into exile in Holland. Berlin was in chaos. From a balcony of the Reichstag, Philip Scheidemann, a leader of the Social Democratic Party, exuberantly (but with no authority whatsoever) announced the formation of the German Republic. (Two hours later the German Communist leader, Karl Liebknecht, proclaimed the German Socialist Republic.) On November 10, the socialists established a government ministry in Berlin and, together with state representatives, called for the election of a National Assembly (Nationalversammlung) to serve as the first legislature and to write a national constitution.

In Vienna, the last Hapsburg, Charles I, abdicated on November 12. The Austrian Empire fragmented into the Austrian Republic (November 13), the Hungarian Republic (November 16), and the United Kingdom of the Serbs, Croats, and Slovenes (November 24), which changed its name to Yugoslavia in 1929.

Armistice. On November 8, a German delegation had already entered negotiations with the Entente. Although it could not win the war, the Entente was determined to win the peace. The Entente would only halt its advance if the Central Powers agreed to renounce the Treaties of Brest-Litovsk and of Bucharest and to withdraw their forces from all occupied territory on the eastern and western fronts. In addition, Germany had to withdraw all forces within Germany to the eastern bank of the Rhine River and deliver most of its locomotives, freight cars, trucks, submarines, and warships to the allies. If Germany refused to accept these terms, the war would be renewed. Germany signed the agreement. It could not do otherwise. At 11:00 A.M. on November 11, 1918, the armed hostilities ceased.

In all, nearly 10 million Europeans died in World War I, and those wounded or taken prisoner were over two and one-half times that number. The economic losses amounted to nearly $400 billion. And yet there was no clear-cut, satisfying military victory. Germany had not even lost any territory to the Allies. It is little wonder that the hostilities continued at the peace table.

Treaty of Versailles. On January 18, 1919, 48 years to the day after the formation of the German Empire, the peace conference began in Paris. The 70 delegates from 27 countries represented only the Entente and their allies. President Wilson came from the United States to meet with David .Lloyd George of England, Georges Clemençeau of France, and Sidney Sonnino and Vittorio Orlando of Italy. Significantly, the Russians were not invited, and the German delegation was told not to arrive until late in April. In the first week, the victors had agreed to establish the League of Nations. With that, the conference turned to drafting the peace treaties.

There was immediate disagreement on just how great a victory the Allies would claim. France wanted Germany's industrial Saar region and also wanted to take the left bank of the Rhine away from Germany. England and the United States objected. Wilson also objected to French and British demands that Germany pay all of their war costs. Italy threatened to leave the conference if its claims for the eastern Adriatic coast were rejected. The discussion of Poland also divided the delegates. But there was general agreement about punishing Germany.

First were the territorial decisions: France received Alsace-Lorraine, Belgium received three cities on its border with Germany, and the Prussian provinces of Posen and West Prussia went to the newly created state of Poland. Poland also got an outlet to the Baltic Sea (Polish Corridor) through the German city of Danzig, which was therefore put under international control; the east German Baltic port of Memel was also taken from Germany. In ethnically mixed areas along the French, Danish, Belgian, and Polish frontiers, residents would vote in a plebiscite to determine which country they would join. All of Germany's colonies were turned over to the League as mandate territories to be administered by one of the Allied powers.

Germany had to accept demilitarization, that is, disarmament and limitation to an army of no more than 100,000 men, all of whom had to be on long-term enlistment (to prevent training of additional soldiers). It could have up to six warships, but no submarines or military aircraft. It could not place any military forces on the left bank of the Rhine or within 30 miles of the river's right bank. The Rhine and all other German rivers were to be open to all international traffic.

Finally, there was punishment. Under Article 231 of the treaty, Germany had to accept the total responsibility for causing the war and monetary payment for the damages, called reparations. These were to compensate the Allies for both military and civilian losses. Germany was to start paying immediately, the total bill would be calculated and announced within two years. The eventual total came to almost $32 billion. Additional payment in kind to the Allies, included surrender of most of its merchant and fishing fleet, new ship production and shipments of coal and other industrial products, as well as the sale of German properties in Allied countries. Germany also had to pay the expenses for the Allied forces occupying the Rhineland.

The Germans were shocked and bitterly angry. Like the other nations, they felt no guilt. They had not lost territory. They had agreed to make a peace settlement based on the Fourteen Points. In their eyes the western Allies had turned an honorable truce into a disastrous defeat for Germany. They repudiated both the war guilt clause and the demand for reparations. Yet threatened by renewal of the war, starved by the British blockade, and in political turmoil, the Germans had no real alternative. The Treaty of Versailles was signed on June 28, 1919, five years to the day after the assassination of Archduke Franz Ferdinand, which had ignited the European powder keg. On July 7, 1919, the German government ratified the Treaty of Versailles. Many of the German people, however, never truly accepted it and were outraged that the government accepted it.

Peace came through separate treaties between the Allies with Germany and with each of Germany's alliance partners (Austria, Hungary, Bulgaria, and Turkey). The Treaty of Versailles, which established the League of Nations, also dictated the terms of the German settlement. Thus, the three great European empires and their dynasties, devastated by war, were destroyed by diplomacy. In their place was a mosaic of ten, newly proclaimed republics.

The German Republic. The peace process was an enormous burden on the new German Republic. Early in January 1919, a Communist extremist group, known as the Spartacists, led an open rebellion in Berlin. The fragile provisional government had to rely on the army to suppress it. The rebellion's leaders, Rosa Luxemburg and Karl Liebknecht, were arrested and died while in police hands. On January 19, as the peace negotiations opened in Paris, elections for the national assembly took place in Germany in an atmosphere of great crisis. The candidates ran under new party labels, but many were carryovers from the former imperial factions. The moderate Majority Socialists (SPD) won 163 seats, the more radical Independent Socialists (USPD) won 22, and the Democrats won 75. The Center had 88, the conservative nationalist parties had 42, and there were 31 delegates from other smaller factions. Due to the fighting in Berlin, the National Assembly opened on February 6 in the city of Weimar to begin drafting a new German constitution. One of its first acts was to elect the Social Democratic leader Friedrich Ebert as the first president of the Republic.

Throughout the spring, while the delegates labored in Weimar, the German domestic crisis continued. The Communists continued their rebellions in Berlin and Munich. They even established a short-lived Soviet Republic in Bavaria in April. The Communists and vigilante groups of former soldiers, called *Freikorps*, clashed openly in the streets. Monarchists assassinated Kurt Eisner, the USPD leader. The French promoted the proclamation of a separatist Rhineland Republic in June, but that, too, collapsed. The Republic's first cabinet, led by Philip Scheidemann, resigned on June 21 rather than sign the hated Versailles Treaty. Hastily, the Weimar delegates voted 237 to 138 for the treaty, and the new cabinet accepted the terms unconditionally on June 23. Britain, however, maintained its blockade (technically an act of war) until July 12.

Weimar Constitution. Following the peace, Germany went through an intense period of constitution writing at the state as well as the national level. The Weimar Constitution reflects an effort to apply the most enlightened political principles to government by the people. It established universal suffrage. The president was directly elected for a seven-year term. The Reichstag was elected every four years from party lists, not territorial districts, in order to give every faction a voice. Reichstag seats were apportioned by the percentage of each party's votes to the national total. A Reichsrat was appointed by the state governments, but could not prevent the Reichstag from acting. The president appointed the chancellor from among the members of the largest Reichstag faction, and the chancellor formed his cabinet from other Reichstag deputies. The Reichstag could give a no-confidence vote and call for a change of chancellor. The president could also dissolve the Reichstag, although he had to call for new elections within sixteen days (Article 25). For the first time, with this cabinet structure, the German government was responsible to the people.

It was a bold new direction for Germany, but the constitution proved to have some weaknesses. First, ballot by party list fragmented the voters and created a number of splinter parties. No single party ever won a clear majority. The chancellors had to worry constantly about building a coalition of parties or else face stalemate or defeat in the Reichstag. Anticipating that, and apprehensive about the postwar turmoil in Germany, the designers added Article 48, which gave the president emergency powers to suspend the legislature and govern by decree. Combined in the wrong hands, these two provisions later helped destroy the Republic. The constitution was adopted on July 31, 1919.

The history of the Weimar Republic can be divided into three distinct phases. First was the period of crisis, 1920–1923, as Germans absorbed the worst impact of the war and the Treaty of Versailles. From 1924 to 1929 was a period of domestic and international rehabilitation, when the Republic appeared to be functioning well. During the third period, 1929 to 1932, the Great Depression wiped out the progress of the previous years and left the country vulnerable to the tactics of Hitler and his fascist party.

Period of Crisis, 1920–1923. The new constitution could not provide stability within Germany. From the moment of the armistice, the extreme right monarchists had denounced the decision as a "stab in the back" of the Empire and the German people. On the left, the Communists demanded the establishment of a socialist state like that ruling Russia. For the next three years, Germany endured almost perpetual upheaval from right and left. In spring 1920, Berlin was seized by 5,000 *Freikorps* troops led by the monarchist Wolfgang Kapp. When the army and police took no action, the Berlin labor unions shut down all transportation and public utilities. This encouraged the civil servants to defy the dictatorship's orders, and the movement collapsed. In the Ruhr, Communist organizers led 50,000 workers in rebellion. When the government sent troops to suppress it, the French invaded, claiming Germany had violated the demilitarized zone. In Bavaria a Putsch led by Gustav von Kahr succeeded and turned that state into a haven for right-wing extremists. One was the leader of the newly formed National Socialist German Workers Party (NSDAP), Adolf Hitler. Together with General Ludendorff, he later led his own abortive Munich Putsch in 1923 (see the later sections, Hitler and the Nazi Party). There were so many crises between March, 1920 and the end of 1923, that President Ebert dismissed seven successive cabinets.

By far the worst episode was the Ruhr crisis of 1923. Claiming that Germans had defaulted on reparations payments, French armies marched into the Ruhr in January to take control of its coal and iron industries. Chancellor Cuno reacted by canceling all reparations deliveries and ordering government officials and laborers alike not to cooperate with the French. Germans in general cheered this defiance, and there was passive resistance throughout the region. It was a grand gesture, but it sent the German economy spinning. Prior to the crisis, the value of the deutschmark had already fallen from 8.9 to over 190 marks to the dollar. When the government had to add support for the workers in the Ruhr to all its other obligations, the currency crashed.

In August 1923 President Ebert appointed Gustav Stresemann as chancellor. Stresemann formed a "grand coalition" government that called off the passive resistance on September 26. For a while the free fall of the currency continued. By November 1923, the value of the mark had collapsed to 4.2 billion to the dollar, and the government printing presses were running day and night to churn out new bills. The inflation devastated wage earners and those on fixed incomes. Communist rebellions in Thuringia and the Hitler Putsch in Bavaria were reflections of the utter chaos of the economy. Stresemann's government implemented a currency reform by issuing the new Rentenmark. This currency was theoretically based on the mortgage value of all national lands and industry. The new bills replaced the old deutschmarks at an official rate of 4.2 to the dollar. Slowly the economy began to stabilize. The rebellions subsided, Hitler went to jail, and peaceful political competition replaced the street fighting. The Republic seemed, at last, to be functioning effectively. It even appeared to have created political consensus.

Stresemann served as chancellor for only 100 days before his cabinet fell. But his leadership in resolving the crisis won the favorable attention of the Versailles powers. Thereafter, until his death in 1929, Stresemann continued to serve as Germany's foreign minister. His strategy was to try to demonstrate that even with the best good faith effort, Germany could not meet the reparations requirements. This accommodating policy of "fulfillment" softened the attitude of the victors and led to the rehabilitation of Germany within the international community.

Period of Rehabilitation, 1924–1929. Stresemann succeeded in opening productive diplomatic relations with England, the United States, and France. Indeed, until then, Germany and Soviet Russia had both been treated as outcasts. In 1922, when the victors called an international economic conference in Geneva, the two rejected nations were allowed to observe, but not participate, in the discussions. Unhappy with this isolation, the Soviet and German diplomats went off together and designed the Treaty of Rapallo (1922). They gave each other full diplomatic recognition, agreed to resume trade, and mutually canceled debts. This agreement only outraged the treaty powers and convinced them that Germany and the Soviet Union were totally untrustworthy.

Stresemann's policy of fulfillment turned this around. His major effort was to revise the Versailles requirements with respect to reparations, foreign military occupation of Germany, and German disarmament. His strategy was to be reasonable and conciliatory and to try to divide France and England over the issues. The first breakthrough was the Dawes Plan for reparations. The British and French, whose economies had also been ruined by the war, needed the reparations payments in order to repay their war loans from the United States. In 1924 Germany agreed to a payment schedule presented from a committee headed by Charles Dawes, president of the First Bank of Chicago. It started with payments of 2.5 billion marks annually, rose to 6.25 billion marks in four years, and thereafter was indexed to German economic recovery. In return, Germany received some $200 million in loans from American banks to help restart its economy.

During the next five years, the Germany economy showed remarkable improvement due to these American loans. Production in virtually all of the basic industries reached or exceeded the prewar levels, with a similar effect on wages and profits. There was an urban building boom and introduction of new technologies. The great prewar industrial firms prospered, aided by the formation of cartels to control production and prices. As the economy increased, social unrest and labor disputes decreased. New technology displaced many workers, but government welfare was able to cover them. Significantly, however, this infusion of capital spurred recovery but not long-term investment. The new prosperity was only skin deep.

Stresemann next engineered the Locarno Treaties (1925). Germany guaranteed the existing frontiers with France and Belgium and promised to accept arbitration for the ongoing disputes with Poland and Czechoslovakia over its eastern frontiers. France signed treaties with Poland and Czechoslovakia to guarantee German compliance. Even when the war hero General von Hindenburg was elected president in 1925 after Ebert's death, there was no disruption in the improving relations. The spirit of good will led to Germany's admission to the League of Nations in 1926, with a permanent seat on the council, and to the withdrawal of Allied occupation troops from Germany in January of 1927. The culmination of this "era of good feeling" was the idealistic Kellogg-Briand Peace Pact of 1928. Signed in Paris by over twenty nations, this agreement renounced war as an instrument of foreign policy. Germany signed the pact in 1929. The final fruit of Stresemann's diplomacy was the Young Plan. This plan, designed by American Owen Young, reduced German annual reparations payments to 2.5 billion marks and scheduled them for the next 59 years. The payments would be divided among the United States, France, and Britain for the first 35 years, then go to the United States alone thereafter. Many in Germany objected to this century-long burden and to the failure of the fulfillment policy to resolve the border disputes in the east or to secure German rearmament. Prosperity alone did not dispel German anger over the Versailles Treaty.

While Stresemann pursued this peaceful reconciliation with the West, German relations with the Soviet Union left his true intentions open to doubt. Even prior to Rapallo, the German army had been secretly conducting training and other military activities in Russia, and it is probable that Stresemann knew of these connections. In 1926 he negotiated the Berlin Treaty with the Soviet Union. It reaffirmed the Rapallo agreement and pledged neutrality if either were attacked by a third party. These good relations permitted the military contacts to continue. Some have accused Stresemann of deliberately betraying the Versailles Treaty. It is more likely that as a German nationalist, he did not want to betray his country. Although he was the Weimar Republic's greatest statesman, he remains controversial, in light of Germany's subsequent military buildup under Hitler.

The Depression. On October 3, 1929, Gustav Stresemann died. Three weeks later, the American stock market crash occurred, with devastating impact on the German economy. New American loans stopped abruptly; others were recalled. Germany was unable to pay back the loans and equally unable to maintain welfare payments to the unemployed. Efforts to raise capital by laying off government workers and raising taxes increased the economic distress while splitting the government and deadlocking the Reichstag. Without effective leadership, the government lost credibility.

By 1930 the German banks had begun to fail, and the drop in foreign trade led to factory closings. Unemployment skyrocketed. President Hindenburg named the Center Party leader, Heinrich Bruening, as chancellor in March. His inability to win socialist support for drastic economic measures paralyzed the Reichstag and deepened the crisis. In the elections of September 1930, the voters turned to the extremist parties. The Majority Socialists (SPD) won the largest constituency with 24 percent, but the National Socialists (Nazis), with 107 seats, won over 18 percent and the Communists (KPD), with 77 seats, won over 13 percent, to become the next largest factions in the Reichstag. No major party commanded enough support to build a workable coalition. In fact, the parties worked to prevent legislation rather than to pass it, and the Reichstag was paralyzed. Once again there was fighting in the streets, especially between the Communists and the Nazis. Increasingly, Hindenburg governed by his emergency powers under Article 48 of the Constitution. The cabinet was helpless. Parliamentary government had failed.

End of the Weimar Republic. The Depression crisis destroyed what was left of the Weimar Republic between 1930 and 1932. Industrial production had dropped by 50 percent and foreign trade by 61.5 percent. The unemployed joined political parties and took to the streets, often in combative semimilitary auxiliary units—the Storm Troops (Sturmabteilung/SA) of the Nazis, the Red Front of the Communists, the Reichsbanner of the socialists and the nationalistic Stahlhelm. All of these blamed German weakness on the Republic and vowed to replace it. Although the SA and the Red Front were banned, they defied authority and continued their activities in other guises.

Only Hindenburg, the great monarchist war hero, stood between the Republic and the extremists. Yet in the presidential elections of March 1932, even he could not win a majority vote. He polled 49.6 percent, Hitler won 30.1 percent, and the Communist candidate, Ernst Thaelmann, won 13 percent. In the runoff election, Hindenburg defeated Hitler, but the general elections of July 1932 returned 230 Nazis, making them the largest faction (37.4 percent) in the Reichstag, and 89 Communists.

Hindenburg refused to name Hitler as chancellor. He named Franz von Papen, an aristocratic former officer and diplomat, instead. Hindenburg had violated the constitution, because Papen held no Reichstag seat. Papen, in turn, appointed the "cabinet of barons," aristocratic conservatives who also were not in the Reichstag. Although Hindenburg and his "new conservatives" were trying to avoid turning over power to the Nazis, this action introduced a form of presidential government that paved the way for Hitler's takeover.

Hitler and the Nazi Party. Adolf Hitler was born in Braunau am Inn, Austria, in 1889. A mediocre student, he wanted to be an artist, but showed no talent. He left Austria for Munich in 1913, and joined a Bavarian regiment when the war broke out. He rose to the rank of corporal, serving as a courier on the western front. He received several decorations for bravery. Without roots in either Austria or Germany, Hitler found a home in the army and a passionate cause in German nationalism. When he learned of William's abdication and the impending armistice, he experienced a bout of hysterical blindness, no doubt related to his fury over Germany's humiliation. He blamed the enemies of the Empire, the socialists and democrats, and added his own personal hatred of Jews to the mix. After he was discharged from the military, he worked for the army as a lecturer against leftist radical movements. He was also assigned to observe and report on a small political faction known as the German Workers' Party (DAP). He joined the party in 1919 and soon became its major spokesman. In 1920, under his influence, the party changed its name to National Socialist German Workers Party (NSDAP), the Nazis. He had an extraordinary talent for public speaking, and party membership began to grow.

In fiery speeches attacking the Versailles Treaty and the Weimar government, Hitler attracted a following. His tirades against disarmament even gained him support from the army. General Ludendorff himself marched beside Hitler on November 9, 1923, in the so-called Beer Hall Putsch in Munich (named for the location where the action was planned). The three-day (November 8–11) action was a total failure. Hitler was tried and convicted for this action, but given only a five-year light sentence. He served only nine months at Landsberg Prison before parole, just long enough to write up his political ideas in his famous book, *Mein Kampf* (My struggle). Imprisonment did not change his mind on the issues; it did convince him that the best way to put them across was through legal means. Once released, he set out to build his party into a major political force.

In the years that followed, Hitler and the Nazis became the lightning rod for attracting a wide range of groups that hated the postwar settlement. His very negativity brought him new followers daily. Thus Hitler was anti-Versailles, antireparations, antirepublican, antisocialist, anti-Communist, anti-Semitic, and anti-Slav. He attracted conservatives and nationalists, workers and the middle class wiped out by the Ruhr crisis and the Depression, militarists and anti-Semites, expansionists who wanted to recover the eastern land to subjugate the Poles, and those who wanted to unify Germany and Austria. He merged their hatreds into a national movement. A brilliant propagandist, Hitler was one of the first politicians to understand the impact of the new technology of radio. He used the microphone like an evangelist and followed up his forceful speeches with energetic personal appearances all over the country, made possible by the airplane. Alfred Hugenberg, owner of a major newspaper, gave him financial support and editorial space. While gaining a national audience, Hitler organized his party for effective local action, dividing it into districts, or *Gaus*, and promoted the formation of the paramilitary Storm Troops to put teeth into the party messages. This, then, was the party that won the most seats in the July 1932 election, and this victory was why Hitler demanded to be named chancellor. Perhaps Hitler's growing strength justified Hindenburg's destruction of the parliamentary system of government through refusing to appoint him.

"Cabinet of Barons." Papen tried to remedy the situation by dissolving the Reichstag and calling new elections in November 1932. These cut the number of Nazi seats to 196 but raised the number of Communist seats to 100. The two extremist antigovernment parties held over 50 percent of the 584 seats. Papen resigned in December, and Hindenburg turned to Kurt von Schleicher, a conservative general, an official in the army ministry, and a known political schemer. Schleicher believed he could control the Nazis by offering a cabinet post to the party's second in command, Gregor Strasser. Both Strasser and Hitler rejected the invitation. Meanwhile, behind Schleicher's back, Papen opened discussions with Hitler. If Hitler agreed to let him serve as vice chancellor, Papen would persuade Hindenburg to make Hitler chancellor. This would give the government substantial backing in the Reichstag, and Papen was certain he could control the Nazi leader. Hitler also asked that Nazis be appointed to two other positions: Wilhelm Frick as minister of internal affairs (which controlled the police), and Hermann Goering as minister without portfolio and Prussian minister of internal affairs. With extreme reluctance, President Hindenburg consented. Hitler became chancellor on January 30, 1933. On March 23, Hitler established his dictatorship.

Causes of the Failure of the Weimar Republic. The failure of the Weimar Republic was a tragedy for Germany and for Europe. Some have blamed that failure on an antidemocratic nature of German society. Yet that cannot be the total story. Germany fought valiantly, and harder than some other nations, to make the new, more democratic system work. Italy went fascist with the government of Benito Mussolini in 1922. Poland, which was recreated by the Versailles Treaty, became a dictatorship under Marshal Joseph Pilsudski in 1926. Yugoslavia could manage neither a republic nor a monarchy, and succumbed to a dictatorship in 1929.

We must look first at the Treaty of Versailles. The peacemakers of the early twentieth century ignored the lessons of their predecessors, Metternich and Bismarck. They claimed too great a victory. By excluding Germany from the negotiations, they gave the German people no stake in maintaining the imposed peace. Their refusal to negotiate after the armistice, the maintenance of the British blockade of German ports, the "war guilt" clause, and the reparations demands all made the Germans, from reactionaries to radicals alike, seek ways to revise the peace. This weakened the Republic from the start.

The economic devastation of Europe was another cause. Britain and France had paid for the war by loans from the United States. They did not have sufficient production to repay them. Germany and Austria had paid for the war by bonds and had bled their economies dry. They had neither the capital to rebuild nor enough to pay the reparations. The chain of new states in eastern Europe had never had independent economies. They had to start from scratch to develop systems of currency, banking, and industrial management, not to mention a whole new infrastructure of transportation and supply centered around their own cities. Russia, previously one of Europe's largest commercial markets, was building a socialist economy and was excluded from the diplomatic and trade negotiations of the western capitalist states.

The Ruhr crisis of 1923 exposed the vengefulness of the peace treaty, and Stresemann was able to soften that somewhat with the policy of fulfillment. The Dawes Plan of 1924, with its superficial circulation of funding, showed how little anyone understood the war's deep disruption of the economy. The Depression shattered illusions of prosperity and democracy around the world. Germany crumbled, like many other countries, and sought the most expedient remedy. For Hindenburg, it was government by decree. The German voters thought it was Adolf Hitler.

7

Hitler and the Second World War

Adolf Hitler came to power legally on January 30, 1933. Ironic as it seems, in hindsight, President von Hindenburg actually restored the Weimar constitutional process by appointing Hitler, the leader of the largest party in the Reichstag, as Germany's chancellor. Papen and the other conservative nationalists of the "cabinet of barons" advising Hindenburg felt certain that they could control Hitler. His Nazi Party would have only two other members in the cabinet. Events proved otherwise.

In his first radio address to the German people, on February 1, Hitler called for new elections in March. He asked for four years to turn the economy around and to end the Social Democrats' control of the Reichstag, which had led the country into ruin. He promised to protect Germany from Bolshevism and to break the chains imposed by the Versailles Treaty. In the upcoming election campaign, Hitler had several important advantages: the visibility of his office, a vigorous party propaganda machine led by Joseph Goebbels, and, through control of the police force, the opportunity to unleash his party's Storm Troopers into the streets without danger of arrest.

Reichstag Fire. On the night of February 27, 1933, the Reichstag building went up in flames. When Hitler first learned of the blaze, he is reported to have exclaimed, "Now I have them!" Hermann Goering,

Hitler's close confidant, president of the Reichstag, and Prussian minister of internal affairs, immediately blamed the fire on Communists who, he said, were starting another revolution. That night over 4,000 members of the Communist Party were arrested and all publications of the Communist and Social Democrat parties were banned for two weeks, which were the weeks before and after the election. Then Hitler persuaded Hindenburg to sign a decree declaring a state of emergency and suspending parliamentary government. A young Dutchman, Marinus van der Lubbe, was arrested for the arson. He claimed sole responsibility for the fire as a protest against both Nazism and capitalism, and he was convicted for the crime. But Hitler's determined conversion of the event into a national crisis is more significant than the actual reasons behind the fire.

Enabling Act. Hindenburg's decree of February 28 was the actual start of Hitler's dictatorship. It opened the way for the arrest of over 10,000 leftists and for a Nazi campaign of intimidation and street fighting against other parties, unhindered by the police. The Nazis polled over 17 million votes on March 5, but still did not obtain an absolute majority in the Reichstag. They won 288 seats and their nationalist allies, 52 seats, giving them a numerical majority of 16 in the 647-member house. Since the government did not permit the 81 elected Communists to take their seats, however, the Nazis' working majority was far greater. In an atmosphere of crisis and Nazi threats, the new Reichstag (with the exception of the Social Democrats) voted to pass the Enabling Act of March 23. This act transferred all legislative authority from the Reichstag to the chancellor's cabinet and gave it authority to suspend constitutional civil liberties for the duration of the emergency. Even though it destroyed the Weimar Constitution, Hitler's dictatorship also came into effect by superficially legal, legislative means. The Enabling Act gave Hitler dictatorial powers only until April 1, 1937, but these powers remained in effect until 1945.

Nature of the Nazi Dictatorship. Hitler had risen to prominence by a strategy of consolidating factions opposed to the government. He well knew the ability of the naysayers to paralyze government. One of his first strategies was to eliminate all possible opposition. This policy was called coordination (*Gleichschaltung*), and it was applied to both national and state levels of government, to political parties and pressure groups, and even to the Nazi Party itself.

Throughout the spring of 1933, the Nazis moved to eliminate all other parties and monarchist organizations. Through dissolutions and government actions, by July 14, 1933, the Nazi Party was the only legal party in Germany. The paramilitary units of the leftist parties—the Reichsbanner and the Red Front—were banned; the conservative Stahlhelm was incorporated into the Nazi Storm Troopers (SA). The last Reichstag election in the Hitler era took place on November 12, 1933: the 661 elected deputies were all Nazis.

Similarly, the independent trade unions were abolished in May 1933. The workers had to join the Nazi Party German Labor Front, which banned all strikes and required compulsory arbitration. Workers cooperatives were also absorbed by the party.

Independent state governments were abolished in January 1934. The Prussian government, the last stronghold of the Social Democrats, had been put under martial law by the Papen government in 1932 because of the street fighting between the socialists and the Nazis. The states became, instead, departments of the national government with appointed governors (*Statthalter*). Most of those men were also Nazi Party district leaders (*Gauleiters*) with personal allegiance to Hitler. The state legislatures (*Laender*) were dissolved and state laws replaced by national, or Reich laws. The Reichsrat was abolished in February 1934. Germany was, for the first time in its history, a totally unified national state. Yet there was a duality of control shared between the government and the Nazi Party that was never quite clear.

Ominously, Hitler's anti-Semitism also emerged in the early days of his regime. By the Civil Service Law of April 7, 1933, all non-Aryans, as Jews were identified, could be terminated from government offices at all levels, municipal through national. Non-Aryan teachers and other semipublic employees could also be terminated. Other religions were regulated as well. In July 1933 all the Protestant churches were combined in a new Evangelical Church headed by a government appointee. A concordat (treaty) with the Vatican that same month gave the Catholic Church freedom to run its own schools and organizations on the proviso that there would be no political speeches from the pulpit. Some Protestant ministers refused to be regulated by the Evangelical Church, and formed the German Confessional Church. Many of them, including Pastor Martin Niemoeller, were arrested and put in concentration camps.

To reinforce his control, Hitler appointed Joseph Goebbels the minister of popular enlightenment and propaganda. Goebbels immediately took control of the entire print and broadcast media, of public performances and celebrations, and of the creative arts. He created a single ideological voice by banning opposition press and imposing a variety of restrictions on the editors of the remaining publications. The editors became, in effect, spokesmen for the Nazi Party.

Hitler also eliminated rivals within the Nazi Party, especially those in the socialist wing of the party and the more militant members of the Storm Troopers (SA). On June 30, 1934, the famous Night of the Long Knives, small parties of Nazis invaded the homes of the targeted party members and killed them. These purges were carried out by Hitler's personal bodyguard, the elite, black-shirted Schutzstaffeln, known as the SS. This body of over 50,000 men was under the direction of Heinrich Himmler. It is estimated that there were as many as 1,000 victims that night, although Hitler only admitted to 77. One was Gregor Strasser, a founder of the party. In the next few days, 85 SA leaders were also murdered by the SS, including their leader, Ernst Roehm, and some of the regional leaders. Some non-Nazis also were killed, including two army generals and a prominent Catholic political leader. Even former Chancellor von Papen was arrested, although he was not shot. These acts revealed to the shocked nation the brutality of the Nazi dictatorship.

The final step in Hitler's takeover came on August 2, 1934, when President von Hindenburg died. On the day before his death, Hitler had decreed his own succession as the leader and head of state. He preferred to use the term "leader," or "Fuehrer," rather than "president," which he associated with the Republic he detested. In a plebiscite held shortly thereafter, 38.9 million German voters endorsed his new office; only about 5 million voted no or cast spoiled ballots in protest. In his new authority, Hitler then required the armed forces to swear loyalty to him personally, not to the state or constitution. Although the army was the one sector of society that might successfully have resisted the Nazis, Hitler kept reassuring them from the outset that one of his major goals was German rearmament. That gained their compliance.

Hitler's Subordinates. Hitler called his regime the Third Reich, the third German Empire, and projected that it would endure for 1,000 years. He did not directly control many of the functions of his government. He worked through a group of lieutenants who shared his beliefs and followed his orders without question. Heinrich Himmler, head of the SS and secret police, Hermann Goering, World War I flying ace and prime minister, and Joseph Goebbels, the propaganda minister, were the party henchmen most closely identified with Hitler. But his inner circle also consisted of men charged with specific functions within the Third Reich. Walther Darré was the minister for agriculture, responsible for increasing production and creating a new order of loyal peasantry; Robert Ley headed the labor front, in charge of keeping workers passive and productive; Baldur von Shirach directed the Nazi youth organizations, with their efforts to indoctrinate the young with Nazi true belief; Hjalmar Schacht, who had helped Stresemann establish the Rentenmark, became the first minister of economics. For the most part, these men were chosen first for their loyalty to Hitler and the party, and then for their competence.

Hitler's Goals. Hitler's main goals were to prepare for rearmament and for German world domination, as projected in *Mein Kampf*. That meant pulling industry and agriculture out of the Depression and converting it to modern military production in support of a new, greater army. Hitler was not a socialist. He had no wish for the state to take over industry, but he insisted that it serve the state. The ultimate goal was self-sufficiency, so that Germany would not be vulnerable in the future as it was in World War I.

In 1934 the government implemented a Four-Year Plan, directed by Hermann Goering, to reduce unemployment and increase productivity, with the goal of preparing Germany for war within four years. It called for a series of public works projects and a labor service agency to help the unemployed find jobs. One notable result of this was the construction of a great 7,000-kilometer highway system, the Autobahn, which also had military utility. Business and industry were given tax incentives to hire more workers and to reinvest their profits into projects of expansion or of research and development. It was a modern system of "pump priming," and it raised the number of employed workers in Germany from 12.7 million in 1932 to 18.3 in 1936, virtually full employment. In order to promote militarily strategic production, the government controlled and subsidized imports. Most of the raw materials necessary for war—oil, rubber, and some steel—came from abroad. The government subsidized the development of synthetic oil and rubber, but they were very expensive. The government also offered contracts guaranteeing profits or, as with the Hermann Goering mining works, went into production itself. Productivity did increase dramatically: steel production grew from 7.6 to 22.7 million tons by 1938, and coal production increased from 236 to 381 million tons during the same five-year period. Although taxes went up during this period, much of this government spending created a growing deficit.

When employment went up, so did prices. But real wages declined. The workers did have job security, however, and some of the public works projects resulted in significantly better housing and living conditions. The state supervised every aspect of the workers' lives, from wages to welfare, from savings plans to their leisure activities and compulsory indoctrination in the Strength through Joy (*Kraft durch Freude*) organizations. Yet after the devastating economic crises of the 1920s, many felt that the loss of job freedom and labor organization was not too high a price to pay.

Police State. Those who resisted *Gleichschaltung* and Nazi control faced the full brunt of the party's judiciary control and concentration camp system. The Nazi Party's Intelligence Service (Sicherheitsdienst, or SD), established in 1931, ferreted out the opposition. After the creation of the state secret police (Gestapo) in 1933, enemies of the state could be taken into custody and sent to the camps. The Storm Troopers were the first to control the camps, but the SS took control after June 1934. The prisoners were subjected to brutal work schedules, indoctrination, and torture for resistance. Many died of the conditions in the camps, and others, while trying to escape. Over 25,000 political prisoners were already in custody by the beginning of 1934. Dachau was the first of these political camps, Sachsenhausen, Buchenwald, and Lichtenburg were the other camps utilized in the prewar period. Political prisoners and criminals were indiscriminately mixed in these camps. Many prisoners were used as forced labor in industry.

Fascism. Political scientists use the term "fascist" to define Hitler's regime. The term originated with the name of Benito Mussolini's political party in Italy, the Fascisti. Basically, the fascist state was a dictatorship that took away individual liberty and free enterprise in order to harness both labor and industry to meet the dictator's goals. The elections, if there were any, were restricted to plebiscites, where people voted yes or no on questions to ratify government actions. Because they were also police states, voting against an issue or not voting at all were ways to express resistance. In fascist ideology, the individual had worth only as an obedient servant of the state. The three most prominent European fascist states were Italy, Germany, and Spain, all of which were extremely conservative, nationalistic, and militaristic in outlook. The governments of General Hideki Tojo in Japan (1940–1944) and of Juan Perón in Argentina (1943–1955) were also fascist in nature.

Anti-Semitism. There were almost half a million Jews in Germany in 1932, and most of them were fully assimilated into German society. During the second Empire the Christian-Social "Anti-Semite" Party of court chaplain Adolf Stoecker gained as many as 16 seats in the Reichstag in

1898, but never posed a serious threat to the safety of the Jewish community. Anti-Semitism is a persistent theme in European history since antiquity. In the past, however, anti-Semitism had been religious in nature, based on the Christian accusation that the Jews had killed Christ. But Hitler's pathological personal hatred of the Jews was framed in racial, not religious terms. It was based on the scientifically false arguments that Germans were an Aryan "master race," destined to control the "inferior races" so they would not become a biological threat. To the Nazis, these "inferior" peoples included Jews, gypsies, and the handicapped. They were slated for elimination. Slavic people, especially the Poles, were also deemed inferior, and they were to become slaves of the Germans, who would take over their territories as new living space (*Lebensraum*) for a growing German population.

Nuremberg Laws. The Civil Service Law of 1933 forced Jews out of government, educational, and judicial positions. Shortly thereafter the government urged a boycott of Jewish businesses. The Nuremberg Laws of 1935 (named for the site of the Nazi Party Congress where they were announced) began the systematic destruction of the German Jewish community. By the Reichs Citizens Law, Jews lost their German citizenship, retaining only a "resident" status. A Jew was racially defined as anyone with one Jewish grandparent, whether or not the individual practiced the religion. This increased the number of people threatened by these laws to almost two million. The Law to Protect German Blood and Honor criminalized Jews who married or had sexual relations with non-Jews or even employed non-Jewish women under the age of 45 years. Jews were excluded from a wide range of occupations and lost the right to have non-Jews as clients or customers. Ghettos were established, and thereafter no Jew could attend a public school, theater, or cinema. In some places they could not even use the public streets. On November 9, 1938, government-organized anti-Jewish riots swept across Germany, desecrating synagogues and destroying over 7,000 Jewish shops. Jews were beaten and killed, and over 30,000 were sent to concentration camps. This Night of Broken Glass (Kristallnacht) demonstrated that Nazi propaganda had elevated anti-Semitism into a deadly mass movement. By the late 1930s Jews were required to sell any of their remaining property at artificially low prices set by the state.

Many German Jews chose to emigrate, but the Nazis made that very difficult. The 16-page application had to be submitted in six copies, accompanied by a recent photograph and all applicable birth, marriage, citizenship, and residency certificates, a recent character reference, and tax receipts. The applicants had to submit an inventory and evaluation of all personal goods they were taking with them—to be taxed at 100 percent of their value—and of all remaining property, which was transferred to the state. Of the 685,000 Jews resident in Germany (including Austria after the annexation), about 375,000 remained. Most of them refused to believe that their state would turn against them.

Hitler's Diplomacy. Having destroyed the Weimar Republic, Hitler moved toward his second stage: overturning the Treaty of Versailles. He wanted to eliminate the restrictions on Germany, not just reform them as Stresemann had attempted to do. This meant restoring Germany to its 1914 boundaries and rearming in strength sufficient to carry out his projected conquests of eastern Europe and beyond. He had informed the German General Staff of these goals in the first week of his chancellorship. Historians divide Hitler's foreign policy into two periods. For the first five years, 1933–1938, he worked mainly through diplomacy. However, he did not negotiate his diplomacy during this period: he preferred to act by a form of diplomatic decree, simply announcing Germany's policy as a way of creating an impression of resolute strength. Thereafter, from 1939 to 1945, he used military force to implement his policy.

Resignation from the League of Nations. Hitler's early diplomacy was decisive and confrontational. In October 1933, well before the death of President Hindenburg, Chancellor Hitler protested that the Allies were not treating Germany as an equal. Refusing to negotiate on this basis, he withdrew Germany from both the international conference on disarmament and from the League of Nations. To prove to the shocked world his support for these actions, he conducted a plebiscite that demonstrated overwhelming popular support for abandoning the hated League. Then he concluded a ten-year nonaggression and friendship treaty with Poland in January 1934. In July 1934 a Nazi Putsch in Vienna assassinated Austria's chancellor, Engelbert Dollfuss. When the movement collapsed, thanks to pressure by Italy and Yugoslavia, the German government disavowed any connection with it. But support to the Austrian Nazi party continued. In the next week, President Hindenburg died, and Hitler became the Fuehrer.

Rearmament. In January 1935 Hitler was further strengthened by a plebiscite in the Saar to determine whether it wanted to go to France or to Germany. France had campaigned vigorously to win support to annex this important industrial region, but the predominantly German population voted overwhelmingly to rejoin the Reich. This significantly increased Germany's military potential. So France sought security in a mutual assistance pact with the Soviet Union. Hitler used this implied threat of encirclement as a reason for renouncing the disarmament clauses of the Versailles Treaty in March and reinstating the military draft to build an army of 36 divisions. France, Britain, and Italy met at Stresa to discuss the situation, but could not reach agreement. Although the League condemned Germany's actions, and France and Soviet Russia renewed their alliance, Britain reversed its tactics. In mid-June it agreed to an Anglo-German naval agreement that limited the size of the German navy to 35 percent of the British fleet. In these nimble moves, Hitler had separated France from England and received British affirmation of German rearmament.

Renunciation of the Locarno Pacts. In 1936 Hitler went even further. In March he renounced the Locarno Treaties guaranteeing Germany's postwar western frontiers. Again the League denounced this shocking action, but Britain would not vote for sanctions. It was a time of international turmoil, with Italy invading Ethiopia and Spain embroiled in civil war. Hitler took advantage of this split among the western nations and sent German troops back into the Rhineland. This clearly violated the Versailles Treaty. The German generals had strongly advised Hitler against remilitarizing the Rhineland. They were sure that it would provoke armed reprisals from France. They warned that the German army was not yet up to the challenge. But France took no action.

The Rome-Berlin-Tokyo Axis. Having loosed Germany from its World War I fetters, Hitler then set about building an alliance system for the next war. In July 1936 Germany and Austria signed an agreement assuring the independence of Austria. In October, as Mussolini was about to send Italian forces to attack Ethiopia, the two fascist states agreed to a Rome-Berlin Axis. Italy, like Germany, had long wanted to overturn the peace settlement. Italy had gotten little of the territory promised it by the 1915 Treaty of London. Popular resentment at being so cheated had helped raise Mussolini and his Fascist Party to power in 1922. His campaign against Ethiopia was an overtly aggressive act against another sovereign member of the League, and resulted in strongly worded sanctions imposed by the League. They failed to deter the Italians. Hitler also extended German diplomatic recognition to General Francisco Franco of Spain, who was leading a civil war against the faltering Spanish Republic. Japan joined the Axis powers in November 1936 in a declaration of solidarity against Communism. Fascist solidarity was evident in the military support that both Italy and Germany provided to help Franco win the Spanish Civil War. It was in Spain that the

German air force (Luftwaffe) practiced the precision bombing techniques it later used in World War II.

Appeasement. By 1937 it was clear that the League guarantees and sanctions had no practical effect against the aggression of Japan against China or of Italy against Ethiopia. Germany clearly posed the next threat. Many nations tried to build security by arranging bilateral treaties, similar to the Rome-Berlin Axis. At the end of the year the British tried to sound out German intentions, and see if there were a way to resolve them peacefully. Historians call this strategy appeasement, and many have blamed it for opening the way to World War II. In fact, that war could not have been avoided, since Hitler firmly believed that war was the only way to restore German glory and achieve German goals. And with most of Europe still struggling with the Depression, it was highly improbable that any elected government could have gained enough votes to take military action against the determined fascists. Appeasement was, therefore, a necessary evil in light of the weakness of the League of Nations, a stalling tactic while trying to prepare for the inevitable conflict.

***Anschluss* with Austria.** In February 1938 Austrian Chancellor Kurt von Schussnigg was summoned to meet with Hitler in his south German retreat at Berchtesgaden. Hitler demanded that Schussnigg bring Nazis into his cabinet and pardon Nazis imprisoned after the 1934 Putsch attempt. Schussnigg complied, appointing Nazi Arthur Seyss-Inquart as minster of interior (with control over the police). Shortly thereafter, Austrian Nazis took to the streets, creating a state of virtual rebellion. When Hitler broadcast a speech on February 20 promising to protect Germans outside of the Reich, Schussnigg called for a plebiscite on Austrian independence from Germany. (Only "yes" ballots were to be distributed.) Hitler sent German troops to the Austrian border, then demanded Schussnigg's resignation and the postponement of the plebiscite. Although Schussnigg resigned, German troops invaded Austria on March 9, 1938. Hitler himself rode triumphantly with the troops into Vienna on March 12. The Austrians put up no resistance, and the following day Seyss-Inquart announced Austria's union (*Anschluss*) with Germany. Italy, Britain, and France protested, but took no action.

Sudeten Germans. A second crisis followed immediately in Czechoslovakia. This young country, led by two great presidents—Thomas Masaryk (1918–1935) and Eduard Benes (1935–1938)—was one of the few states to sustain a republican government in the interwar period. It was a difficult task, complicated by the coexistence of three competing ethnic groups: the Slovaks in the agricultural east, the Czechs in the industrial west, and a minority of (formerly Austrian) Germans in the mountainous industrial region known as the Sudetenland. The Sudetenland lay along the length of Czechoslovakia's frontier with Germany. Predictably, there were Nazi agitators among the Sudeten Germans. Konrad Heinlein led the nationalistic Sudeten-German Party, which was largely financed from Nazi Germany. By 1935 it was the second largest political party in the Czech parliament.

After Hitler's promise to protect Germans outside the Reich, and the *Anschluss*, Heinlein published his Carlsbad Programs demanding full equality of Germans with Czechs and autonomy for Germans with the Czech Republic. The government offered to recognize the minority rights of the Germans, but would not concede full autonomy. The *Anschluss* had, in fact, wrapped the Reich around the vulnerable western half of Czechoslovakia. During the summer, while the British mediator Lord Walter Runciman tried to bring about a peaceful settlement within Czechoslovakia, Hitler ordered new fortifications along the Czech frontier. He sent 750,000 men on army maneuvers along the border in August.

Czech Crisis. In the first week of September, the Sudeten Germans walked out of the negotiations with the Czech government and began staging violent demonstrations for the right of political self determination. On September 12 Hitler echoed that demand in a speech from Nuremberg. To defuse the crisis, British Prime Minister Neville Chamberlain flew to Germany and had a face-to-face meeting with Hitler. They met in Hitler's mountain retreat at Berchtesgaden, and in this relaxed hideaway, Hitler told Chamberlain that Germany planned to annex the German Sudetenland of Czechoslovakia and was willing to go to war to do so. Shaken, Chamberlain returned to London, where he met with French Premier Edouard Daladier. Runciman was there as well, as the men discussed plans to force Czechoslovakia to meet Hitler's demands. France and England promised to guarantee the remaining Czech territory. It seemed the only possible way to avoid war.

The Czech government gave way to the diplomatic pressure of the great powers. Chamberlain then flew back to Germany on September 22, only to find that Hitler had raised the price of peace. He wanted immediate transfer of the Sudetenland, with all its assets, to Germany, and a plebiscite for the other Germans in Czechoslovakia. Stunned, Chamberlain rejected these demands and returned to London on September

24. The Czechs called up their army, and the western powers, including the United States and Italy, all appealed to Hitler to negotiate. He finally agreed to this on September 28.

Munich Agreement. On September 29, a conference on the Czech crisis took place in Munich. Together, Chamberlain, Daladier, Hitler, Mussolini, and their aides reached agreement. No Czech representatives were present. Although the Soviet government had offered to aid Czechoslovakia, it was not invited to Munich, either. By the Munich Agreement of September 29, 1938, Czechoslovakia would evacuate the Sudetenland within two weeks so Germany could annex it; a plebiscite would be held in other areas with a German minority to determine their future. France and Britain would guarantee the remaining state. Italy and Germany said they would only guarantee the remaining state after territorial claims suddenly made by Poland and Hungary had also been settled. Both of those countries had denied the Soviet Union's request to send troops through their territory to aid Czechoslovakia, in the event of war.

The press was filled with smiling pictures of weary diplomats. Chamberlain arrived back in London and waved a copy of the agreement to the crowd, telling them that it guaranteed "peace in our time." But there were many dissenting voices shouting, "Appeasement," criticizing the diplomats for destroying one of the last democracies on the continent. The debate went on, while Germany annexed over 10,000 square miles of land with some 3.5 million inhabitants (including a significant Czech minority). Germany also got the highway transit rights through the remaining Czech state to reach the Oder and Danube Rivers. Hungary and Poland took sizeable pieces of territory. All that remained of Czechoslovakia was a tiny rump state, weakened by ethnic conflict. Its name was changed officially to Czecho-Slovakia.

There was a flurry of anxious and important-looking agreements following the Munich agreement: Italy with England, Soviet Russia with Poland, Germany with France—all assuring good intentions and willingness to prevent conflict. Yet these seemed to acknowledge the inevitability of war.

Destruction of Czecho-Slovakia. In mid-March 1939, in response to a request from Slovakia's premier, Monsignor Josef Tiso, Germany annexed the rest of Czecho-Slovakia, which became the Bohemian and Moravian protectorates. Hitler rode into Prague on March 14. None of the powers opposed the move. Yet this action was quite different from the first Czech crisis. Then, Hitler could claim he was protecting German minorities. In March 1939, Hitler expanded German control to fundamentally non-German territory. It was blatant aggression. A week later his forces had annexed Memel on the Baltic. None of the powers who had guaranteed Czecho-Slovakia took any action to stop the Germans. Britain and France did announce in March that they would protect Poland. The Munich Agreement was the height of appeasement. By invading Czecho-Slovakia Hitler had shown its futility. Yet the guarantee of Poland seemed like an empty promise.

During the summer of 1939, France, Britain, and the Soviet Union held diplomatic talks in the effort to find a mechanism to prevent German aggression against Poland. Joseph Stalin, the Soviet dictator, knowing of Hitler's hatred of Communism and Slavs, wanted a concrete military agreement. He was justifiably skeptical about the previous British and French acts of appeasement. He also wanted the right to send his armies across Poland to attack Germany to keep it from invading the Soviet Union. The French and British did not trust the Communist leader, and the Poles rejected his demand outright. Meanwhile, Hitler was preparing for decisive action.

Polish Crisis. At the beginning of April 1939, Hitler ordered his generals to prepare for Case White, the invasion of Poland. For months, Nazi sympathizers had been agitating among the German minority in Poland and creating incidents in Danzig. Their complaints of discrimination and demands for self-determination echoed those that had destroyed Czecho-Slovakia. Hitler demanded a free hand in Poland to "protect" the German minority. German armies now confronted Poland along their historical frontiers and from Slovakia in the south. Hitler wanted to separate Stalin from France and Britain. He did so by opening up trade negotiations with the Soviet Union, but Poland was discussed as well. On August 21, 1939, came word that an agreement was pending. France and Britain felt deserted and betrayed by Stalin. They repeated their determined pledges to protect Poland. On August 23, Germany and the Soviet Union signed the Non-Aggression Pact, promising not to join any action that directly or indirectly threatened either power. In a secret part of the treaty, they agreed to divide Poland between them, should there be war. The conquered territory would begin to add the *Lebensraum* that Greater Germany demanded. The Soviet Union would regain territory lost in World War I.

This surprising agreement among declared enemies stunned the world. It gave Japan an excuse to leave the Rome-Berlin-Tokyo Axis agreement, which had been based on the solidarity of fascists against Communists. It placed Poland in an utterly defenseless position. As Hit-

ler repeated his demands on Poland, diplomats around the world urged
him to negotiate. Poland agreed to mediation. But Hitler, emboldened
by appeasement, regarded Chamberlain and Daladier as "miserable
worms" and "cowards." He was determined to go to war in Poland, and
the Non-Aggression Pact made the action virtually danger free. Desperate, Poland mobilized its forces on August 30.

Germany Attacks Poland. In the dawn hours of September 1, 1939,
Hitler launched the invasion of Poland. Although Italy called for negotiations, England and France refused to meet unless Germany withdrew
from Poland. On September 3 the two western powers declared war on
Germany, and World War II began.

Hitler's rearmament program had built a military power based on the
latest technology. Thus German tanks, motorized troop carriers and aircraft swept over 1.7 million men across Poland. It was a lightning-quick
war, a *Blitzkrieg*: German forces crossed western Poland in 18 days.
Although Warsaw held out bravely, it was flattened by German strategic
bombing. The Soviet Union hurriedly invaded on September 17. Warsaw
fell on September 27, and Hitler and Stalin divided up Poland two days
later. Germany annexed over 72,000 square miles with over 22 million
inhabitants. The Soviet Union took an even larger territory, over 77,000
square miles and some 13 million inhabitants.

The war unleashed Hitler's rabid racism as well. Within Germany, the
incurably ill and mentally handicapped were assembled and put to death
in specialized institutions. In Poland, the Slavic political leaders suffered
the same fate. Then attention turned to the Jews. Poland had Europe's
largest Jewish population, approximately three million before World War
II. They were rounded up from villages and towns and then compacted
in urban ghettos in cities like Warsaw and Lodz. German farmers moved
into these evacuated Polish territories, and many "Aryan-looking" Polish
children were taken for "Germanization." Polish Jews had to wear a
yellow star on their clothing and surrender their goods. In the crowded,
disease-ridden ghettos, they were slowly starved and eliminated due to
the lack of adequate food and medicine. This was the beginning of
Hitler's plan to systematically exterminate Europe's Jews, the Holocaust.
This combination of overwhelming military power and determined racism is one of the most devastating characteristics of Germany's conduct
of World War II.

"Phony War." During the first year of the war, Germany and the Soviet Union cooperatively disposed of eastern Europe. After dividing Poland, Stalin imposed Russia's might on Estonia, Latvia, and Lithuania,

then went after Finland. In the bitter Russo-Finnish War (November 1939–March 1940), Finnish resistance exposed weaknesses in the Soviet army, but could not hold off the inevitable. The Soviet Union was expelled from the League of Nations, but it conquered Finland and took territory nevertheless. Although technically in a state of war with Germany, France and England were still not ready for full-fledged combat. Some historians have called this period the "Phony War." Others, comparing it with Hitler's campaigns, have called it the *Sitzkrieg*, the "sitting war."

German Invasion of Scandinavia. Early in 1940, England and France mined the waters around Norway to keep them out of German control. The Germans marched into Denmark and launched airborne forces to the Norwegian coastal cities in March 1940. Little Denmark was quickly overwhelmed and accepted military occupation. The Norwegians resisted, and Anglo-French troops landed to help them, but were forced to pull out. The superior German forces prevailed. In April 1940, King Haakon VII escaped to London and the Germans set up a puppet government. In 1942 Vidkun Quisling became Norway's fascist dictator.

Fall of France. On May 10, 1940, German forces attacked Luxembourg, the Netherlands, and Belgium on the way to France. This attack was unannounced, and also lightning swift. German pinpoint bombing of central Rotterdam flattened all but the shell-scarred city hall. Queen Wilhelmina of the Netherlands fled to England, and her country surrendered on May 14. The Belgian armies were collapsing as a British Expeditionary Force landed to help them. By May 28 they were trapped on the beaches of Dunkirk, being strafed and bombed by German planes as hundreds of small British boats braved the firestorm to ferry the soldiers to waiting ships. Nearly 340,000 British and French troops were evacuated, but over 30,000 men and all their equipment were lost. German forces pressed on and took Paris on June 17. The French government fell. The new premier, Marshal Henri-Philippe Pétain, signed an armistice with the Germans on June 22, 1940. Germans occupied northern France. On July 9 Pétain moved the capital to Vichy, south of the Loire River, and established an authoritarian government friendly to Germany. When French general Charles de Gaulle declared resistance to the Germans, he received diplomatic support from Britain. On July 3 and 4, the British destroyed French naval ships in Algeria and other ports in order to prevent them from falling into German hands. With the Germans fast overtaking France, Mussolini invaded from the south, declaring war on both France and England. The Rome-Berlin Axis remained in place.

Battle of Britain. Throughout the summer of 1940, German planes attacked England and German forces prepared to invade from the French channel islands. As Germans attacked English airfields and war plants, British planes bombed German industrial cities in the Rhine and Ruhr valleys. The Germans declared a blockade of Britain in an effort to isolate it, but Britain and the United States signed a lend-lease agreement on September 2. In exchange for 50 American destroyers, Britain gave the United States 99-year leases on Atlantic military bases from Canada to British Guiana. The United States, although not at war, began plans to build a two-ocean navy and to draft and train men for the armed forces.

Despite their devastating bombing runs, the Germans were unable to defeat the British Royal Air Force. Nor could they enforce the blockade, which American convoys penetrated to resupply the beleaguered islands. In June 1941 Hitler called off the air war in order to prepare for the invasion of Russia. Winston Churchill summed up the bravery of the Royal Air Force pilots, saying, "Never have so many owed so much to so few."

Balkan Campaigns. While Germany was preoccupied on the western front, the Soviet Union turned south to demand territory from Rumania. Hitler and Mussolini agreed that Rumania, with its rich oil fields at Ploesti, should be defended against the Soviet army. German troops were sent there on October 8, 1940. Although Stalin sent his foreign minister, Vyacheslav Molotov, to Berlin to negotiate, both Rumania and Hungary joined the Axis powers. But Italy's campaign in Yugoslavia and Albania was going badly, so German forces were sent there as reinforcements. Yugoslavia joined the Axis in March 1941, and the German troops next invaded Greece. They entered Athens at the end of April. With these advances, the British were pushed out of many of their Mediterranean naval bases, falling back to North Africa and the Middle East.

Russian Front. In 1940, after the Soviet action against Rumania, Hitler decided to prepare Germany to conquer Russia. He ordered his generals to draw up plans for Operation Barbarossa, with an expected invasion date of May 1941. The need to disperse troops to the Balkans and North Africa held up the invasion, causing great uneasiness among the German generals. They doubted that Germany was ready for such a major campaign. But after all the victories on the western front, Hitler was confident. On June 22, 1941, Germany, aided by Italy, Rumania, Hungary, and Finland, invaded Russia with some three million men. The battlefront was over 2,000 miles long. The German *Blitzkrieg* moved up to 50 miles per day into Soviet-occupied Poland, the Ukraine, and the Black Sea region By September the German forces were besieging Moscow.

War with the United States. In April 1941, Japan and the Soviet Union concluded a nonaggression pact of their own. Japan had already taken Manchuria, which bordered on Siberia, and was preparing to widen its own conquests into China and Southeast Asia. Between December 6 and 8, 1941, Japan unleashed attacks against China, British Hong Kong, Malaya, and the American naval base at Pearl Harbor in Hawaii. The following day, United States president Franklin Roosevelt immediately asked Congress to declare war on Japan. On December 11, 1941, Italy and Germany, respecting the weakened Rome-Berlin-Tokyo Axis, declared war on the United States. The American military was not yet up to full force. The immediate effect of the entry of the United States into the war was to increase supplies to England and the Soviet Union. This helped both the British navy and the Russian Red Army continue their pressure on the Germans.

African Campaign. When Italy had declared war in 1940, it had its eye on British territories in North Africa. In the fall 1940, Italian forces moved from Ethiopia into British Somaliland and from Libya into Egypt. The British counterattacked, pushing the Italians back and invading both Ethiopia and Libya. The Germans sent in reinforcements in April 1941. General Erwin Rommel led the seasoned Africa Corps in a determined campaign to recover Italian losses. Rommel's forces pushed back the British for six months, until the British sent General Bernard Montgomery to oppose him in October 1942. One month later, American General Dwight Eisenhower led combined American and British forces into Morocco and Algeria They took over Vichy French posts there and arranged an armistice. Although the Germans then occupied the rest of France, the French forces in North Africa continued to help the Allies.

The Holocaust. By 1942, the Axis had most of Europe under its control. Spain, Portugal, Switzerland, and Sweden maintained their neutrality, but they did not challenge German or Italian authority. In northern Europe, from France across to the front lines in Russia, the German occupying forces imposed Hitler's vicious racial campaign against the Jews. Generally they worked with local collaborators who were willing to identify and round up Jews. In Poland the Jews were placed into ghettos until concentration camps could be built. In western Europe the Jews were rounded up and sent, by closed freight cars, to labor camps or to the eastern concentration camps. The Jews of Germany's Balkan allies suffered a similar fate. In the Soviet Union, volunteer Mobile Killing Units, called *Einsatzgruppen*, drove into towns and villages, rounded up the Jews, and shot them. There were several sweeps, and hundreds of thousands were killed in this manner. In January 1942, at a conference at Wannsee, leaders of the SS spelled out their plan to industrialize the extermination procedures that we now call the Holocaust. Specially designed killing facilities with gas chambers and crematoria were developed. Jews and other victims were cycled through them for elimination. Train tracks and schedules, building supplies and manpower were all allocated for this deliberate genocide. This was Hitler's Final Solution, and it made concentration camp names such as Auschwitz, Treblinka, Bergen-Belsen, Sobibor, and Dachau forever infamous. The Holocaust was responsible for the death of some six million Jews and great numbers of prisoners of war, political prisoners, intellectuals, and other "undesirables," such as gypsies, Jehovah's Witnesses, homosexuals, and the physically and mentally disabled. Two-thirds of European Jewry were killed by the Nazis and their collaborators between 1938 and 1945, most from conquered territories. The local populations surrendered their Jews in hope of milder treatment from the German conquerors. The Holocaust was, like the carefully planned invasions, an integral part of Nazi aggression in Europe.

Resistance to Hitler. Within the German police state, resistance was scattered and sporadic. There were few opportunities for resistance groups to coordinate their activities. One such effort was the so-called White Rose movement at the Catholic University in Munich. Led by Hans Scholl, this student group worked mainly through pamphlets and secret meetings. Its leaders were taken and beheaded as traitors early in 1943. Another form of resistance was that of Adam von Trott zu Stolz, a member of the German Foreign Office who sought assistance from abroad to build and develop a resistance movement. He and other members of the predominantly civilian Kreisau Circle wanted to plan a new Christian state to succeed the Third Reich. They were caught and hanged in 1944. The most famous resistance conspiracy was that of the military, led by Colonel Claus Schenk von Stauffenberg. With a group of other officers, he plotted to assassinate Hitler during a military staff meeting. He planted a bomb underneath the conference table on July 20, 1944, but the blast failed to kill the Fuehrer. The conspiracy was exposed, and its members were executed. All of these actions only served to intensify police state activities. By the end of the war, over 11,000 Germans had been executed for resistance to the Nazi regime.

There were successful resistance movements outside of Germany that carried out sabotage and espionage behind German lines. In France, the resistance movements coalesced around the Free French headed by Charles de Gaulle. A number of German Communists who had found asylum in the Soviet Union organized the National Committee to Free Germany.

The Axis in Retreat. In December 1942, at the Battle of Stalingrad, the Russians finally stopped the Germans. The 17-month-long siege of Leningrad broke in January 1943. After months of fighting from street to street, the Russians held Stalingrad in February, with 80,000 Germans killed or captured. Along a front line that ran from the Baltic Sea to the tip of Greece, the Germans retreated throughout 1943 and 1944.

In the west the Allies defeated the Germans in North Africa by May 1943. There were nearly one million Germans casualties on that front. In July General Eisenhower led Allied forces from Africa into Sicily, taking the island by the end of the following month. On September 2, they pushed on into Italy, which surrendered the following day. German troops kept fighting, however, and it was not until June 4, 1944, that the Allied forces entered Rome. Two days later a massive Allied force landed on the beaches of Normandy, opening the western front. Once again, Germany was fighting a two-front war. Germany's eastern allies began to surrender to the Soviet Army. Rumania in August 1944, Estonia and Bulgaria in September, Latvia and Yugoslavia in October, Hungary in February 1945. By early 1945, the Allied forces under Eisenhower in the west and the Soviet forces under Marshal Georgi Zhukov in the east were preparing to attack Germany itself.

Allied Diplomacy. The Germans were holding fast in Tunisia when, from January 17 to 27, 1943, President Roosevelt, British Prime Minister Winston Churchill, and French resistance leader General Charles de Gaulle met at Casablanca, Morocco. They knew of the German defeat at Stalingrad and were optimistic about the African campaign. They agreed that they would press the Axis powers for unconditional surrender, although they did not announce the policy at that time.

In February 1945, Churchill and Roosevelt traveled to meet Stalin in Russia's Black Sea port city of Yalta. At this meeting the "Big Three" decided that defeated Germany would be disarmed, de-Nazified, demilitarized, and divided into four zones (including a French zone), zones for the victorious Allies to occupy under the direction of an Allied Control Council. Berlin, located in the Soviet sector, was to be divided into four zones as well, with free access guaranteed by the Russians. In view of the Soviet control of eastern Europe, the Big Three agreed to give Poland the German territory east of the Oder and Neisse Rivers, approximately 27 percent of prewar Germany. The German populations would be deported from Poland, Czechoslovakia, and Hungary back to Germany. There were still issues outstanding, and the statesmen agreed to meet again when the war was over.

Defeat and Surrender. The end came quickly. In January and February 1945, the Russians blasted the German forces in Poland. By February 20 they were 30 miles from Berlin. The going in the west was somewhat slower, but Allied forces found a bridge over the Rhine still standing at Remagen, and crossed it on March 7. American forces reached the Elbe River early in April, while Soviet forces were subjecting Berlin to a devastating bombardment. As the German armies collapsed, Hitler ordered the destruction of German industries to prevent them from falling into Allied hands. But his orders were ignored. He accused the Germans of cowardice and weakness, saying they deserved defeat. On April 29 he wrote his "Political Testament," declaring his total innocence and blaming the war on Jews and the European powers who supported them. On April 30 Adolf Hitler committed suicide in Berlin. He named Admiral Karl Doenitz to succeed him, with Joseph Goebbels as chancellor. When the Russians refused to negotiate with Goebbels, he too committed suicide, taking his family with him.

Berlin fell to the Russians on May 2, 1945. German troops began to surrender along the southern and western battlefronts. General Eisenhower accepted the surrender of the German forces on May 7 in the French city of Reims; the Russians had a similar ceremony in Berlin-Karlshorst on May 8.

8

From Occupation to Sovereignty, 1945–1949

Europe lay shattered and exhausted in the summer of 1945. Over 35 million civilians and soldiers died in the war. The Soviet Union alone lost nearly 20 million; Poland lost about 3 million, and Germany had approximately 4.5 million dead. In addition, 5.1 million Jews perished in the Holocaust, over 90 percent of them in Eastern European countries which turned their Jews over to German occupying forces. Some 3 million Polish Jews alone met their death in this way. There were actually more civilian than military deaths in this war, for the first time in history. In Central and Eastern Europe nearly half of the urban housing was destroyed, and 75 percent of the rural homes were caught in the battle zones. Intense aerial and artillery bombardment had destroyed railroads, canals, bridges, harbors, and industrial plants and equipment. The economy was in a state of virtual collapse across the continent. Agriculture was at a standstill.

Stunde Null. The Germans called it Zero Hour. Between 50 and 60 percent of all their buildings were destroyed. In Berlin, for example, nearly 85 percent of the industry was destroyed or dismantled. More than 25 percent of Germany's housing was destroyed, with a higher proportion in cities like Hamburg, where over 50 percent of the housing lay in ruins. Transportation was also demolished. Some 10,000 locomotive engines and over 112,000 freight cars were destroyed. Railroads, canals, and bridges had been targeted by bombing raids, then further damaged by retreating German armies to slow the Allied advance. The entire merchant fleet was destroyed. Roads and streets were filled with shell holes and rubble. Water and sewer systems were destroyed. The average diet available provided only 40 percent of minimum daily requirements. Fuel and clothing were simply not available.

Refugees and Expellees. Toward this disaster zone streamed nearly 16 million German refugees, fleeing from former German lands east of the Oder-Neisse line or expelled from other European countries where they had once been members of a German minority. It was the greatest migration in history. About 3 million never made it at all. Of the rest, some 5 million settled in the eastern zone administered by the Russians; 8 million headed toward the three western zones of occupation. There were also about 8 million nationals from other countries who had been in German labor and concentration camps. These expellees and refugees made Germany's immediate postwar population approximately 20 percent larger than it had been during the war. The nearly 8 million Allied troops occupying Germany further strained the resources of the devastated land.

Occupation Zones. For the two weeks immediately following the surrender, Admiral Karl Doenitz remained in place as the nominal head of the German government. Then he, the members of his government, and other prominent Nazi leaders were arrested. They were imprisoned, pending trial by an International Military Tribunal for crimes against peace and humanity. On June 5 the occupying powers announced that Germany, based on its December 31, 1937, frontiers, had been divided into four zones of occupation. The Soviet Union controlled the region east of the Elbe River, which was centered on Berlin. On July 1, 1945, American troops, which had thrust into areas of Thuringia and Saxony within the Russian zone, pulled back to the west. The British took the northwestern sector, with the Rhineland city of Cologne and the Elbe port city of Hamburg. The Americans had the southwestern sector, with the great cities of Frankfurt and Munich. The French had an hourglass-shaped western sector, centered on the Rhineland city of Koblenz in the north and Freiburg in the south. Berlin was similarly divided. An Inter-Allied Control Council, made up of one commandant appointed by each of the four powers, served in a joint administration of the city.

Potsdam Conference. From July 17 to August 2, 1945, the Big Three leaders of the United States, Britain, and the Soviet Union met at Potsdam, in the Soviet zone just outside of Berlin, to discuss arrangements for coordinating their administration of Germany. Two of the leaders were new: Harry Truman had become the American president after Roosevelt died in April 1945; Winston Churchill's government was voted out during the conference, and he was replaced in Potsdam by Britain's new prime minister, Clement Attlee. They were hosted by Stalin.

The Potsdam Conference continued the discussion begun by the Big Three at Yalta (in the Crimea peninsula) in February. It was influenced by the reality that the Soviet armies were in control of Eastern Europe. Some historians have charged that President Roosevelt, at Yalta, and President Truman, at Potsdam, gave the Eastern European countries away to the Russians. The fact is that the Western powers never had control of these regions, and did not intend to fight Russia for them.

The Potsdam agreements envisioned that the four great powers would cooperate in Germany, in a "condominium" government, so to speak:

> German militarism and Nazism will be extirpated and the Allies will take in agreement together, now and in the future, the other measures necessary to assure that Germany will never again threaten her neighbors or the peace of the world. It is not the intention of the Allies to destroy or enslave the German people. It is their intention that the German people be given the opportunity to prepare for the eventual reconstruction of their life on a democratic and peaceful basis. If their own efforts are steadily directed to this end, it will be possible for them in due course to take their place among the free and peaceful peoples of the world.[2]

The Allies agreed that each power was responsible for the political and economic recovery in its own zone. Germany would be completely demilitarized and disarmed. Organizations that reflected Germany's military traditions were prohibited. All vestiges of Nazism were to be obliterated: Nazi leaders, supporters, and high officials would be arrested and tried; all Nazi Party members in any public office would be removed. The Allies permitted Germany no production of munitions, ships, or aircraft. Any production of strategic metals and chemicals was to be strictly controlled. The economy was to be treated as a single unit, but decentralized and regulated to break up monopolies. There would be prompt restoration of basic agriculture, transport, housing, and utilities to make sure that the needs of the occupying forces, refugees, and German people were met. Each of the Allies was entitled to reparations so long as Germany remained self-supporting. In addition, the Soviet Union would receive some of the industrial equipment from the western zones in exchange for basic commodities from the eastern zone.

The Potsdam accords also recognized some significant territorial changes. The East Prussian region around the city of Koenigsberg went to the Soviet Union, and all other territory east of the Oder and Neisse Rivers went under Polish administration, pending the final determination of Poland's western frontier. The territory transferred to Polish hands had accounted for over 20 percent of Germany's prewar agricultural production, and made the remainder of the state, impacted with refugees, vulnerable to malnutrition and even to pockets of starvation.

Germany also ceased to have any diplomatic representation abroad, and all of its foreign relations were conducted by the Allies. All records were turned over to the Allies. German nationals could not leave German territory without specific authorization from one of the occupying authorities.

Administration of the Soviet Zone of Occupation. When the Potsdam agreement was implemented, significant differences began to emerge in the administration of the occupied zones. The Russians clearly came with a plan and with a group of German Communists-in-exile to help implement it. Walter Ulbricht was their most prominent leader. The Russians set up the Soviet Military Administration for Germany (SMAD) headed by Marshal Zhukov, which, in turn, created offices to manage the zone. Established within two months after the surrender, these functional offices were each directed by a local German and one of the Soviet-trained German Communists. On June 11, SMAD issued an order calling for the formation of political parties. Four antifascist political parties were recognized: the Communist, the Social Democratic, the Liberal, and the Christian Democratic. In April 1946 the Social Democrats and Communists merged to form the Socialist Unity Party (SED). Wilhelm Pieck, the Communist Party (KPD) leader, and Otto Grotewohl, the Social Democratic Party (SPD) chief, cochaired the new party.

The Russians began immediately to take reparations, dismantling existing factories, claiming inventories, and herding livestock, loading it all on trains and trucks for shipment to the Soviet Union. Because of the ruined transportation system, however, much of the industrial equipment never made it to Russia, and rusted on railroad sidings. The remaining plant and equipment was seized by the government, without compensation, and declared to be state property. Banks and their assets were seized as well. A political referendum in Saxony in June 1946 affirmed this action, and the zone government assumed responsibility for the management of the economy. SMAD also implemented land reform, seizing some 8.3 million acres without compensation to former Junker owners and redistributing it in small plots to farmers. Some land was retained for large state agricultural cooperatives (VEGs). This created over 220,000 new 17- to 20-acre holdings for farmers and refugees, and allowed some 165,000 others to increase the size of their acreage.

Education was centralized for the zone, and teacher training started immediately. Nazis were purged from the classrooms at all levels. New curricula were introduced oriented around Soviet-style socialist ideology and Marxist-Leninist concepts of party democracy.

Western Occupation Zones. Procedures in the western sectors contrasted sharply with the centralized approach of the Russians. The French closed their zone off to the rest of Germany and began immediately shipping most of its industrial production to France. As after World War I, the French occupying forces began a campaign to win the Saar. They built a new school system that featured aspects of French practice and culture. Because France had not been included in the Potsdam Conference, it felt no obligation to uphold the agreements made there. French occupation officials resisted British and American efforts to centralize and coordinate administration of communication, finance, and foreign trade of the western zones.

The British set up offices to manage economic affairs and divided their zone into three administrative districts: Schleswig-Holstein, Lower Saxony, and North Rhine–Westphalia. Appointing officials with Nazi-free records, the British reestablished local government and political parties within each district, but delayed zonewide political activity until 1946.

The Americans established the Office of Military Government (OMGUS) headed by General Joseph McNarney and General Lucius Clay. They were responsible for the occupation forces, but policy decisions were handled from Washington. The American Joint Chiefs had drafted an order—JCS-1067—that established a hard-line military control in the region, but growing tensions among the occupying forces made it difficult to implement. By September 1945, the Americans gave the Germans permission to form political parties. The zone was divided into three administrative regions: Bavaria, Baden-Wuerttemberg, and Hesse.

It was readily apparent from the outset that four-power administration was not going to work in Germany because the Allies could not agree on how to do it. They were divided between punishing Germany and restoring it. Ideology played a role as well. The Western powers feared

Communist control in the Eastern zone, and the Russians regarded Nazism as a direct outgrowth of monopoly capitalism. In March 1946, Winston Churchill warned the world about an "iron curtain" that had descended across the continent of Europe. Thereafter, the Allied Control Council became virtually ineffective. Four-power talks in the spring of 1946 and in 1947 could not produce implementation of the Potsdam agreements.

Emergence of Political Parties. Postwar political parties appeared first in the Soviet zone. The Communist Party formed first, on June 11, 1945, in response to the Soviet decree. The Social Democrats organized on June 15 in Berlin, as the "united voice of the German working class." By October, however, Social Democrats in the western zones, led by Kurt Schumacher, wanted their own party organization, and the party split into two factions. The party's Central Committee, in Berlin, later joined with the Communist Party to become the Socialist Unity Party (SED).

In the western zones, political parties first appeared in the late summer of 1945. The Christian Democratic Union (CDU) had roots in the prewar Catholic Center Party. In the new era, however, it unified Catholics and Protestants in a political movement that was basically conservative and federalist. The first group formed in Cologne in July 1945, then expanded to other localities and restructured itself at a September meeting in Frankfurt. By December, at Bad Godesberg, the local parties agreed on the name Christian Democratic Union. The party's leading personality was Konrad Adenauer, the 70-year-old Mayor of Cologne, who became the party's chairman early in 1946. Initially, the party founders had wanted to nationalize the major industries, but the United States authorities vetoed that concept. With strong influence from the trade unions, the party developed the concept of the "social market economy," that is, free enterprise but with responsibility for the well-being of the citizens. Ludwig Erhard, a professor of economics and advisor to the American commandant, is credited with defining this policy.

In Bavaria the Christian Social Union (CSU) formed in October 1945. Like the CDU, the CSU was interdenominational, conservative, and federalist. Its insistence on autonomy reinforced the latter two perspectives, however. The two parties often acted in concert, but never merged.

The prewar liberals also organized parties under the occupation. The Liberal Democratic Party (LDPD) first formed in Berlin during July 1945, led by Wilhelm Kuelz. Here again, the western zones wanted their own organization. In Baden and Wuerttemberg, Theodor Heuss and Reinhold Maer founded the Democratic Peoples' Party (DVP) in July 1945. In September the Party of the Free Democrats (FDP) organized in Hamburg. Other liberal organizations grew in the American and British zones. The liberals stood for free enterprise and the elimination of church influence on affairs of state. The formation of the SED in the Russian zone ended the autonomy of the LDPD, and the western liberals finally coalesced into a separate Free Democratic Party (FDP) in December 1948, with Theodor Heuss as chairman.

De-Nazification. In accordance with the Potsdam agreement, the Allies carried out de-Nazification, although the procedures were different in each zone. The Russians removed former Nazis from government and education positions. The Americans required all suspects to answer a 131-item questionnaire, which helped classify them into five categories ranging from "most guilty" to "sympathizer," with punishments appropriate to each category. The French held judicial proceedings; the British turned the process over to the local German administrations they had appointed.

Nuremberg Trials. Despite their disagreements in other areas, the four Allies were united in their determination to prosecute the Nazi leadership. On August 8, 1945, they agreed on a statute to establish an International Military Tribunal to try 22 Nazi leaders for conspiracy to break the peace, breaking the peace, aggression, war crimes, and crimes against humanity. They chose Nuremberg, site of the Nazi Party congresses, as the location for the proceedings. The trials began in November 1945 and continued to October 1, 1946. The defendants included the leadership of the most infamous Nazi Party organizations and government organizations and the supreme army command. Although Hitler, Goebbels, and Himmler had all committed suicide, there were others to hold accountable for Nazi brutality. Twelve men were sentenced to death, including: Hermann Goering, Marshal Wilhelm Keitel, chief of the army command; Wilhelm Frick, secretary of internal affairs; and Julius Streicher, publisher of the rabid anti-Semitic paper, *Der Stuermer*. Goering committed suicide before his death sentence could be carried out. Seven others were sentenced to prison, for terms of from ten years to life. They served their terms in Spandau Prison in Berlin. Rudolf Hess, Hitler's deputy, the last prisoner in Spandau, died in August 1987. Franz von Papen, the former chancellor, and Hjalmar Schacht, the economic wizard, were acquitted.

Bizonia. In an atmosphere of growing tension among the occupying powers, the Americans acted unilaterally, in May 1946, to stop reparations delivery to the Russians. The Russians retaliated by halting shipment of vital agricultural products to the west. By the end of the year, thousands of Germans were dying of starvation, and the costs of the occupation were skyrocketing. These early stages of what became known as the Cold War had a profound impact on German recovery. As the Soviets and the Americans grew more distant, each side became more willing to return power to the German sector it controlled. Talks at the foreign minister level during 1946 did not break the distrust. On September 6, American Secretary of State James Byrnes stated it was time for the Germans to be trusted with building their own democratic state. The United States invited France and Britain to develop joint economic policies for their zones. When France declined, the Americans and British agreed to unite their zones on January 1, 1947, into Bizonia. With its Economic Council, 104-deputy Parliamentary Assembly, and 16-member Council of States, this new administrative unit gave considerable responsibility for managing affairs back to the 39 million Germans in the region. The Russians gave their zone a similar structure in February 1948. The French eventually turned Bizonia into Trizonia in April 1949.

Cold War. By 1947 the tensions between Western Allies and the Soviet Union led to overt diplomatic confrontation on an international level. The Russians supported local Communist uprisings in Greece, Turkey, and Iran, areas formerly within the British sphere of influence. But the British could not afford to maintain their imperial forces any longer. The Americans assumed the burden, and with the Truman Doctrine, declared that the United States would provide economic and military assistance to nations wishing to ward off Communism. Agreeing to this plan to contain Communism, the American Congress voted some $400 million in March 1947 to assist Greece and Turkey. This policy, clearly aimed at Soviet expansionism, divided Europe and announced the beginning of the Cold War. At the council of foreign ministers then meeting in Moscow, peace treaties were drafted for signatures from Italy, Rumania, Hungary, Bulgaria, and Finland. Most of these were outside of Western control. In Germany, however, where Western interests were involved, it was not yet possible for the powers to agree on a peace treaty for a united German state.

Marshall Plan. In June 1947, the American secretary of state, George C. Marshall, gave the commencement address at Harvard University. In it, he issued an invitation to the nations of Europe: if they would collaborate on a plan for the economic recovery of Europe as a whole, the United States would provide resources and technical assistance to help carry it out. Although the Soviet Union and its satellite states in Eastern Europe rejected the invitation on July 2, 16 Western European nations met 10 days later to begin drafting the European Recovery Program (ERP). The western zones of Germany were included in the plan, which drew the frontiers of the Cold War right through the middle of the occupied nation.

In 1948 the American Congress approved the Marshall Plan and appropriated funds for European reconstruction. Unlike the Dawes and Young plans following World War I, the Marshall Plan required structured and coordinated investment in basic industry and agriculture, and the transportation infrastructure. It included provisions for housing in order to consolidate the workforce in industrial centers. To start the recovery, the plan also provided emergency food and raw materials. Germany received roughly $1.4 billion of the $17 billion in Marshall Plan aid appropriated between 1948 and 1952. Implementation of the plan ended the controls on West German industrial production levels and provided the opportunity for full use of Germany's managerial and technological skills as well as the large available workforce.

The Russians walked out of the Allied Control Council in March 1948, accusing the Western powers of breaking the Potsdam agreement for four-power administration of the German economy. As a correlation to the Marshall Plan, Britain, France, Belgium, the Netherlands, and Luxembourg signed the Brussels Treaty in March 1948. This established a 50-year alliance of economic and military cooperation. In May of that year, the first meeting of the Congress of Europe took place and began discussions on the potential for a European Union.

Berlin Airlift. In order to implement the Marshall Plan in Germany, the Western Allies announced a reform of the currency used in their zones in June 1948. The value of the new deutschmark was pegged to that of the American dollar. The Russians followed with their own currency reform, and thereafter the official currencies defined the practical border between the eastern and western regions of Germany. In protest of the reforms in the west, the Russians stopped all traffic traveling to and from the west to Berlin by road and by rail. Berlin lay some 120 miles within the Soviet zone. The Americans, British, and French refused to be denied access to the beleaguered city, and began a massive airlift of vital supplies. Using air corridors from Hamburg, Hanover, and Frankfurt am Main, some 195,000 planes flew approximately 1.5 million tons of vital supplies. At the height of activity, one plane landed every three minutes. The Russians claimed sole authority over the city in November, but the other powers rejected that contention. The Berlin Blockade lasted eleven months, until May 1949. It cemented the cooperation between the western zones of Germany but spelled a serious division in the city of Berlin. The Western military governments formed a three-power command and authorized elections for mayor of West Berlin. On December 5, the Social Democrats won two-thirds of the vote, and Ernst Reuter became lord mayor.

West Germany: The German Federal Republic. With the Frankfurt Documents of July 1, 1948, three Western occupying powers authorized the state (*Laender*) presidents in their zones to draw up a constitution for a West German federal state. In September 1948, a Parliamentary Council of 65 representatives of the state legislatures began meeting in Bonn to write the constitution. The powers then signed the Occupation Statute on April 8, 1949, in which they agreed to recognize self-government in West Germany. On May 8, 1949, four years after the German surrender to the Allies, the Basic Law was approved by the Parliamentary Council in West Germany. On May 23, shortly after the ending of the Berlin Blockade, the Basic Law of the German Federal Republic was adopted. The structure of the government has been described in chapter 1. The city of Bonn was designated as its capital. In August, elections for the Bundestag brought a narrow victory to the Christian Democrats (139 seats) over the Social Democrats (131 seats). Konrad Adenauer (CDU) became the first chancellor of the Republic, heading a conservative coalition of the CDU and FDP. Theodor Heuss (FDP, 52 seats) was elected president. The new government was convened in September 1949. It signified the official division of Germany into two units.

East Germany: The German Democratic Republic. In March 1949, during the Berlin Blockade, the Russians authorized the People's Council, formed in 1947, to draft a constitution for a Democratic Republic in East Germany. On October 7, 1949, the People's Council formed the Provisional People's Chamber, the legislature of the German Democratic Republic, and issued the state's new constitution. It provided for a People's Chamber (Volkskammer) as the sole source of state legislative authority. The Volkskammer elected the members and chairman of the Council of State, a 16-member body that served as head of state. The Volkskammer elected the chairman of the National Defense Council, the president, prosecutor general and judges of the Supreme Court, and the Council of Ministers, which directed the political, economic, cultural, and social matters of state. As in West Germany, the president had limited powers. Within the Volkskammer, parliamentary committees dealt with policy issues and prepared bills for deliberation by the full legislature.

The Volkskammer elected Wilhelm Pieck president of the Republic and Otto Grotewohl the prime minister. Walter Ulbricht, the deputy prime minister, also exercised considerable political influence.

People's Assemblies were elected at the village, city, and regional levels. The constitution proclaimed equal, universal, direct, and secret elections of candidates approved by their fellow employees or work teams. Only nominees so approved could stand for election. The candidates for any of the legislatures, from the local to the national level, were listed on a ballot prepared by the National Front, the political organization coordinating the activities of the SED and the Democratic Bloc, which consisted of the Democratic Farmers' Party, the National Democratic Party, and the Confederation of Free German Trade Unions. To run the elections, the National Front worked with the general secretary of the SED, chairman of the Council of State, and the chairmen of the Democratic Bloc.

The division of the former German Reich into two sovereign states was complete. It marked the failure of the Potsdam agreement to settle the affairs of Germany. In the decades to come, both states and all of the occupying powers would proclaim the goal of reunification of Germany, but each expected to do so on its own terms.

NOTES

1. Raul Hilberg, *The Destruction of the European Jews* (New York: Holmes & Meier, 1986), p. 339.

2. Keesing's Research Report, *Germany and Eastern Europe since 1945 from the Potsdam Agreement to Chancellor Brandt's "Ostpolitik"* (New York: Charles Scribner's Sons, 1973), p. ?

9

The German Federal Republic, 1949–1990

Western Cold War rhetoric often designated East Germany as a mere satellite or colony of the Soviet Union, while identifying West Germany as an alliance partner of the United States. In fact, neither state was fully sovereign in 1949. Both continued to host occupying forces. Both were recognized by their patrons as sovereign states by 1955 and made part of regional alliance systems. Each became a symbol of one of the competing political and economic systems — the free enterprise, democratic system of Western Europe, and the centrally planned Communist Party regimes of Eastern Europe. Nowhere was the competition between the two systems more visible than in Berlin, which remained under four-power military authority long after the founding of the two states. It is remarkable that despite these burdens of compliance and competition, each developed a relatively stable and productive government, even though they were not equally stable and productive.

After the founding of the Federal Republic in West Germany in 1949, a three-power civilian High Commission replaced the military occupation government and retained considerable control. In this chapter we examine the western German Federal Republic (Bundesrepublik Deutschland, BRD). Its history is distinguished by the fact that it had swifter success in revising the occupation regulations than its eastern counterpart.

The Adenauer Years, 1949–1963. Konrad Adenauer fully understood the tasks he faced as the Federal Republic's first chancellor. The first was to demonstrate that the Federal Republic was a firmly rooted, sustainable democracy. The second was to win full sovereignty and true partnership within the Western bloc. Adenauer combined the offices of chancellor and foreign minister during the crucial period of 1951 to 1955; he worked to convert West Germany from a former enemy into an ally in the eyes of the West. His third task was the reunification of Germany under the auspices of the Federal Republic.

After the nightmarish collapse of the Weimar Republic and the Third Reich, Germans were uncertain about the future; most had not envisioned a divided Germany. West Germans accepted the new situation as a necessity. Adenauer's leadership, therefore, played a crucial role in shaping the new state and in building support for it. He was well up to the task. Fiercely independent, he had been dismissed from office by the Nazis in 1933 and again by the occupying powers in 1946. As chair of the Parliamentary Council and the CDU party, he had broad political contacts among both the Germans and the Allies. Conservative, seasoned, and determined, he dominated those in the other government offices. So strong was his control that some Germans characterized the period of the 1950s as a "chancellor democracy" and his subordinates as a "shadow cabinet." While many Germans objected to Adenauer's controlling style, the 14 years of his five terms as chancellor (September 15, 1949, through October 16, 1963) provided continuity of policy and vision, which reassured the Allies and the Germans alike.

Theodor Heuss. The first president of the Federal Republic, Theodor Heuss, had been a member of the German Democratic Party since the founding of the Weimar Republic. As a Reichstag representative, he courageously voted against the Enabling Act in March 1933. After the war he was elected to the Landtag in Wuerttemberg and helped found the Free Democratic Party, which he chaired. Like Adenauer, he served on the Parliamentary Council. His willingness to lead his party into the CDU/CSU coalition in 1949 helped give the new government a stable majority in the Bundestag. Heuss was unanimously elected to a second term in 1954 by the National Convention. The Bundestag was prepared to pass a constitutional amendment to permit him a third term in 1959, but he declined to serve. A confirmed and popular democrat, Heuss invested the presidency of the new Republic with a statesmanship and credibility that complemented the forceful Adenauer administration.

Nazi Past. The new Federal Republic faced enormous challenges. While the occupying forces had dealt with the prominent Nazis, it was still true that most Germans had supported the Hitler regime at some point. Outspokenly anti-Nazi, Adenauer condemned those who had committed criminal acts. But he believed that reconciliation with "fellow travelers" had to take place. Accordingly, the Nazi Party was outlawed in the Federal Republic. But Adenauer accepted the support of individuals with a "brown past" when they accepted the new political system. He even appointed some to office. Many felt that the Bonn government did not actively pursue Nazi criminals or confront the Nazi past. Adenauer preferred to commit former Nazi sympathizers to the new regime rather than let them contribute to a neo-Nazi movement.

Anti-Semitism. The Bundestag passed legislation to punish anti-Semitism severely. The Federal Republic assumed the responsibility for compensating individuals and groups that were victims of the Nazi political, religious, and racial persecution. There were laws compensating Jewish victims, although only about 30,000 members of the former German Jewish community remained after the war. On September 27, 1951, the chancellor and the Bundestag unanimously agreed to pay reparations to the State of Israel on behalf of the victims of the Nazi regime. A reconciliation agreement with Israel was signed on September 10, 1952, that provided for the payment of 3 billion Deutschmarks over the following 12 years.

The Refugee Problem. During the inaugural years of the Republic, some 10 million refugees, Germans expelled from other lands or displaced from the eastern territories, had to be accommodated. They comprised approximately 16 percent of the population. The resident Germans resented the strain that the newcomers put on housing and public welfare; relations between the two populations were tense. The refugees formed their own political party, the Association of Those Expelled from Their Homelands and Deprived of Their Rights (Bund der Heimatvertriebenen und Entrechteten), known as the BHE. Adenauer perceived that this disgruntled group was a danger to the Republic's stability. He worked to resolve the issues it raised. As a good faith gesture, he added a member of the BHE to his cabinet during the early 1950s.

At first the government had to assign refugees housing in private homes. Thus, one of the first problems to be tackled was housing. The first Public Housing Act of April 1950 led to the construction of over 1.8 million units within six years. Subsequent legislation in 1953 and 1956 continued this policy, the second assisting some private as well as public housing units. Rent controls were also put in place and remained effective until the 1960s. In addition, laws were passed to help compensate refugees for a portion of the losses they had suffered when they were forced out of their former homes.

Five Percent Law. There were 36 political parties fighting for election in 1946. In a further effort to strengthen parliamentary democracy, the Bundestag passed the Five Percent Law in 1949. To be entitled to a seat in the Bundestag, a party had to secure 5 percent of the national vote. This eliminated the possibility that small parties would splinter the legislature as they had in the Weimar era. Some small parties lost their Bundestag seats when this law went into effect in the 1953 elections. Small parties remained active in state elections, however.

Social Market Economy. It was also crucial to find employment for the swollen work force. The government helped settle refugees in the industrial areas of the Rhine, Ruhr, and Wuerttemberg. With the Marshall Plan, most caps on industrial production were removed, and the German "economic miracle" began. Ludwig Erhard, the minister of economic affairs (1949–1966), was the architect of the new social market ec↓nomy. He insisted on a laissez-faire policy toward business and industry, a free and competitive marketplace without cartels or government regulations.

At the same time, the government guaranteed the stability of the currency and provided for the security and welfare of the workers and those who were unable to work. Social welfare programs amounted to 36.5 percent of the national budget in 1951; this figure had risen to 42 percent four years later. In 1955 some 20 percent of the population still received some form of assistance. Many, including the Social Democrats, called for reform of the social insurance system. After a long public and political debate, the Bundestag in 1957 adopted a measure significantly raising retirement pensions and providing some cost of living adjustments. This reduced the welfare rolls.

Workers' Codetermination. The influential German Federation of Trade Unions was made up of approximately five million workers in 16 trade and industrial unions. One of its most insistent union demands was for codetermination, the right to participate in management. The Codetermination Law of April 1951 required that the board of directors of every public coal, iron, or steel company include one manual and one salaried worker and three other members nominated by the concern's workers. A follow-up law in July 1952 extended the requirement to include trade union nominees on the board of every joint stock company, although not direct worker membership. This recognition of workers' rights helped secure labor peace in the early days of the Republic.

"**Economic Miracle.**" As a result of all these factors, the German economy took off. A few statistics help explain its dramatic and sustained growth. In 1949, overall industrial production stood at about 90 percent of the 1936 level (the last normal prewar year). By 1953 it was at 158 percent of the 1936 level.[1] Unemployment, which stood at over 8 percent in 1950, fell to under 1 percent by 1961. Between 1953 and 1960, the gross domestic product (GDP), the total value of all goods and services produced, rose over 60 percent. Prohibited from investing in costly rearmament, West Germany produced industrial, consumer, and export goods that helped satisfy European demands long postponed by the war. The catalyst of Marshall Plan aid helped form a strong, diverse, and lasting base for West German prosperity. When the Korean War began in June 1950, other countries converted some of their industry into military production. This improved the market for German goods. Ironically, the standard of living in Germany was higher than that of some of its former conquerors. By 1955 West Germany was the world's third largest industrial economy.

Adenauer's Foreign Policy. Like Stresemann in the Weimar Republic, Adenauer sought to end Allied restrictions on Germany as quickly as possible. He used two strategies successfully: reconciliation with France and integration of Germany into the Western economy. His first success came in the diplomatic sphere. In November 1949, the Petersberg Agreement between West Germany and the Western powers allowed the Republic to establish diplomatic consulates overseas and to join international organizations. In 1950 the Western powers accorded West Germany full diplomatic privileges and agreed to recognize the Federal Republic as the legitimate authority for all of Germany. In July 1951 France, Britain and its Commonwealth allies, and the United States officially ended their state of war with Germany. In 1951 West Germany became a full member of the Council of Europe. Although the Council of Europe had no legislative authority, it brought Germans together with delegates from other nations to discuss matters concerning the region and make recommendations to the individual states.

Schuman Plan. France wanted compensations for West Germany's reentry into the diplomatic arena. One of Adenauer's greatest achievements was reconciliation with France. In return for the Petersberg Agreement in November 1949, he agreed to the Ruhr Authority establishing economic control of this important industrial region by a consortium of the Benelux countries (Belgium, Luxembourg, the Netherlands), France, Britain, and the United States, although the territory remained German. This part of the agreement was very controversial within Germany. Kurt Schumacher, leader of the SPD, branded Adenauer the "Allied chancellor" in protest. Nonetheless, Adenauer next supported the plan of the French foreign minister, Robert Schuman, to expand the regional scope of this cooperation into a European Coal and Steel Community (ECSC). The Benelux, Italy, France, and the Federal Republic signed the Schuman Plan in April 1951, and it went into effect in June 1952. Within the next four years, coal production in the ECSC rose 23 percent, and iron and steel, 145 percent. This farsighted program was the first step toward the eventual European economic union.

European Security. On April 4, 1949, ten West European nations, the United States, and Canada signed the North Atlantic Treaty (NATO). The signatories agreed that an attack on any one of them was an attack on all, and a cause to use any means to repel the attacker. A permanent council was formed, with three separate command groups, and provisions were made for a permanent international military force. When, in 1950, the Korean War raised fears for the security of both Asia and Europe, the United States wanted to add a military force from the German Federal Republic to the NATO armies in Europe.

The French initially objected out of concern for their own security if Germany rearmed. But in October 1950 their premier, René Pleven, proposed a plan for a European Defense Community (EDC), which defined an acceptable level of German participation. Germany would provide military units limited to 1,200 men, but no artillery. The military command would be international, thus preventing Germany from having a separate army. Negotiations opened in Paris among France, West Germany, Italy, and the Benelux.

Bonn Treaty. Adenauer used this occasion to address the occupation statutes. Without consulting his cabinet or the Bundestag, he met with the three Western powers in December 1950. The result was the Bonn Treaty, which was to repeal the occupation statute and end the authority of the Allied Control Council. The status of Berlin was unchanged by this agreement, and the three powers retained their authority for German reunification. The treaty was to come into effect with the ratification of the EDC. Some West German public opinion was strongly against rearmament and any agreement that would threaten reunification. Led by the Social Democrats, the opposition protested that it would take a constitutional amendment to permit rearmament and the military draft. Adenauer persisted. In May 1952 the Bundestag ratified the Bonn Treaty. The French National Assembly finally rejected the EDC treaty in August 1954, however, and the future of the Bonn Treaty was in doubt.

The 1953 Elections. The Social Democrats voiced outspoken criticism that Adenauer's policies endangered German reunification. Their election platform for the 1953 elections focused on the issues of reunification and defense. However, their major spokesman, Kurt Schumacher, had died in 1952. During June 1953, labor strikes and political unrest in East Germany were suppressed by Soviet armed force. This made Adenauer's defense policy more attractive. German voters gave the CDU over 45 percent of their votes, and the SPD, 28 percent. National politics shifted to the right.

NATO and the Western European Union. After the failure of the EDC, a conference on European security began in September 1954. The Benelux, France, Britain, Italy, and West Germany agreed to authorize West German rearmament under NATO regulation. They further agreed to form the Western European Union (WEU), which would work together with NATO to maintain regional security. To achieve this agreement, Adenauer agreed to French demands to place the Saar basin under European control. On May 5, 1955, Germany proclaimed its sovereign independence. Four days later—just ten years after the unconditional surrender—the Federal Republic of Germany became a member of NATO.

Trade Relations with East Germany. Despite the growing separation between the two Germanys, some economic cooperation remained. The Frankfurt Accords of October 8, 1949, permitted trade between the two new states. A subsequent agreement in September 1951 defined trade agreements for the Federal Republic and West Berlin, with the Democratic Republic and East Berlin, and these remained in effect until the 1990s. For purposes of trade, the western and eastern deutschmarks thereafter had equivalent value, and all transactions were handled by the two state banks, the Bundesbank in the west and the Staatsbank in the east. Both states defined this commerce as internal, not foreign, trade. East Germany purchased machinery, electrical supplies, and chemicals from the west; West Germany purchased textiles and clothing, agricultural and wood products, lumber, and minerals from the east.

The German Question. Despite the success of trade agreements, relations between the two German states deteriorated. In virtually every instance, the west initiated changes and the Soviet Union and the Democratic Republic reacted with parallel actions. When West Germany accepted Marshall Plan aid from the United States, the Soviet Union formed the Council for Mutual Economic Assistance (COMECON) in January 1949 with the Eastern European nations: Bulgaria, Czechoslovakia, Hungary, Poland, Rumania. COMECON also worked for economic integration of industry and trade within its region, but without the investment of funds that characterized the Marshall Plan. When the Federal Republic joined NATO in May 1955, Russia and its allies formed the Warsaw Pact military alliance in the same month. It is clear, therefore, that Soviet policy makers felt that the status of Germany had a direct impact on Russian security. The integration of the two German states into these regional alliances weakened hopes in both Germanys for reunification.

Adenauer decided to try to achieve unification by direct negotiations. Bypassing East Germany entirely, he traveled to Moscow in September 1955. In addition to reunification, he wanted to secure the return of the thousands of German prisoners of war still in Russian hands. Since the death of Stalin in 1953, the Russians had become more conciliatory with the West. They agreed to release the prisoners, and even ignored Adenauer's testy statement that the Federal Republic did not agree to the changes made in the German frontiers after 1945. Moscow accorded the Federal Republic full diplomatic recognition and agreed to the exchange of ambassadors.

The Hallstein Doctrine. The Soviets had given the East German state full diplomatic recognition in 1954. The Bonn government insisted that it was the sole legitimate successor to the sovereignty of the total German nation. On September 23, 1955, the Federal Republic announced that it would sever diplomatic relations with any nation having diplomatic relations with the East German state. Named for Adenauer's foreign policy advisor, Walter Hallstein, this doctrine effectively cut the Federal Republic off from the nations of the Soviet bloc. As an occupying power, the Soviet Union was, of course, exempted from this West German policy.

Subsequent events strengthened Adenauer's hand. The Saar plebiscite gave a majority vote for return to Germany. The Bundestag voted for universal military service for the federal army (Bundeswehr), previously made up of volunteers. The Soviet suppression of the Hungarian uprising in October 1956 helped Adenauer refute Social Democratic objections to rearmament. In 1957 the Saar officially joined the Federal Republic. In March 1957, the European Coal and Steel Community nations signed the Rome Treaty founding two new European institutions: Euratom, for research and development of peaceful atomic energy, and the European Economic Union, to create a common internal trade market not subject to the tariffs and regulations of foreign trade. Europe's most advanced industrial nation, Germany, benefited from lowering of tariffs. In exchange, it agreed to French demands to provide subsidies to farmers in the Union. These successes helped Adenauer and the CDU/CSU win the 1957 elections. For the first time in German legislative history, one party had received an absolute electoral majority.

Berlin Ultimatum. As West Germany became more firmly integrated into the Western alliance, the Russians sought to assert their position in all-German affairs. In March 1952 Joseph Stalin called for a conference to establish an all-German government. Under the Russian plan, united Germany would have complete economic autonomy, the right to build and maintain a military defense force, and full membership in the United Nations. It would, however, give up the lands east of the Oder-Neisse line and be barred from joining any military alliance. Occupation forces would be withdrawn within the year following the conclusion of the treaty. The Russians even agreed to all German elections under four-power supervision. The Western allies turned down the Soviet bid, insisting that the peace treaty should be signed first and that a sovereign Germany should be able to enter alliances thereafter if it wished. Adenauer insisted that no German government would ever give up its rights to lands east of the Oder-Neisse line.

In the years following this overture, the East Germans addressed a number of notes to the Adenauer government raising the possibility of a confederation of the two states. The chancellor and his Western Allies continued to reject these initiatives. The Russians ran out of patience. On November 10, 1958, Soviet Premier Nikita Khrushchev proclaimed that the Western powers no longer had a right to remain in Berlin. On November 27, he demanded that Berlin become a demilitarized free city, and called for a conference to achieve this within the next six months. Failing that, the Soviet Union would help the Democratic Republic annex the city. The NATO Council rejected the Soviet ultimatum in December 1958. Khrushchev responded in January 1959 with the proposal for a new peace treaty, envisioning two German states and a demilitarized Free Berlin. This proposal was connected with the Rapacki Plan, introduced by Poland, for a demilitarized and nuclear-free zone in central Europe. Both were rejected by West Germany and its allies.

The Wall. Yet economic rather than political issues opened the widest breach between the two German states. In 1949 some 130,000 East Germans had fled to the west. The pace of defection rose during the 1950s to a peak of 330,000 after the public unrest in 1953. As the East German government intensified the implementation of socialism, many of its citizens "voted with their feet" for economic opportunity in West Germany. Almost 200,000 left in 1960, and the pace intensified in 1961. On August 13, 1961, the East German government completed the construction of a wall dividing Berlin and sealing it off from the west. It also closed the frontier with the Federal Republic. West Berlin's Mayor Willi Brandt appealed to the American president, John F. Kennedy, to guarantee the security of West Berlin. Kennedy came to the city and gave his famous and fervent "Ich bin ein Berliner" speech to show American resolve. (The literal translation of these words is "I am a jelly doughnut," but the delighted Berliners knew what he meant.) The Berlin Wall revealed the economic weakness of East Germany. But it was a major defeat for Konrad Adenauer, for it also pointed out the weakness of his diplomacy with the East.

Adenauer and the CDU/CSU won the 1961 election despite an erosion of support. To secure a stable majority, Adenauer formed a coalition with the FDP. They joined on the condition, however, that Adenauer retire in 1963, when he turned 85. The next two years were bittersweet for *der Alte*, "the old one."

The *Spiegel* Affair. The low point of Adenauer's final years began on October 10, 1962, when the newsmagazine *Der Spiegel* sharply criticized the Bundeswehr and Adenauer's defense policy. *Der Spiegel* was published by Axel Springer, a press mogul who had often criticized the government. On October 26, its Hamburg editorial offices were raided by the police. Files were confiscated, and the federal attorney charged the editor and publisher of the magazine with treason. This blatant violation of press freedom caused massive public uproar and a split in the government coalition. The FDP ministers withdrew from the cabinet. Adenauer had to admit that the government had violated press freedom. The defense minister, Franz Josef Strauss, lied about his participation in the affair. In the new cabinet he had to form in December 1962, Adenauer excluded the previous ministers of defense and of justice.

German-French Treaty. Adenauer's last triumph was the conclusion of the Elysée Treaty between Germany and France in January 1963. He and Charles de Gaulle, the French president, agreed on regular consultations over foreign policy, the economy, trade, defense, and a program of youth cultural exchanges. This treaty marked the end of centuries of hostility. On that sweet note, Adenauer relinquished the chancellorship on October 15, 1963.

Chancellor Ludwig Erhard (CDU), 1963–1966. The author of West Germany's "economic miracle" was the CDU/CSU choice to succeed Adenauer. He had been the minister for economic affairs since the first Adenauer cabinet. As chancellor he had to mend the split with the FDP caused by the *Spiegel* affair. He also had to cope with Franz Josef Strauss, the new CDU leader, and with Adenauer, who remained active in the CDU and constantly fought his protégé's policies. In particular, Erhard's foreign policy favored easing tension with the eastern countries. In December 1963 the West Berlin City Senate was able to negotiate an agreement with the Democratic Republic to permit West Berliners to visit relatives in East Germany over the Christmas holidays. Some 1.2 million individuals passed through the wall between December 19, 1963, and January 5, 1964. This arrangement was extended by additional agreements into 1966. Approximately 4.3 million passes were issued in all.

In March 1966, Erhard sent a peace feeler to the Warsaw Pact nations. They rejected it because it contained no relaxation of the Hallstein Doctrine isolating East Germany. Meanwhile, Charles de Gaulle was taking France out of NATO in order to conduct a more independent policy. The CDU divided over the way to deal with France and NATO. Some, like Erhard and his foreign minister, Gerhard Schroeder, wanted to maintain the "Atlantic" orientation. Others, like Franz Josef Strauss and Konrad Adenauer, wanted to retain close relations with France. This conflict was complicated by an economic recession, which began in 1966 and rapidly led to a budget crisis. Unemployment rose from 0.4 percent in 1965 to 3.5 percent in early 1967. The coalition fell in October 1966 when the FDP ministers resigned. State elections in Hesse and Bavaria during November 1966 signaled the ominous rise of the right radical National Party, which campaigned on economic issues. Erhard resigned as chancellor on November 30, and the CDU opened negotiations with the SPD to form a new coalition. On December 1, Kurt Georg Kiesinger became chancellor of the new coalition government.

The Grand Coalition: Chancellor Kurt Georg Kiesinger (CDU), 1966–1969. The Grand Coalition was controversial, to say the least. Kiesinger, who had been nominated by Strauss, was a former Nazi who had served in Hitler's Foreign Office. The Social Democrats held nine of the ministries, their first entry into the new government, and many of their constituents accused them of selling out. The coalition inherited the diplomatic and economic problems of the Erhard chancellorship. The most urgent problem was the economy. The minister of economics was Karl Schiller, a Social Democrat. His Stability Law of June 8, 1967, required both national and state governments to develop measures to assure full employment, stability of the currency, a positive foreign trade balance, and overall economic growth. Unions, management, and local government worked together to resolve problems. The economy recovered. Inflation dropped; the gross domestic product almost doubled between 1960 and 1968.

Right-Wing Parties. During the economic crisis a radical right began to emerge. The Deutsche Reichspartei (DRP), founded in 1946, had been excluded from the Bundestag by the Five Percent Law. By 1949 the Socialist Reichspartei (SRP), organized on the Fuehrer principle, began winning seats in the state legislatures of Lower Saxony and Bremen. After the Federal Constitutional Court banned it in 1952 as a neo-Nazi organization, many of its members joined the DRP. In 1964 the National Democratic Party (NPD) split off from the DRP. Some of this activity was stimulated by the Auschwitz trials, from 1963 to 1966, of the former SS members who administered the death camp. While most Germans deplored the records of the former SS concentration camp guards, others said it was time to end the persecution. A small minority denied the Holocaust, or characterized it as Allied propaganda. They were attracted to the neofascist protest movements. These groups mixed nationalism, racism, and expansionism with aggressive campaigning in state elections. Although they never gained Bundestag seats, they became an ominous presence in German state politics.

The 1968 Student Revolt. Influenced by activist student movements in the United States and France, leftist German students organized to make political demands. The Socialist German Student Union, Sozialistische Deutsche Studentenbund (SDS), was one of the most outspoken. Students protested many issues, from the Vietnam War to the visits of foreign dignitaries. By the late 1960s, many of their marches and protests became violent, especially in Berlin. The police often reacted with force. Students across Germany exploded when one of their number, Benno Ohnesorg, was killed by the police. Another student, Rudi Dutschke, was wounded by a member of the radical right. The coalition government introduced an Emergency Law that would permit use of army troops to put down riotous demonstrations as threats to the "free democratic order." The law went into effect in June 1968, although it was little used. Its provision for an emergency form of cabinet raised serious objections.

Other radical protest groups formed in the 1970s. The Red Army Faction (RAF) actively promoted revolution. This underground group, headed by Andreas Baader and Ulrike Meinhof, led a terrorist movement until the capture of Baader and Meinhof in June 1972. The RAF prompted the passage of the law banning government employees from membership in any antidemocratic organization. Many protested that this was unconstitutional; it was seldom applied.

The Greens. Not all these movements were violent. In the late 1970s, some of the protest movements began warning about the potential dangers of nuclear power and other environmental pollution, earning them their distinctive name. They entered local elections and gained seats in over half of the West German states. They formed a national party in 1979 when they wanted to run a slate of candidates in the European Parliament election. Although they won no seats, they began to attract the attention of the postwar generation and students to environmental issues.

Chancellor Willi Brandt (SPD), 1969–1974. The one bright note for the Great Coalition government was the economic recovery. That had been designed by the Social Democrat Karl Schiller, and the SPD centered their election campaign around it. The election of September 28, 1969, gave the CDU/CSU 242 Bundestag seats, the SPD 224 seats, and the FDP the deciding 30 seats. The SPD chairman, Willi Brandt, who had been foreign minister in the Great Coalition, asked the FDP to join in a coalition government. On October 20 Brandt became the first Social Democratic chancellor of the Federal Republic. The coalition also helped elect Gustav Heinemann, a Social Democrat, as the new federal president.

Under Adenauer and the Great Coalition, the West Germans had tried to deal with Eastern Europe without recognizing East Germany or relinquishing claims to the lands east of the Oder-Neisse line. While Russia had extended diplomatic recognition to West Germany, little else had been achieved. Walter Ulbricht, the East German leader, had successfully kept the Warsaw Pact nations from dealing with the Federal Republic.

Moscow Treaty. Brandt's foreign minister was Walter Scheel of the FDP. Their Social-Liberal government changed the direction of German diplomacy. Over furious opposition from the CDU/CSU, Brandt and Scheel pushed through a new foreign policy that became known as the East Policy, Ostpolitik. They began by initiating talks with Moscow and Warsaw in January 1970. Brandt and DDR Minister President Willi Stoph met in March and May 1970—the first formal discussions between the two German governments since 1947. The first fruit of the Ostpolitik was the Moscow Treaty, which Brandt and Soviet Premier Alexei Kosygin signed on August 12, 1970. Both states agreed to abandon the use of force in their relations with each other and to recognize the territorial integrity of all European states in their existing boundaries, including the Oder-Neisse line. As a clarification, Foreign Minister Scheel added a statement that the treaty in no way contradicted the Federal Republic's wish to pursue German unification by means of peaceful self-determination.

Warsaw Treaty. On December 7, 1970, Brandt and the minister president of Poland, Josef Cyrankiewicz, signed the Treaty of Warsaw. Both states recognized the Oder-Neisse line as the western frontier of the People's Republic of Poland and the territorial integrity of the existing Polish and German states. They relinquished all claims against each other as well as the use of force and agreed to the exchange of ambassadors. After Brandt had signed the treaty, he laid a wreath on the monument honoring the Jews sacrificed in the Warsaw Ghetto. The act was construed by many as a recognition of the many lives lost to Nazi oppression.

Four-Power Agreement on Berlin. While in Moscow, Brandt indicated that the Moscow Treaty would have difficulty in the Bundestag unless some agreement were reached on Berlin. When Walter Ulbricht was deposed in East Germany, in May 1971, a major obstacle to reconciliation was gone. On September 3, 1971, the four powers signed an agreement recognizing the special relationship between West Berlin and the Federal Republic and guaranteeing the free movement of people and goods between the two regions. The Western powers agreed that West Berlin was not a part of the Federal Republic and that to continue four-power control over the city should be continued. In recognition of the successful Ostpolitik, Willi Brandt received the Nobel Peace Prize for 1971.

Basic Treaty. The most significant product of the Ostpolitik was the Basic Treaty of December 21, 1972. The two German states each recognized the sovereignty of the other and agreed to develop friendly relations. The treaty ended the Hallstein Doctrine. In 1973 the Federal Republic established diplomatic relations with Bulgaria, Czechoslovakia, Finland, Hungary, and Bulgaria. Both German states joined the United Nations in September 1973. The following year, they exchanged diplomats, although not at the ambassadorial level.

Domestic Reform. The Brandt government also introduced a number of domestic reforms that improved education and increased retirement pensions. The voting age was lowered to 18, adding 2.5 million new voters to the rolls. The Factory Constitution Act of 1971 gave workers more rights in the business management of their employers. All of these were passed over opposition from the CDU/CSU. Under this coalition, the federal army grew to be second only to the French army in Western Europe. Despite these reforms, domestic unrest continued.

The year 1972 was one of turmoil for the Brandt government. The eastern treaties barely made it through the Bundestag, his SPD party divided over economic policy, and the minister of economics, Karl Schiller, resigned. The terrorist attacks on Israeli athletes at the Munich Olympic Games only compounded the air of crisis. The president called for Bundestag elections, which were held in November. Brandt's popularity helped the SPD take 45.9 percent of the vote, defeating the CDU/CSU (44.8 percent) for the first time. The Brandt government signed the Treaty of Prague with Czechoslovakia in 1973, voiding the 1938 Munich Agreement, recognizing their mutual border, and denouncing the use of force against each other. But in April 1974 it was revealed that Brandt's personal assistant, Guenther Guillaume, was an East German spy. Brandt resigned the chancellorship on May 6, 1974, although he retained his Bundestag seat and the chairmanship of the SPD.

Chancellor Helmut Schmidt (SPD), 1974–1982. The Bundestag elected Helmut Schmidt, the SPD defense minister (1969–1972) and minister of economics (1972–1974), as Brandt's successor. He selected Hans-Dietrich Genscher (FDP) as his foreign minister. The new government had 11 SPD and 4 FDP members. They took over just as the world oil crisis set off soaring inflation. Schmidt's solution was to turn to nuclear power. This raised protests from the Greens and others. With its flexible pensions and welfare programs, West Germany weathered the storm better than many other European countries. But social unrest continued.

Schmidt signed the Helsinki Agreements of the Conference of Security and Cooperation in Europe (CSCE) in 1975. These called for improving human rights and increasing the freedom of movement throughout Europe. This helped Schmidt carry the Bundestag elections in 1976. The CDU candidate for chancellor was Helmut Kohl, a moderate. He was backed with the full force of the Axel Springer press and the untiring efforts of Franz Josef Strauss for CSU victory in Bavaria. The FDP conducted an outspoken campaign against Strauss. Although the CDU/CSU gained 48.6 percent of the votes, the SPD/FDP coalition retained power with a majority of only 10 seats.

After the election the SPD began to move toward a more worker-oriented policy. Schmidt found himself losing support within his own party, despite its support for his detente policy. A new Workers' Co-Determination Law of July 1976 required any firm with more than 2,000 employees to provide for representation of workers and union members on the board of directors. Both owners and unions remained unsatisfied by this compromise. In addition, German women had begun to organize around a measure to legalize abortion. The Schmidt government put through a controversial measure that permitted medical abortion during the first trimester if the mother's life were endangered by continuation of the pregnancy.

The 1973 oil crisis had dampened the West German economy and created a condition of level productivity with rising inflation, stagflation. By 1981 production was down and unemployment was 1.3 million. Meanwhile, Japanese competition made inroads on electronics and consumer good sales. In the crisis, Germans began to protest the increasing numbers of foreign "guest" workers, *Gastarbeiter*, in West Germany. By 1972 there were over two million of them. They were unskilled workers who came mainly from Turkey, Yugoslavia, and Italy. Many had brought their families. This put pressure on schools and social services in the cities where they settled.

Schmidt's foreign policy was also faltering. His meetings with Soviet leaders and Erich Honecker, the new DDR president, were friendly, but did not result in major gains. Meanwhile, the Soviet Union began an adventurous foreign policy, supporting revolution in Angola and Nicaragua and invading Afghanistan in 1979. It also started replacing obsolete middle-range rockets in Eastern Europe with new SS-20 rockets. Schmidt tried a dual-track foreign policy of building defenses while pursuing detente. But the Americans and British felt detente wasn't working. The more conservative CDU favored calling for a stronger line toward the east. The SPD wanted more tax support for workers and less for defense. The Social-Liberal coalition broke apart. In October 1982, Schmidt lost a no-confidence vote in the Bundestag. Helped by the FDP, Helmut Kohl, the CDU leader, was elected to replace him. Kohl took office on October 1, 1982.

Chancellor Helmut Kohl (CDU), 1982–1998. Thanks to his good relationship with Hans-Dietrich Genscher, the FDP leader and foreign minister in the Schmidt cabinet, Kohl had won the democratic party away from the Social Democrats. But he needed more than parliamentary maneuvering to secure his cabinet. On March 3, 1983, the Bundestag elections took place. The SPD ran Hans-Jochim Vogel, the moderate former minister of justice, as their candidate for chancellor. In the face of economic problems and concern about the Soviet Union, the electorate swung to the right. Kohl and the CDU/CSU won 255 seats, an increase of 18 seats. The SPD and FDP both lost seats to the newly active Green Party, who gained 5.6 percent of the national electorate for the first time, and 28 seats in the new Bundestag. Kohl's cabinet retained Genscher as deputy chancellor and foreign minister, but the CDU held all but two of the other ministries.

The Kohl government had some early crises to weather. The Social Democrats and the Greens raised unwavering objections to the November 1983 agreement to permit the deployment of intermediate-range nuclear missiles in Germany. A bribery scandal swirled around the minister of economics, Otto Graf Lambsdorff, resulting in his resignation in June 1984. Further investigation into contributions to the political parties embarrassed the CDU/CSU, FDP, and SPD and also tarnished the federal president, Karl Carstens (CDU, 1979–1984). The coalition's choice for president, Richard von Weizsaecker, was elected in 1984. He proved to be very popular and was reelected, without opposition, in 1989.

In 1985, the Federal Republic commemorated the Fortieth anniversary of Germany's surrender with mixed emotions. The SPD celebrated the end of Nazi rule; the CDU considered the surrender the beginning of the Soviet oppression of East Germany. Many regretted that it marked the beginning of a divided Germany. President Ronald Reagan's visit to Germany irritated many when he visited a concentration camp and then the military cemetery at Bittburg, where some SS graves were located.

These issues made inroads on the 1987 Bundestag elections. The CDU/CSU lost 21 seats and nearly its worst showing since 1949 (234 seats). The SPD lost 9 seats. The parties on the left surged. The FDP gained 12 seats and the Greens' faction grew from 28 to 44 seats in the hard-fought election.

The biggest challenge began to unfold in 1989. Mikhail Gorbachev's call for open discussion, glasnost, and restructuring, perestroika, in the Soviet Union, raised expectations for change within East Germany. As Erich Honecker's Communist government cracked down on East German protesters, non-Communists began to take part in the governments of Poland and Hungary. A flood of East Germans escaped to the West through Hungary in July and August. The West Germans had little to do with the rapid and surprising collapse of the Honecker government in the fall. Kohl's greatest contribution was his diplomacy with Mikhail Gorbachev. By assuring him that a united Germany would not develop atomic, biological, or chemical weapons and would remain under NATO constraints, Kohl secured Gorbachev's agreement to let unification take place. The opening of the Berlin Wall, on November 9, 1989, symbolized the first step toward unification.

Things moved rapidly after that—more rapidly, perhaps, than the West Germans had anticipated. East German elections in March resulted in a victory for the coalition of parties favoring unification. The two governments worked out a treaty to unify the economy as the first step. Signed on May 18, 1990, it went into effect the following July 1. The Unification Treaty, to incorporate the five East German *Laender* into the Federal Republic and to consolidate Berlin and make it the national capital, was signed on August 31, 1990. It went into effect on October 3, 1990, which was designated a national holiday.

The four powers agreed to let the two German states work out the mechanisms for unification to be approved by the four powers. These Two Plus Four deliberations paved the way for the former victors to end their role in Germany. Kohl met with Gorbachev in July to review the issues. On July 12, 1990, the Two Plus Four agreement was signed. It authorized German unification, confirmed the existing territorial borders, and ended Allied authority over Berlin and the new unified state. The two German states each confirmed Poland's borders and relinquished any further claims on Poland. Thus, 45 years after the unconditional surrender, a united Germany, with full sovereignty, stood firmly in the center of Europe.

NOTE

1. William S. Boas, Wilhelm Grotkopp, Heinrich Spieker, and Dorothea Kempff, eds., *Germany 1945–1954* (Cologne, Germany: Boas International Publishing Co., n.d.), p. 171.

10

The German Democratic Republic, 1949–1990

The German Democratic Republic (DDR) perceived itself as an entirely new German state, the first German workers' and farmers' state. It claimed foundations in the traditional working-class Social Democratic and the Communist Party protest movements and their resistance to Hitler. The DDR rejected responsibility for the collapse of the Weimar Republic, the war, and the Holocaust. It celebrated the liberation of Germany by the Soviet armies in 1945 and the collaboration with the Soviet Military Administration (SMAD) against the "fascist" parties. It accepted Soviet plans for building a socialist economy with state ownership of the means of production. As the middle ground between the two powerful Cold War blocs, the Democratic Republic was subject to considerable political and economic pressures.

The Pieck/Grotewohl Years, 1949–1954. On October 7, 1949, the German Democratic Republic was established by a proclamation of the People's Council, which reconstituted itself as the Provisional Volkskammer, the People's Chamber. On October 10, the parliaments of the five East German states—Mecklenburg, Brandenburg, Saxony, Saxony-Anhalt, and Thuringia—formed the provisional Laenderkammer, the Council of States as the upper house of parliament. Later, in 1952, the five *Laender* were dissolved and replaced by 15 districts, including East

Berlin. (The Federal Republic and its occupying powers refused to recognize East Berlin as a part of the German Democratic Republic. The upper house was dissolved in 1958.)

Together the two chambers elected Wilhelm Pieck, a German Communist who had spent the Hitler years in exile in the Soviet Union, as the first president, a largely ceremonial office. Otto Grotewohl, a former Reichstag member and leader of the Berlin Social Democrats, headed the predominantly Communist cabinet, the Council of Ministers. Walter Ulbricht, another exiled Communist who had returned to Germany with the Soviet army in 1945, served as the deputy chairman of the Socialist Unity Party (SED), and had considerable influence. Also on October 7, the East German political parties joined together in the National Front, dominated by the SED. A State Security Service, Staatssicherheitsdienst (SSD), and the Ministry of State Security maintained a network of police and agents to control opposition groups. Once this government was in place, the Soviets dissolved their military government and replaced it with a civilian control commission. The Democratic Republic was a one-party state with little opportunity for political dissent.

Walter Ulbricht. As the leader of the group of Communist Germans-in-exile who returned with the Soviet armies in 1945, Ulbricht was a founder of the Communist Party in East Germany. He carried that leadership into the SED in 1946 and served as a member of its Central Committee. He was elected to the Volkskammer in 1949. From 1950 to 1953, he was the general secretary of the SED. From this position of strength and close association with the Russians, he was able to dominate the government and effectively remove rivals from power. He is considered the most significant political leader in the DDR between 1950 and 1971. He influenced both the Stalinist way in which the economy was developed and the close adherence to Soviet foreign policy. Like Adenauer, he provided continuity in political and economic direction, which helped stabilize the Democratic Republic in its formative years. East Germany developed the strongest economy within the eastern bloc under his leadership. When Wilhelm Pieck died in 1960, an executive committee replaced the office of president. Ulbricht became chairman of the Council of State and remained in that position until his death in 1973.

Nonrecognition by the West. On October 7, 1949, the day the East German Republic was founded, Konrad Adenauer denounced it as illegal because it was not based on free elections. The western Allied High Commission refused to acknowledge that the DDR represented all Germany or even eastern Germany. The West German Hallstein Doctrine of

1955 served further to isolate the DDR from other non-European countries. Until the Basic Treaty of 1972, the West identified the Democratic Republic only as occupied Germany or the Russian Zone. The result was that the Democratic Republic was dependent on the Soviet Union to represent its interests abroad. Of necessity, it was a dedicated and loyal ally of the Soviet Union. The West, nonetheless, criticized the DDR for its satellite status within the Soviet orbit.

In 1946 East Germany had a population of approximately 17.3 million, about 28 percent of the total German population. It was a very homogeneous state, with a small minority of ethnic Sorbs and a minuscule Jewish minority. Its territory of 107,173 square kilometers was roughly 36 percent of the territory under four-power control. Due to the confiscation of prewar property from affluent owners, the majority of the population was classified as workers and farmers. Many from the former middle class fled to the west. The East German elite consisted of the principal party leaders at all levels and key government personnel. Membership in the SED was important for advancement, but stayed under 15 percent of the total population.

East German Social Conditions. Within East Germany, de-Nazification had the function of removing known former Nazis from positions in the economy and replacing them with Communists. The Nazi and Junker enterprises and estates were confiscated and placed under state control.

Workers in the Democratic Republic were organized in the Free German Trade Union Federation, Freier Deutscher Gewerkschaftsbund (FDGB). Working through smaller unions for the various trades, the FDGB incorporated workers from all levels, manual trades through white collar positions. Every enterprise with 20 or more workers had to have a union. There was a hierarchy within the union, ranging from local to national levels. The highest-level positions were held by SED members. The FDGB was not a grassroots organization. It was most effective in coordinating government policy directives across the workforce.

The youth of the Democratic Republic were organized into the Free German Youth organization, Freie Deutsche Jugend (FDJ), founded in 1946. Other youth organizations were not permitted. The FDJ provided recreational facilities and cultural, athletic, and entertainment programs for young people between the ages of 14 and 25. Although membership was voluntary, there was strong pressure to join, especially since the organization controlled the entrance exams for the university and for scholarships. The government worked through the FDJ to instill political values and integrate the young people into the socialist perspective. The initiation rites for those joining the organization were semireligious in nature, although the individuals pledged themselves to the state rather than to the church. Many of the youth leaders remained in influential positions as members of the SED.

Women were also organized in East Germany. The Democratic Women's League of Germany, Demokratischer Frauenbund Deutschlands (DFD) was founded in 1947. It helped obtain a constitutional provision for the equality of women and campaigned for women's rights. It supported the government's efforts to move women into the workforce and encouraged women to enter the universities and politics. The government provided day care centers and educational incentives for women, together with paid educational leave.

The majority of East Germans who practiced their faith, roughly half of the population, were Protestants. Roman Catholics accounted for less than 10 percent of the population, and other religions, less than 1 percent. From the outset, the government discouraged religion and forbade the formation of religious youth groups and religious instruction in the schools. Yet the Lutheran Church was the only organization within East Germany to retain any independent organization. Despite opposition to the regime by some pastors, the churches experienced little persecution. Moreover, the churches were able to retain loose ties with religious organizations in West Germany. The formation of the organization of East German Evangelical Churches, Bund der Evangelischen Kirchen in der Deutschen Demokratischen Republic, in 1968 was an effort to more closely associate the Lutheran movement with the East German government.

Economic Recovery. East Germany did not participate in the Marshall Plan. Indeed, the Soviet Union was still extracting reparations from the region while the West began investing in the Federal Republic in 1949. In the predominantly agricultural East, the land reform carried out during the occupation was designed to help hold people on the land and provide food for the recovering industrial centers. Although housing was desperately needed, it was low on the budget priority list. The units built were state owned and rent controlled. Many were massive high-rise blocks hastily built of preformed concrete and difficult to maintain.

Planned Economy. The government set to work on a Five-Year Plan, along the Soviet model, to rebuild the local economy. East German planning was synchronized with the COMECON organization, established by the Soviet bloc nations in 1949 after they had declined to join the

Marshall Plan. COMECON coordinated regional planning, but did not infuse it with resources as the Marshall Plan did in the west. Recovery in eastern Europe was considerably slower than that in the west due to widespread war damage and the lack of new investment capital. The conversion of the local economies to centrally planned socialist systems was disruptive and delayed the recovery process.

To facilitate central planning, the East German government nationalized much of the industry that had remained in private hands. These and the other state-owned concerns were converted into Publicly Owned Enterprises, Volkseigene Betriebe, VEBs. They made up some 75 percent of the industrial sector.

Five-Year Plans. Economic planning was the responsibility of the SED, which set the goals; the Council of Ministers, which enacted them; and of the State Planning Commission, which coordinated the plan's design and implementation by the government agencies. Once the plan was adopted, each of the enterprises had specific goals it had to meet. The first Five-Year Plan (1951–1955) focused on doubling the capacity of industry and on overcoming the losses through war damage and reparations. The plan focused on energy, heavy industry, and chemical and machine manufacture, at the expense of consumer goods. Shortages in raw materials kept the plan from fulfilling its stated goals and prevented the second Five-Year Plan from being implemented until 1958. Nevertheless, the plan resulted in improvement.

When the second Five-Year Plan, for 1956–1960, was approved, it continued the emphasis on industrial production quotas, calling for an increase of over 50 percent. There was a new emphasis on technology and the introduction of nuclear power generating facilities. In addition, the government tried to get the remaining privately held firms to share ownership with the state on a fifty-fifty basis.

This system of planning goals continued through the end of the regime, although planning was changed to an annual basis in the 1960s. Using 1950 as the base index year (1950 = 100), the gross domestic product (GDP) rose from 100 in 1950 to 173 in 1955. By 1965 the index had risen to 321. Between 1955 and 1965 the average monthly salary of an East German worker rose from 439 marks to 640 marks. In 1985, the GDP index stood at 801, and the average monthly salary at 1,140 East German marks.

Although East Germany benefited from the industrial complex in the Leipzig region, it had neither the diversity nor the size of the West German workforce. It had large deposits of brown coal (lignite) for energy, supplemented by Russian oil. Its major products were electronics, optical goods, and machine tools, which it sold mainly to the COMECON countries. Once trade with the Federal Republic was regulated, East German products also made their way into the west through the Common Market. Although its economy lagged far behind that of West Germany, East Germany enjoyed the highest standard of living of all the Soviet bloc countries, and ranked within the top 20 of the world's industrial economies for much of its existence.

By 1960 all but about 10 percent of industrial production was through VEBs. Nevertheless, the economy began to slow down in the 1960s. The government's planning schedule was changed to the Seven-Year Plan in 1959, and this was revised in 1963. The new plan called for an 85 percent increase in productivity.

Collectivization of Agriculture. In 1959 the government, backed by heavy SED pressure, began collectivizing agriculture. This reversed the land reform policy of 1945, in which small farms were encouraged in order to get agriculture going again. The Agricultural Production Cooperatives, Landwirtschaftliche Produktionsgenossenschaften (LPG) brought over 85 percent of cultivated land under their control. There were state-owned farms, cooperatives based on communal use of land, cattle cooperatives, and collectives in which all land, livestock, and machinery were owned by the organization, with a small plot allowed for private use. The average yield of agricultural crops, measured in tons per hectare (1 hectare = 2.47 acres), increased slowly. For example, wheat production averaged 2.6 tph in 1961–1965 and 3.6 tph in 1976–1980; potato production averaged 16.6 tph in 1961–1965 and 17.5 tph in the 1976–1980 period. Joining a collective was, technically, voluntary, but there was considerable party pressure to help the plan.

Ulbricht Dictatorship. Thanks to the National Front, the 1957 elections in East Germany gave the SED almost 100 percent of the vote. Ulbricht and Pieck remained in power. When Pieck died in 1960, the office of president was abolished and Ulbricht took over as chairman of the new executive committee of the Council of State. It consisted of 23 members appointed by the SED for four-year terms. It had full legislative and executive powers, including diplomatic authority. As first secretary of the SED, Ulbricht now controlled both party and state. He also chaired the new National Defense Council, which placed him in control of the armed forces. Grotewohl remained as prime minister, with limited responsibilities.

Workers' Emigration and the Berlin Wall. The government pressures on the working class resulted in hundreds of thousands of East German workers emigrating to West Germany. This was not a sudden development. Emigration had begun after the introduction of the first Five-Year Plan, with over 10,000 men, women, and children leaving monthly. With the additional demands for productivity and collectivization, the number of defections increased to 149,000 in 1959 and 199,000 in 1960. By that time more than 2.5 million individuals had gone west, most of them under 25 and in the prime working ages. It was at that point that Ulbricht decided to build the wall that locked workers into the Democratic Republic. Construction on the wall in Berlin ended on August 13, 1961. Traffic between East and West Germany was restricted to seven crossing points. Eventually, a similar 830-mile barrier sliced apart the two German nation.

New Economic System. Despite rigorous efforts to fulfill the economic plan, East German productivity declined in the early 1960s. Again taking his cue from the Soviet Union, Ulbricht implemented the New Economic System (NES) in 1963. This relaxed centralization, putting planning on an annual instead of a five-year basis. While the central authorities identified the goals, the actual planning and implementation was developed by the Associations of Publicly Owned Enterprises, Vereinigungen Volkseigener Betriebe (VVBs). The NES called for planning decisions based on profitability and salaries based on performance.

Ulbricht also brought new blood into the upper echelons of the SED by putting new emphasis on leadership with technical and managerial skills. The state's early support of education and training had increased the professional level of the SED's membership. Many of those with university or trade school training were placed in positions responsible for planning and managing the VVBs. These economic and political reforms were among the first to be implemented in the Soviet bloc. They stabilized the East German economy throughout the decade. But by 1968 the economy went into another decline. Ulbricht introduced the economic system of socialism, which again relied on centralized planning. The first plan focused on increasing high-technology industries of chemicals, electronics, and plastics. The new quotas proved impossible to meet and were abandoned in 1970.

Soviet Orbit. Much of East German history was determined by its relationship to the Soviet Union. On March 5, 1953, Joseph Stalin, the Soviet leader, died. His successor, Georgi Malenkov, initiated a new economic program for the Soviet Union emphasizing the production of consumer goods. The East German government copied this plan in its

New Course by raising the production quotas for industrial workers. The results were strikes and public protests in virtually every industrial city. Workers demanded an end to the Stalinist programs of the Ulbricht regime and called for economic reforms. Combined police and Soviet army forces turned out against the workers. On June 17, East Berlin workers battled Soviet tanks with stones. It was a losing battle, and approximately 500 of the protesters lost their lives.

Sovereignty. In 1954, when the Soviet Union had completed extracting reparations, it granted formal sovereignty to the German Democratic Republic. It shut down its Control Commission in Berlin and arranged for the East German government to buy back the SAGs, the industrial enterprises that it claimed under the occupation. This was one of the few instances where events in East Germany actually preceded the parallel event in West Germany, which did not become sovereign until 1955.

Police and Military Forces. The Soviets had permitted the East German People's Police, Volkspolizei, to carry military-grade weapons as early as 1948, but the East German constitution prohibited rearmament. As in the west, the constitution was amended in 1953 to permit remilitarization, but no formal action was taken until 1955. After West Germany joined NATO, East Germany became a member of the Warsaw Pact. In that year the Ministry for National Defense, led by General Karl-Heinz Hoffman, established the National Peoples Army. At first, some units of the Volkspolizei were redesignated as military forces and so armed. The target was a force of 170,000 men, all technically classified as volunteers since there was no legislation to impose a military draft. The Russians did not permit a unified army in East Germany. Instead, there were a number of small specialized militarized forces. The largest was the Border Police, with 50,000 men; the Security Alert Police had 30,000 men. Other police units, like the Factory Guard, the Railroad Security, and the District Police, were smaller than 10,000. A Workers' Militia of 350,000 and the youth of the Sports and Technical Crafts organization all received considerable military training and were available as reinforcements. Meanwhile, the Russians maintained, at German expense, a large military force in East Germany, headquartered in Potsdam.

Opposition to Ulbricht. In 1956, when Soviet leader Nikita Khrushchev denounced Stalin in his Secret Speech to the Twentieth Communist Party Congress in the USSR, many expected that Stalinist policies would be abandoned across the Communist bloc. Indeed, there were voices in the East German SED that called for such reforms. Among them were three outspoken professors, Wolfgang Harich, Ernst Bloch, and Robert Havemann. They and others called for a more humane form of socialism. But Ulbricht stilled them and purged the party's ranks. The professors were dismissed from their posts; Harich was sentenced to 10 years in prison, and Bloch fled the country. Harich went to the West after completing his sentence. Havemann decided to stay in East Germany, but was stripped of all his offices. He lived in virtual isolation until his death in 1982. A number of once prominent SED leaders suffered similar punishment.

Constitution of 1968. In 1967 the People's Council appointed a commission to write a new constitution to reflect the transformation of the society into a socialist state. The document received 94.5 percent approval by plebiscite and went into effect on April 9, 1968. The new constitution gave the working class and the SED the leadership of the socialist state (the 1949 document had stipulated "the people"). It proclaimed state ownership of the means of production. It pledged the DDR to international socialism under Soviet leadership. It did not significantly change the state structure.

Ulbricht's Foreign Policy. Ulbricht kept East Germany firmly under the Soviet wing for the duration of his tenure in office. Since the West did not recognize the DDR, he worked to assert East German leadership among the other Warsaw Pact nations. His outlook was ideological, and he saw little prospect in reconciliation, detente, with the West. His Ulbricht Doctrine aimed at arranging bilateral mutual assistance treaties within the Eastern bloc and preventing those states from dealing with West Germany until it recognized the Democratic Republic. He signed treaties with Bulgaria, Czechoslovakia, Hungary and Poland during 1967. He thoroughly condemned the Czech uprisings in 1968 and urged intervention by Soviet and Warsaw Pact nations to suppress it.

Detente. But while Ulbricht maintained his hard line, things had changed in West Germany. Following Adenauer's retirement, his successors, Ludwig Erhard (1963–1969) and Willi Brandt (1969–1974), sought ways to improve their relations with the Soviet Union. Brandt's Ostpolitik had replaced the Hallstein Doctrine. In August 1970, West Germany and the Soviet Union signed the Moscow Treaty, in which the Federal Republic recognized the Oder-Neisse line and the USSR agreed to a nonaggression pact. With the 1970 Warsaw Treaty, West Germany and Poland came to a similar agreement. The Four-Power Agreement on Berlin in 1971 recognized the unique status of West Berlin, separate from the Federal Republic, but guaranteed free access to it by the West. When

Ulbricht resisted Russia's pressures for this softer line, he lost Soviet support. On May 3, 1971, the SED replaced him as first secretary of the SED Central Committee with Erich Honecker. Ulbricht remained chairman of the Council of State until his death in 1973, but Honecker exercised the real political power. The two German states finally acknowledged each other in the Basic Treaty of 1972 and exchanged diplomatic representatives. In September 1973, the two German states joined the United Nations. East Germany had finally escaped the isolation imposed by the Western nations. By 1975 the Democratic Republic had established diplomatic relations with 119 countries.

Erich Honecker, Chairman of the Council of State, 1971–1989. The new SED first secretary was a working-class, lifelong Communist. After Hitler seized power, Honecker fought in the resistance until his capture and sentencing to 10 years in prison. He began his return to power as a member of the SED Central Committee and as the leader of the Free German Youth. He became a member of the Council of State in 1971. Honecker's domestic program, called the Main Task, was basic Marxist-Leninist socialism—central economic planning and increased industrial productivity—but this time with more emphasis on workers' needs for housing, maternity leaves, day care, and higher retirement pensions. By 1972, with the creation of 11,000 new nationally owned enterprises, the state converted the remaining industrial sector, mainly food and textile concerns, to socialism. The Strategy for the Development of the National Economy in the 1980s, adopted by the Tenth SED Congress in 1981, once again called for expanding the economy by intensifying labor and technological productivity.

The 1974 Constitution. These new policy directions were codified in the constitutional revisions of 1974. The Democratic Republic declared itself to be "forever and irrevocably connected" to the Soviet Union and dropped references to a united German nation. Honecker also strengthened the position of the Council of Ministers, giving it more authority than the Council of State, which had been supreme under the previous constitutions. The Volkskammer had 500 members elected from a unified National Front list. Using a formula established in 1963, the SED, as the largest party in the National Front, always held 127 seats in the Volkskammer. The trade unions (FDGB) held 68 seats, the other political parties each had 52 seats, and various organizations, such as the Free German Youth, the Women's League, and the Cultural League had smaller allocations. Because the SED led the unions and organizations, the SED control of the Volkskammer far exceeded its elected representation. Until 1979 the 66 representatives from East Berlin were delegated by the city council; thereafter they were elected directly.

Foreign Relations. The Democratic Republic, following the Soviet lead, was active in providing assistance to third world countries in the effort to gain support for the socialist bloc. Using treaties and intergovernmental agreements, after 1970 the DDR helped developing countries set up over 700 enterprises, all of which were state owned. Students from these countries were accommodated at the universities and technical schools, and technical experts went abroad, armed with socialist ideology as well as their expertise. The emerging countries helped elect the DDR to a rotating seat on the United Nations Security Council for the 1980–1981 term.

German-German Relations. Honecker's policy of separation, *Abgrenzung*, emphasized the distinctions between East Germany and West Germany. With this new perspective, the Democratic Republic reclaimed its German past, recognizing, for example, King Frederick II of Prussia (Frederick the Great) as a model for enlightened centralized authority. This policy emphasized the ideological and economic differences between the two states and moved away from earlier commitments to reunification. Symbolically, the word "German" was stricken from the title of many organizations, and the term "German nation" was absent in the 1974 constitution. The SED was designated as a "Communist" party. The DDR signed a new friendship and mutual assistance treaty with the Soviet Union on October 7, 1975, affirming East Germany's close association with the USSR. This was a cold response to West Germany's Ostpolitik, but one more pronounced by the government than supported by the East German population at large.

Despite *Abgrenzung*, there was increasing contact between the two German states. Thanks to the transit agreement of 1971, millions of West Germans and West Berliners visited in the East, and trade between the two states picked up considerably. Both governments worked carefully to preserve good relations through the tensions of the worldwide oil crisis of 1973, the missile crises of middecade, and the Soviet invasion of Afghanistan in 1979. Honecker and Schmidt met in 1981, and Franz Josef Strauss visited East Germany in 1983. In 1983 and 1984, the Bonn government provided nearly 2 billion DM in credits to the DDR in exchange for permitting East Germans to visit family in the west. In 1986 the first German-to-German partner-city pacts were signed; there were more than 40 of these arrangements by 1988. In 1987 Honecker visited the Federal Republic capital of Bonn, the first East German head of state to do so.

No major agreements were discussed, but it appeared as though both governments were ready to maintain the normal diplomatic relations between two sovereign states.

Human Rights Issues. In 1975, 33 European nations, the United States, and Canada met in Finland and agreed to a set of principles known as the Helsinki Agreements. These established three basic concepts: the security of the existing states and their territories; cooperation in economic, technological, and environmental affairs; and protection of the human rights of their citizens. With no binding means for enforcement, the Helsinki Agreements were perceived at the time as more symbolic than real. In fact, they were a time bomb. When coupled with popular expectations raised by the proclamation of glasnost and perestroika, they led to the development of popular movements unprecedented in Eastern Europe, movements that eventually brought down the Soviet Union and its allied socialist governments.

Within the Soviet Union, the Jews began demanding the right to emigrate and ethnic minorities called for more autonomy. In Poland there were demonstrations against government-imposed price hikes, and the shipbuilders of Gdansk called for recognition of their independent Solidarity trade union. In East Germany, when the Helsinki Agreements were first signed, some 120,000 individuals demanding freedom to travel applied for permits to emigrate; they were denied.

But by the 1980s the East German economy began to decline. Most of its foreign trade was with the Eastern bloc, which was technologically behind the West. Centralized planning had stifled innovation and investment in new or improved products. Rising production costs for energy and raw materials made East German goods less competitive on the world market. Increasing government pressure for higher productivity led to a growth in absenteeism and poor workers' morale. In 1984 small groups of East Germans began to take over foreign embassies and demand the right to emigrate. In 1986 Honecker announced that the new economic plan would concentrate on the most modern technologies—computers, nuclear energy, lasers, and robotics. Funds were diverted from other industries in order to promote these high priorities. Living conditions deteriorated, and criticism of the regime became more overt. On August 13, 1986, the twenty-fifth anniversary of the building of the Berlin Wall, protest demonstrations sputtered throughout East Berlin.

January 15 was the anniversary of the 1919 murder of Karl Liebknecht and Rosa Luxemburg, the founders of the German Communist Party. This was, routinely, an official day of commemoration in the German

Democratic Republic. On January 17, 1988, a counterdemonstration took place in Berlin. Marchers demanded the democratic freedoms that Rosa Luxemburg had called for. Others demanded the freedom to travel abroad. The government reacted with force, arresting 120 individuals and sentencing them to months in prison. Another 54 were declared traitors and expelled to the west.

The East German Evangelical churches had long been critics of the regime. In 1978 they had denounced the introduction of compulsory military training in the secondary schools. In March 1984, the Evangelical Synod called upon the government to improve the standard and climate of living in the DDR. In July 1987, the East German Catholics called their first national meeting and demanded an end to the discrimination against practicing Christians. In January 1988, the churches denounced the harsh government treatment of the demonstrators. Some 2,000 people attended protest services in Berlin. They claimed the right to speak in the name of all who stood for peace and freedom, Christian and non-Christian, who were suppressed by the regime. Other demonstrations in Dresden called for civil liberty and human rights. Honecker only took a harder stand. In January 1989, he denounced the civil liberties movement as "extremist intemperance" and asserted that the "wall which protects us from fascism" would remain in place for the next 50 to 100 years.

Mikhail Gorbachev. During the 1980s the Soviet Union went through a prolonged leadership crisis. Leonid Brezhnev, first secretary of the Communist Party and head of the Soviet state since October 1964, died in November 1982. He was succeeded by Yuri Andropov, who succumbed to kidney failure in February 1984. His successor was Konstantin Chernenko, an old Communist warhorse who died of emphysema in March 1985. The new Communist Party chief was Mikhail Gorbachev, a protégé of Andropov's. At 54 years of age, he belonged to a new generation of party leaders.

In the mid-1980s, the Soviet Communist Party comprised approximately 7 percent of the population, but had enormous control over political, economic, and social affairs. Gorbachev issued a call for opening up discussion of national issues, glasnost, and the transformation of the party, perestroika, to make it a more dynamic organization capable of solving national problems. Gorbachev intended this discussion to take place within the Soviet Communist Party. The peoples of the Soviet Union, however, interpreted glasnost and perestroika as an opportunity to raise demands and seek other, non-Communist directions for resolving them. The Western nations interpreted glasnost and perestroika as the basis for demanding democratic reforms throughout the Eastern bloc. The consequences for East Germany and other Warsaw Pact nations were revolutionary.

Cracks in the Wall. In May of 1989, in the growing spirit of detente, representatives of the Austrian and Hungarian governments met at their mutual frontier and authorized the demolition of border fortifications. That summer hundreds of East German tourists, who were permitted to travel in Warsaw Pact countries, flocked to the Federal Republic embassies in Warsaw, Prague, and Budapest, pleading for asylum. On August 24 the Hungarians opened their border. The dam had broken. By October 25 some 24,500 East Germans had fled through the Hungarian gateway.

In response to the uproar, some of the small East German parties tried to act. The Liberal Democrats, led by Manfred Gerlach, called for change. Baerbel Bohley, who had been arrested in the 1988 demonstrations, announced the formation of the New Forum Party on September 10. Another opposition party, Democracy Now, formed shortly thereafter. Workers called on their unions to demand reform. At this time, the thrust of their demands was for reform, there was little overt call for revolution.

Without acknowledging these defections, the government celebrated the 40th anniversary of the German Democratic Republic on October 7, 1989. Mikhail Gorbachev stood on the podium as an honored guest. To a city festooned with anniversary posters, the 77-year-old Honecker proclaimed his nation to be a "bulwark against imperialism." But thousands of East Germans demonstrated behind barricades in the streets of Berlin, Leipzig, Potsdam, and Dresden, demanding freedom to travel, free elections, and other reforms. They chanted "Gorbi, Gorbi," in an appeal to the Soviet chief to help the reform process. When police used force to quell the demonstrations, the East Germans responded passively, and world opinion lashed the Honecker government. In Leipzig on October 9, the monthly peace prayers attracted over 70,000 to a candlelight vigil. They faced down the police, chanting "We are the people; we're staying here."

The End of Honecker and the Berlin Wall. The SED leadership met in emergency session on October 10. Many called for reform and resigned when Honecker refused their demands. But on October 18, the SED deposed Honecker, electing Egon Krenz as the new general secretary. Krenz made a television address announcing the change, *die Wende*, but called for a renewal of socialism. On October 24 Honecker was dismissed from the Council of State and as the Minister for National Defense. Krenz was elected to head the Council of State, although there were a number of no-votes in the Volkskammer. By the end of the month, the peaceful, candlelight demonstrations in Leipzig were attracting 100,000 participants, and the movement had spread to other East German cities. They were often joined by defectors from the police and East German armed forces. Significantly, Gorbachev had ordered the Russian troops to remain in their barracks; he wanted the Eastern European governments to resolve their own problems. As the movement grew, SED leaders deserted the party. The Czechs opened their borders on November 3. Krenz gave in. On November 8 he legalized the New Forum Party. On November 9, 1989, he lifted all travel restrictions, and the Berlin Wall crumbled and fell before the battering of the joyful demonstrators and chisels of souvenir-hunters. Only short protected sections of it remain today in Berlin.

Kohl's Ten-Point Plan. In the Bundestag, on October 8, Chancellor Kohl offered the East Germans economic help if they reformed their economic and political systems. On November 13 the Volkskammer elected Hans Modrow to head the government until new elections could be held. Kohl surprised the Bundestag with a Ten-Point Plan, on November 28, for collaboration with East Germany. It would begin with communications and transportation. Once the East German constitution was changed, the Federal Republic would help introduce a market economy in the east. Ultimately, there would be cooperative arrangements that with free elections, could lead to a German federation. He left open the question of whether this would lead to reunification, recognizing that this was a European issue.

Round Table. On December 1 the Volkskammer voted to end the privileged position of the SED. Two days later Krenz and the SED leaders resigned their party posts; Honecker and Erich Mielke, head of the hated state police, Stasi, for over 30 years, were expelled by the SED. The party disintegrated after mass resignations. It was reconstituted by the relatively unknown Gregor Gysi as the Party of Democratic Socialism (PDS). Krenz resigned as chairman of the Council of State on December 6, leaving Hans Modrow to head a caretaker government. At this point the opposition movements claimed their rights. There were new parties, such as the New Forum, founded in September, Democracy Now, established on October 1, and Democratic Awakening, formed in mid-December.

And the old parties—the CDU, the Liberal Democrats, the National Democratic Party, and the Farmers' Party—all broke away from the SED in November to found the United Left. On December 7 the opposition parties met with Modrow in the Round Table to plan the transition: a new constitution and national elections.

On December 19 Kohl and Modrow met in Dresden. Amidst the growing public call for unification, they agreed to work for closer relations between the two states and to call for a conference of the Conference for Security and Cooperation in Europe to deal with the larger issues. As a symbol of this agreement, Modrow opened the Brandenburg Gate on December 22.

The tenor of the public demonstrations became stronger and more insistent. On January 15, 1990, a mob invaded and destroyed the Stasi offices, demanding action against the repressive security police. The state attorney filed charges against Erich Mielke, the deposed minister of state security, the following day.

Unification Issues. From the outset, the four powers that occupied Germany reserved their right to decide on German unification. This principle remained firm, even as each German state acquired sovereignty, and the four ambassadors restated this claim after a short meeting on December 11, 1989. Each German state was a member of an alliance system, so German unification was as much an international as a domestic concern. Many of the smaller European states, not to mention France and Poland, were apprehensive at the creation of a unified Germany, 78 million strong, in Central Europe. When Gorbachev met Ronald Reagan near Malta in December 1989, he warned the American president not to try using force to achieve German unification. In February 1990, representatives of NATO and the Warsaw Pact met in Ottawa, Canada. They agreed on the Two Plus Four mechanism for determining unification: the two German states would reach an agreement, which would be reviewed and acted upon by the four powers that had occupied them. On March 8, 1990, the Bundestag opened the way by formally recognized the existing Polish frontier, and recommended that the two German parliaments issue a joint declaration to that effect following the Volkskammer elections.

Elections. The elections for the Volkskammer on March 18, 1990, were the first free elections in East Germany since 1932. The party lineup was extraordinary. On the right was the Alliance for Germany, a coalition of the CDU, Democratic Awakening (DA), and the recently formed German Social Union (DSU), with Lothar de Maziere as its candidate. The liberals, including the Free Democratic Party (FDP), the German Forum, and the Liberal Democratic Party, formed the Alliance of Free Democrats behind

Hans-Dietrich Genscher. On the left, the New Forum, the Human Rights Initiative (IFM) and Democracy Now formed Alliance 90. By election day, there were 24 parties on the ballot. Their western partners joined in the lively election campaign, although the Round Table denounced the practice. Most, though not the PDS or the SPD, favored rapid unification. Thus the elections were also like a referendum on unification.

The election results gave 48.1 percent of the vote to the CDU's Alliance for Germany, which, coupled with the FDP and Alliance 90, gave 57.3 percent of the vote to parties favoring unification. Yet the SPD and the PDS garnered 21.9 and 16.4 percent, respectively, which reflected a strong sentiment for maintaining East German identity. With Kohl's support, de Maziere ran for premier, but the SPD was reluctant to endorse him. Negotiations dragged on until a new cabinet was formed on April 12. Lothar de Maziere was confirmed as premier in a government consisting of 11 CDU ministers, 7 SPD ministers, and 6 additional ministers from three smaller parties (FDP, CSU, DA). When de Maziere first addressed the new Volkskammer, he praised the East Germans for their peaceful revolution and promised to seek unity under "good, reasonable, and progressive" conditions.

The first step was the negotiation of the Treaty of May 18, 1990, between the Federal Republic and the Democratic Republic to establish Monetary, Economic and Social Union. This established a unified deutschmark under the West German State Bank, Bundesbank, and the social market economy, to become effective July 1, 1990. Thereafter, events moved rapidly. On May 5 the Two Plus Four talks began. The two German parliaments individually recognized the "inviolability" of the existing Polish frontier and renounced all claims against Poland. In July, Kohl met with Gorbachev in Moscow. The Russian premier agreed to unification with the conditions that the Federal Republic would not maintain atomic, biological, or chemical weapons, that its military forces would be restricted to 370,000, and that the former DDR territory would not be incorporated into NATO until all Soviet troops were withdrawn from the area, by 1994. Kohl agreed that Germany would help pay for the repatriation of the Russian troops.

On August 31, 1990, the two republics signed the Unification Treaty. The five eastern German states were incorporated as *Laender* in the Federal Republic; Berlin, consolidated from 23 boroughs, was also designated as a *Land* and the capital of the unified state. The treaty took effect on October 3, 1990, and the anniversary of that day was designated a national holiday, the Day of German Unity. With unification, the Basic

Law was also amended. In particular, Article 23, The Jurisdiction Area of the Basic Law, which listed only the 11 original *Laender* and Greater Berlin, was repealed.

On September 12, 1990, the Two Plus Four Settlement was signed by representatives of the Federal Republic, the Democratic Republic, France, Britain, the Soviet Union, and the United States. The united Federal Republic was recognized and the four former occupying powers acknowledged that their rights and responsibilities for Germany had ended.

11

The German Federal Republic
after 1990

For the second time in its history, Germany has unified its separate states by treaty. But so much has changed since the German princes gathered at the French chateau of Versailles in 1871 to fashion the Second Empire. For over a century, the German people struggled to learn self-government, failing tragically and falling under the authority of conquering states as a result. They learned much from the occupying powers following World War II: the two differing models of government provided options they had not had before. Thus, the 1990 merger was the product of a powerful democratic movement sweeping across Eastern Europe and of the patience and persistence of the East Germans themselves. Like their countrymen in the west, they chose republican government in a capitalist state. It was absolutely unprecedented that a sovereign state would surrender itself in such a peaceful and productive manner.

Yet it is clear that the turning, *die Wende*, meant a turn to the right. Freedom from Communist rule gives those in the newly incorporated Laender only a minority voice in the mainly conservative Federal Republic. Thus, for East Germans, unification has been a mixed blessing. Used to virtually full employment for men and women in state enterprises and amenities such as state-supported child day care, many are unequipped to compete in a competitive market economy of free, private enterprise. They continue to press their social issues politically.

Elections. The new Bundestag was elected on December 1, 1990. There were 662 seats at stake, up from 519 in the 1987 elections. The CDU/CSU gained 319 of them, which Kohl interpreted as a mandate. The East Germans cast over 44 percent of their ballots for the CDU. The SPD made only slight inroads into the east; it held 239 seats in the new Bundestag. The FDP prospered, growing from 48 seats (1987) to 79. The Greens lost significantly, their faction decreasing from 44 in 1987 to 17 in 1990. They held their seats by combining with the Alliance 90 in the east. Although the East German Party of Democratic Socialism (PDS) won 8 seats, it was the only small party to top the 5 percent cutoff. The right radical Republicans won barely 2 percent of the national vote. Curiously, only 78 percent of the electorate voted for the unification Bundestag, down from 84 percent in the previous election.

The Bundesrat expanded to 68 seats with the incorporation of the new states. Saxony, Saxony-Anhalt, Thuringia, and Brandenburg each had four representatives. The smaller state of Mecklenburg-Vorpommern had three. The representation for Berlin remained at four seats.

Changes in State Government. One of the first tasks of unification was for the five new states to write democratic state constitutions. This was not simply pro forma, because the East Germans were accustomed to having social rights, such as the right to work and state-subsidized housing, written into their constitution. This was not the case in West Germany. Ultimately, the definition of social rights was left out of the new constitutions, but the issue remained on the mind of the people in the eastern states. Their constitutions were in place by 1993.

The Unification Treaty designated Berlin as the capital city of the Republic. But Bonn was reluctant to give up its status as government headquarters. There was a lively debate between those who wanted to restore Berlin as the legitimate historical capital and those who felt that Bonn, which was the nerve center of the Federal Republic, should retain its place as a symbol of the new, democratic Germany. This was one issue where the weight of the east Germans played a significant role. Berlin had been their capital, and they wanted a national city that was symbolic of their role in German history. When the Bundestag voted on the issue in June 1991, the east German representatives gave the victory to Berlin. Bonn was designated the Federal City in recognition of its honored role as the West German capital for the 40 interim years. In recognition of national unity, the Bundestag is in Berlin, while the Bundesrat, for the time being, stays in Bonn. Eight ministries keep their headquarters in Bonn, along with some federal agencies.

Economic Adjustment. The economic impact of unification had not been clearly forecast by either of the two German states. Kohl had promised in 1990 that "no one will suffer; everyone will benefit." The economic treaty resolved differences, in theory, but the reality proved more difficult. Much of East German plant and equipment was worn out or obsolete and debt ridden. The federal government pledged to assume the East German debt and to stabilize the regional economy. The plan was to privatize the former state-owned industries by offering them as joint ventures or for outright sale to interested investors in Germany and abroad. The government established the Trust Agency, Treuhandanstalt, to manage these arrangements for some 14,000 enterprises, virtually the entire industrial capacity of the east. Many of these were broken up into smaller firms. When the Treuhand completed its responsibilities in 1995, it had signed some 85,000 privatization contracts, which promised over 200 million marks in investment and 1.5 million jobs. The process was enormously costly, leaving a 270 billion mark debt.

The work of the Trust Agency was controversial, particularly because of the massive unemployment it created. On April 1, 1991, its first director, the West German business executive Detlev Rohwedder, was assassinated by terrorists. In 1995, when the agency was downsized into four successor organizations, many enterprises were shut down as unprofitable, and 60 remained to be sold. The closure of East German industry also resulted in a considerable loss of trade, especially with Eastern Europe.

In addition to reorganization of industry by the Treuhand, the government began investing to upgrade the infrastructure of the east. Over 80,000 housing units went up; roads, railways, bridges, and waterways were constructed and repaired. Considerable expenditure was necessary to deal with the substantial environmental pollution in the east, caused by excessive use of brown coal and poor management of industrial wastes. Many of the workers in the new states were thrown out of work with unification; funds were needed to retrain them, and for social welfare until they could find employment. By the end of 1995, these public expenditures had amounted to some 825 billion marks.

Additional unemployment resulted from removing individuals trained in Communist perspectives from their posts in schools, universities, and the civil service. They were often rapidly replaced by workers from the west, which caused resentment. The younger generation, raised under

Communism, was bitter that, having done well in their training, they were now disqualified by it from working in their chosen fields. In other instances, workers from the west received higher wages or supervisory positions. Pensions in the east were only 82.2 percent of those in the west in 1996. These differences and tensions have created a gap between the workers in the east, Ossies, and those from the west, Wessies. Moreover, many West Germans have been unhappy with the high costs of unification and displeased with the complaints coming from the eastern states.

Because the state had owned all property in the German Democratic Republic, unification introduced an enormous dilemma over the privatization of nonindustrial real estate. Soon there was a flood of claims to homes, commercial properties, and farms from former residents of the five new states. These came not only from those who had fled the post–World War II regime but also from many who had fled the Hitler regime. In some cases, their heirs laid claim to family holdings they felt they should have inherited. The result is a tangled mass of claims and counterclaims, almost impossible to resolve because original land records were destroyed in the war or were long buried in file storage. It will take the courts years and years to resolve these matters. In the meantime, uncertainty about property ownership has had a chilling effect on investment in the region, slowing its economic development.

The costs of unification created substantial budget deficits and mounting inflation. When rent controls were ended in the five new states in 1991, housing costs there increased by as much as 250 percent. Labor unrest grew, especially in the eastern states. At first the government denied the difficulties, but then it joined with labor and management to find ways to resolve them. These talks led, in 1992, to the Solidarity Pact. It imposed a new schedule of taxes and budget cuts to help reduce the deficit while still investing in necessary projects in the eastern states. This plan raised taxes on consumer goods. It also placed a surcharge on wages, 7.5 percent on January 1, 1995. This solidarity surtax has been reduced in stages to 5.5 percent in 1998. Between 1992 and 1995, the average gross domestic product rose 7.3 percent per year. Still, the tide of unemployment rose to nearly 4 million by 1994, some 13.5 percent.

Withdrawal of Soviet Troops. On August 31, 1994, with German President Helmut Kohl and Russian President Boris Yeltsin looking on, the last of the 340,000 Russian soldiers and 210,000 civilian dependents left Germany. In accordance with their agreement, Germany provided some 14.6 billion marks to facilitate this withdrawal, most of which went to building houses in Belarus, Russia, and Ukraine for the returning men and their families.

The Stasi Legacy. Under the former East German regime, the Ministry of State Security, the Stasi, had maintained a force of secret police to stifle opposition. Headed by Erich Mielke, the Stasi augmented its regular staff of some 100,000 with over 150,000 informers and spies. It created a police state, which the Germans were determined to dismantle after unification. In October 1990 the federal government set up a commission to take over and administer dossiers in the Stasi files in order to protect the some six million individuals they covered. Headed by Pastor Joachim Gauck, the commission initially planned to review the 180-kilometer-long cache of files to prosecute Stasi personnel who committed criminal acts. But east German citizens anxiously demanded the right to see what was in their files. They were given access after January 1992. Not surprisingly, these records revealed numerous instances of spying and shocking betrayal. This led to many subsequent accusations and actions against Stasi informers as well as those who had committed crimes. The exposure of Stasi activities has been a painful part of postunification history. Accusations of collaborating with the Stasi cost many individuals their jobs.

In some ways, dealing with the Stasi problem resembles the problems of de-Nazification following World War II. Virtually every German had had to compromise with the Hitler regime at some point; therefore, when de Nazification was carried out, there had to be a distinction between compliance for self-preservation and criminal behavior. It was never a completely clean process. So it is with the Stasi connections. This has resulted in a continuing controversy that has taken on political overtones. For example, Manfred Stolpe, who represented the Protestant church during the DDR, became a leader in the PDS following unification, and minister president in Brandenburg. He is accused by some of collaborating with the Stasi, defended by others as the protector of what little freedom the church retained. There have been similar charges by the CDU/CSU against PDS chairman Gregor Gysi and some of that party's Bundestag delegates.

***Volksdeutsche* and Asylum Seekers.** With unification, Germany experienced another influx of population. Much of it was a result of the instability caused by the collapse of the Soviet system in Eastern Europe. There, democratization was often accompanied by a militant nationalism, and minority populations with German ancestry decided to seek safe haven in the Federal Republic. The Basic Law (Article 33) confers citizenship on "every German," not just those born within the national boundaries. Similarly, it offered asylum to "persons persecuted on political grounds" (Article 16). Some 200,000 individuals claiming German descent, the *Volksdeutsche*, and over 200,000 refugees from civil conflict in Yugoslavia and elsewhere fled to Germany after unification. Those without homes or work received state welfare, further straining the economy. Many Germans resented the expense of this invasion, which competed with funds to invest in urgently needed economic development.

As demand arose for reform of the asylum law, some took matters into their own hands. Groups of neo-Nazis, "skinheads," conservative nationalists, and unemployed youth began to act out against the foreigners. This occurred particularly among the youth and unemployed in the eastern states, although there were also incidents in the southwest of Germany. In 1992 there were over 2,000 violent incidents, like the burning of refugee quarters in Rostock. But there was also considerable public outcry against the "foreigner hate." In Leipzig, where the peaceful public demonstrations against the DDR had begun, a similar effort was made to reduce the hostility against foreigners. Once again, demonstrators stood outside the St. Nicholas Church and in the nearby public square. This time they carried placards reading "Everywhere else I am a foreigner, too." The city of Potsdam held a special summer street fair to try to educate Germans about the benefits of cultural diversity. The Bundestag also took action by passing an amendment to Article 16 of the Basic Law. After July 1993, this amendment redefined the concept of asylum and the procedures for administering it. Any refugee entering Germany from a "safe third country" could no longer claim asylum. The amendment also curtailed cash benefits to asylum seekers. These efforts, coupled with rigorous police action against the most militant street groups, helped reduce the violent activities.

A recent event indicates that the Federal Republic is also dealing productively with the long-standing problem of anti-Semitism. In February 1998 the American Jewish Committee (AJC) opened an office in the newly constructed Mosse Palace on Leipziger Platz in Berlin. This is the only office the AJC has established outside the United States and Israel. Here, on a site formerly covered by the Berlin Wall, the committee works through educational programs to improve German-Jewish relations and to facilitate the growing migration of Jews from Eastern Europe. German Foreign Minister Klaus Kinkel welcomed this "expression of trust" in the Federal Republic and the German people.

Foreign Affairs. Germany's foreign policy in the 1990s focused on strengthening the European Union and helping to link the states of Eastern Europe to it. The European Union signed an Agreement of Partnership and Cooperation with Russia on June 24, 1994. Germany has provided over 90 billion marks to Russia and had extended over 47 billion marks in credit to the Commonwealth of Independent States (former states of the USSR) by 1995. The Federal Republic is also the third largest contributor to the United Nations, paying over 22 percent of the NATO budget. Despite the economic problems at home, the Federal Republic contributed some 11 billion marks to help finance the expenses of the Gulf War against Iraq.

In 1993, at the request of the United Nations, a small transportation unit from the army served in the UN peacekeeping forces in Somalia. This was controversial at home, since the German army had been prohibited from serving abroad. The German Federal Court ruled, in July 1994, that the army could serve in the operations of NATO and the Western European Union or in UN peacekeeping operations. On December 6, 1995, the Bundestag voted to send 4,000 men as part of the UN peacekeeping activities in Bosnia.

European Union. In early 1993, the European Community implemented the European Common Market. This created a barrier-free internal market of 345 million consumers. All but Switzerland and the European Free Trade Association (Austria, Finland, Iceland, Liechtenstein, Norway, and Sweden) joined with the Common Market in the European Economic Area. Efforts to create a common currency began in the 1990s with discussions among the national state banks. On January 1, 1994, the European Monetary Institute began paving the way for a European Central Bank headquartered in Frankfurt, Germany. Negotiations also began in December 1994 to find ways to integrate Bulgaria, the Czech and Slovak Republics, Hungary, Poland, and Rumania into this framework.

The 1994 Elections. In the 1994 elections, the CDU/CSU coalition retained its position as Germany's largest faction, but lost 25 seats in the Bundestag. The FDP suffered even more heavily, losing 32 seats. While the SPD gained 13 seats, the big winner on the left was Alliance 90/The Greens. With a 49-member delegation, they surpassed the FDP by 2 seats. Another major winner was the PDS, the old East German SED in new clothing: it increased its faction from 8 to 30 seats in the Bundestag. Some 79 percent of the eligible electorate participated. The setback to the ruling coalition clearly reflected the economic problems and labor unrest of the early 1990s.

Despite the many problems that emerged as a result of unification, the Federal Republic made substantial progress in the 1990s. Germany ranks third behind Japan and the United States in world market share (17.1 percent) for high technology products. The gross domestic product is increasing steadily at a rate over 2 percent annually, and private consumption and exports are both rising. Unemployment is slowly decreasing, although mainly in the western states. New construction and investment are changing the look of the cities in the five new states, and they are becoming increasingly attractive to tourists and to trade conventions and fairs. For example, in 1995, Germany attracted 114 of the 150 major international trade fairs, hosting over 142,000 exhibitors. This activity generates some 8 billion marks for the German economy. Nearly 200 smaller regional fairs supplement this activity. From June 1 to October 31, 2000, Hanover hosts Germany's first world's fair, the World Exposition EXPO 2000, on the theme "Mankind—Nature—Technology."

Looking Ahead. The Bundestag elections of September 1998 signaled a new leadership for Germany in the twenty-first century. After 16 years, Helmut Kohl and his CDU/CSU government were defeated by the SPD's Gerhard Schroeder and his "New Center." Among the smaller parties there was a slight movement toward the left as well, especially in the strengthened role of the PDS. The radical right groups continued their protest movements over unemployment and immigration but did not gain sufficient constituent support to win seats in the Bundestag. Clearly, economic issues played a significant role in the outcome. At election time, German unemployment stood at 10 percent overall, with nearly double that rate in the eastern states. These political issues are reflected in the makeup of the 1998 Bundestag:

Party Seats	1994	1998
CDU/CSU	294	245
SPD	252	298
FDP	47	44
Greens	49	47
PDS	30	35

At 54, Schroeder grew up in the postwar world and joins Britain's Tony Blair in giving Europe a new, pro-labor outlook after decades of conservatism. A child of the working class, Schroeder has been a career politician most of his adult life. He joined the SPD in 1963 at the age of

19. Earning his high school diploma three years later by attending night school, he continued on to law school, moving up in SPD ranks to serve as president of the young socialists in 1978. He served in the state legislature of Lower Saxony from 1980 to 1986 and was that state's minister president from 1990 to 1998. His centrist, reform-oriented ideas cost him his role as the party's economic leader in 1995 but won him votes from the conservatives in 1998.

The SPD took key positions in the new government, with Oskar Lafontaine as finance minister and Rodolf Scharping as defense minister. Wolfgang Thierse, SPD leader in the eastern states since reunification, was chosen by the party to be the speaker in the Bundestag. In alliance with the Greens, the 1998 government gained a 21-seat majority. Schroeder will preside over the relocation of the German capital to Berlin and the introduction of the new Euro currency to replace the deutschmark.

Kohl's inability to solve the economic problems of German unification contributed to his political defeat. He is the first German postwar chancellor to be voted out of office in a national election. Nevertheless, his legacy is a record of brilliant leadership in both German and European unification.

As the world's third largest industrial economy, the German Federal Republic is well positioned to recover from the enormous economic shock of unification. The development of the European Common Market can only help complete this adjustment process. This, in turn, should help maintain the stability of domestic politics in the twenty-first century.

Notable People in the History of Germany

Konrad Adenauer (1876–1967). Lord mayor of Cologne and a member of the Prussian Landtag (1917–1933) for the Catholic Center Party. Barred from office for his opposition to Hitler, he was in a concentration camp from 1944 to 1945. He helped found the Christian Democratic Union in 1945, and became its leader in the British Sector. In 1949 he became the first chancellor of the Federal Republic, serving until 1963. From 1951 to 1955 he also served as foreign minister. Under his administration the Federal Republic joined the Allies in the Marshall Plan, the European Union, and NATO. Together with French president de Gaulle, he promoted the reconciliation of Germany and France. He resigned from office at the age of 87 and died four years later.

Theobald von Bethmann-Hollweg (1856–1921). The fifth chancellor of the German Empire (1909–1917). He served as Prussian minister of interior and imperial secretary of the interior before being appointed chancellor. After his diplomacy failed to neutralize the Triple Alliance, he led Germany into World War I in August 1914. He always tried to depict Germany as fighting a defensive war. When he refused to endorse unlimited submarine warfare in 1917, he was forced to resign.

Otto von Bismarck (1815–1898). Born to an aristocratic Junker family, Bismarck studied law and was elected to the United Diet in 1847. He was against the revolution in 1848, and his loyalty was rewarded by appointment as the Prussian representative to the German Confederation. There he championed Prussia against Austria. Later he served as ambassador to Russia and France. In 1862 William I appointed him minister president of Prussia to help break the deadlock with the Landtag over the military budget. He won popular support for building the military, and the Landtag conceded. He maneuvered the Austrian-led German Confederation into war with Denmark (1864) to help Prussia gain territory in Schleswig-Holstein, then challenged and defeated Austria in the Seven Weeks' War (1867), which ended the German Confederation. He consolidated the North German Confederation (1867–1870) north of the Main River and served as its chancellor. The confederation entered into defensive alliances with the south German states. He maneuvered France into the Franco-Prussian War (1870–1871), which invoked those alliances and led to unification of Germany by a treaty among the German rulers, excluding Austria. Bismarck was the first chancellor of the German Empire (1871–1890). He conducted a conservative policy, suppressing the Catholics and Social Democrats, while paternalistically wooing the working classes with Europe's most advanced social welfare insurance. Diplomatically, he tried to give Germany the profile of a satiated, peaceful state. He created a complex network of treaties, starting with the Dual Alliance of 1879, to isolate a revenge-minded France and to restrain his allies from entering a war that might involve Germany. He convened and presided over the conference that began the "scramble for Africa." He served all three German emperors, but quarrelled with William II, who accepted his resignation in March 1890. He retired to his estate north of Hamburg, but remained a critical voice in politics until his death in July 1898.

Willi Brandt (1913–1992). Born Herbert Ernst Karl Frahm, Brandt was a socialist and a journalist who used the name Willi Brandt. When Hitler seized power, Brandt fled to Sweden and remained there through World War II. Then he returned to Germany. He was an SPD member of the Bundestag (1949–1957) and mayor of Berlin (1957–1966). Defeated in his bids for the chancellorship in 1961 and 1965, he became vice chancellor and foreign minister in 1966. He was elected chancellor in 1969 and served until 1971, when he resigned due to a scandal caused by the infiltration of an East German spy into the government. In 1971 he received the Nobel Peace Prize for his Ostpolitik, which began the reconciliation with East Germany.

Bernhard von Buelow (1849–1929). The fourth chancellor of the German Empire (1900–1909). He entered the diplomatic service in 1875 and was appointed foreign secretary in 1897. Despite his extensive diplomatic experience, his leadership was characterized by the disintegration of Germany's diplomatic position because of his unwillingness to confront William II. The Triple Alliance of France, Britain, and Russia came into being during his tenure. The Morocco crisis of 1905, the *Daily Telegraph* affair of 1908 and the Bosnian crisis of that same year all demonstrated the hostility of Europe to Germany. He was forced to resign in 1909

Georg Leo von Caprivi (1831–1899). Selected by William II to succeed Bismarck as Prussian minister president (1890–1892) and chancellor (1890–1894). He alienated the Prussians by his education and school policies, which led to his resignation in 1894.

Charlemagne / Karl der Grosse (742–814). Carolingian Frank, descendent of Charles Martel, who consolidated Aquitaine, Burgundy, Provence, Alemania, Thuringia, Bavaria, and Friesland for the declining Merovingian dynasty. His father, Pippin, deposed the Merovingians in 751. Charlemagne became king of the Franks in 768. He led several campaigns, at the request of the pope, against the Lombards of northern Italy. Pope Leo III crowned him Emperor of the Romans on Christmas day 800. He established his capital in Aachen (Aix-la-Chapelle), where he founded an important school. He led brutal eastward expansion campaigns against the Saxons. The Germans recognized him as Charles the Great during his lifetime. He died in Aachen in January 814.

Charles V, The Great (1500–1558). Hapsburg grandson of Maximilian I. Raised in Flanders due to his mother's insanity, he became King Charles I of Spain, Mexico, and Peru in 1516, and heir to the Holy Roman Empire in 1519, although he did not have time to be crowned until 1530. He joined Pope Leo X in opposing Martin Luther, banning Luther and his doctrines at the Diet of Mainz in 1521. He fought four campaigns against Francis I of France for control of Italy. He combatted the Protestant nobility in the Knights' War (1522–1523) and the Schmalkaldic Wars (1546–1547), and put down the Peasants' War (1524–1525). He accepted the Peace of Augsburg (1555) to resolve the Protestant wars, permitting the prince of each of the German states to establish his own religion within his realm. He divided the Hapsburg realm between Spanish and Austrian holdings before he died at the monastery of Yuste in Spain, in 1558.

Clovis (466–511). Salian Frank, who became king of the Merovingian dynasty in 481. He consolidated his rule over all the Franks and expanded his holdings up to the borders of Theodoric's Italy. Converted to Christianity in 498, he was consecrated king of the Franks by Bishop Remigius at Reims, France, in the same year and went on to consolidate the Roman Catholic Church in his kingdom. He died in Paris in 511.

Friedrich Ebert (1871–1925). Member of the Social Democrat Party and Reichstag Deputy (1912–1918). He led the SPD through World War I, supporting defense but calling for peace negotiations and government reform. He was chancellor for a day, November 9, 1918, when William II abdicated, then served as head of the German Republic proclaimed on November 10. He served as the first president of the Weimar Republic (1919–1925) until his death.

Ludwig Erhard (1897–1977). Designed the currency reform for West Germany, and then was appointed minister of economics in the Federal Republic (1949–1963). He presided over the "economic miracle" of West German recovery. He became vice chancellor in 1957 and succeeded Adenauer as the second chancellor in 1963. Although elected in his own right in 1965, he lost a vote of confidence over economic policy in 1966 and resigned.

Ferdinand II (1578–1637). King of Bohemia (1517–1519), Holy Roman Emperor (1519–1537), and king of Hungary (1521–1525). Devoutly Catholic, he tried to restore Catholicism to Protestant Bohemia and touched off the Thirty Years' War. He allied Austria with Bavaria and the Catholic League of Princes. He died in 1637 before the issues were resolved.

Frederick I, Barbarossa (1123?–1190). Hohenstaufen dynasty king of the Germans and Emperor of the Romans (1152–1190). He began the use of the term "Holy Roman Empire." Successful in winning support of the great dukes and the Church, he made numerous campaigns in Italy as well as against the Slavs. He reformed the Empire to establish the electoral system. He was forced to concede autonomy to northern Italian towns by 1183 Peace of Constance. In 1186 he joined Richard I of England and Philip II of France on the Third Crusade, but drowned in Asia Minor in 1190 before reaching Jerusalem.

Frederick I, Hohenzollern (1657–1713). Succeeded the Great Elector as Frederick III, elector of Brandenburg (1688–1701). Emperor Leopold I in 1701 recognized him as king in Prussia, which lay outside the Holy Roman Empire. He was known mainly for his patronage of scholars and the arts.

Frederick II, the Great (1712–1786). As king of Prussia (1740–1786), he was known as an enlightened despot. He broke the Pragmatic Sanction recognizing Maria Theresa as ruler of Austria, and set off the War of the Austrian Succession (1740–1748) by seizing the Austrian province of Silesia. Although nearly bankrupted by that war, he built the baroque palace of Sans Souci in Potsdam in the mode of Versailles, and gave asylum to French Huguenots to help build the town. When Austria, Saxony, and France allied to help Maria Theresa regain Silesia in 1756 (the Diplomatic Revolution), Frederick II allied with England. In the Seven Years' War (1756–1763) that followed, Prussia retained Silesia. Thereafter, Frederick concentrated on centralizing the Prussian government and building law codes and economic structures. He successfully challenged Austria again in the War of the Bavarian Succession (1778–1779). He died at Sans Souci in August 1786.

Frederick III (1833–1888). King of Prussia and German emperor (1888). He gave evidence of liberal tendencies in his youth, and married Princess Victoria, daughter of Queen Victoria, who was said to have influenced him toward a more liberal constitutional monarchy. He was often at odds with Bismarck. When he succeeded to the throne in March 1888, he was in the terminal stages of throat cancer. He ruled only three months before his death in June 1888.

Frederick William, the Great Elector (1620–1688). As elector of Brandenburg (1640–1688), he made an armistice with the Swedish forces fighting the Thirty Years' War and remained neutral through the Treaty of Westphalia (1648). An absolutist, he allied with the Junkers to build the Prussian centralized state in which they served as administrators and military officers. He expanded his territory in 1660 when the Treaty of

Oliva with Sweden gave him full sovereignty over Prussia. He invited the French Huguenots (Protestants) to Prussia when they were expelled from Catholic France. He laid the foundations for the Prussian state.

Frederick William II (1744–1797). King of Prussia (1786–1797) who allied with Austria to help French King Louis XVI in the French Revolution. He gained territory for Prussia in the Partitions of Poland in 1793 and 1795, but lost Rhineland holdings to France in the Treaty of Basel in 1795. Through poor administration, he nearly bankrupted Prussia.

Frederick William III (1770–1840). King of Prussia (1797–1840) who resisted Napoleon, but suffered humiliating defeat and loss of territory in 1806. He launched internal reforms in Prussia that benefited the peasantry and towns. He joined Russia and Austria to defeat Napoleon in the War of Liberation in 1813. He supported the Prussian Zollverein treaties, which unified trade, but as a member of the conservative Holy Alliance, accepted Austrian leadership of the German Confederation.

Frederick William IV (1795–1861). King of Prussia (1840–1861) who called the United Diet in 1847 and promised a Prussian constitution during the Revolution of 1848. But he refused to take the imperial crown from the popular Frankfurt Parliament, and tried, instead, to unite the German princes. Their refusal in 1850 was humiliating. Thereafter he supported reactionary policies in Prussia. Overtaken by mental illness in 1858, he relinquished power to his brother, William, as regent for the remaining years of his life.

Joseph Paul Goebbels (1897–1945). Joined the Nazi Party in 1922 and became its propaganda specialist as editor of its official publication, *Der Angriff.* Hitler appointed him the district administrator (*Gauleiter*) of Berlin in 1926. He was elected to the Reichstag in 1928. Appointed minister for propaganda and national enlightenment in March 1933, he was largely responsible for creating the "Hitler myth." He used this position to attack intellectuals, burning their books; to urge anti-Semitism; and to call for mass commitment to total war. In 1944 Hitler placed him in charge of mobilization. He and his family committed suicide in Hitler's Berlin bunker on May 1, 1945.

Hermann Goering (1893–1946). World War I air ace who joined the Nazi Party in 1922. He headed the Storm Troopers and became one of

Hitler's closest advisors. In 1932 he was president of the Reichstag. In Hitler's dictatorship, Goering was the administrator of the Four-Year Plan, which facilitated rearmament (1934), and commander of the Luftwaffe (1935). Hitler designated Goering as his successor in 1939, but at the end of the war, when he tried to take control, he was dismissed by Hitler from both the party and his government offices. He was tried and condemned to death by the Nuremberg tribunal, but committed suicide by taking poison from an unknown source in October 1946 before the sentence could be carried out.

Otto Grotewohl (1894–1964). Served in the the Reichstag (1925–1933). He led the SPD in East Germany in 1945 and took it into the SED. He served as minister president of the Democratic Republic (1949–1964).

Henry IV (1050–1106). Salian king of the Franks (1056, with his mother as regent) and emperor of the Romans. He used internal colonization to build towns as counterweight to feudal nobility and the Church. He also appealed for popular support during civil war (1073–1075) and quarreled with Pope Gregory VII over the right to invest bishops. When excommunicated by the pope, he apologized in a theatrical manner at Canossa, Italy, in 1077. He gave little support to the First Crusade (1095). His sons rebelled against him, with papal support, and he died in prison in 1106.

Hermann / Arminius (16 B.C.E.?–C.E. 21). Born in the region between the Weser and Elbe, son of a prince of the Cherusk tribe. He trained as a Roman soldier under the rule of Emperor Tiberius. He returned to Germany to organize resistance to Roman efforts to control the right bank of the Rhine. Augustus Caesar thereafter kept Roman forces west of the Rhine. Hermann's troops defeated three Roman legions at the Battle of the Teutoberg Forest in 9 C.E. He failed to unite the German tribes, and was murdered by a tribal rival.

Theodor Heuss (1884–1963). A political liberal, Heuss was a newspaper editor before and during World War I. From 1920 to 1933, he was a teacher. Elected to the Reichstag (1924–1928 and 1930–1933) as a member of the German Democratic Party, he voted against the Enabling Act in March 1933. During the Hitler dictatorship, he offered continuing opposition through the press. After World War II, he served as minister of culture in Wuerttemberg (1945–1946) and as a member of its Landtag (1945–1949). He helped found the Free Democrat Party in 1948 and served as its leader. He helped write the *Grundgesetz* as a member of the Parliamentary Council. Elected the first president of the Federal Republic in 1949, he was unanimously reelected in 1954 but declined to serve a third term.

Heinrich Himmler (1900–1945). After joining the Nazi Party in 1923, Himmler served as one of Hitler's personal bodyguards. He participated in the Beer Hall Putsch. In 1929 he took command of the Party SS. In 1934 he commanded the secret police (Gestapo), and in 1936, the national police force that was responsible for implementing the decrees to exterminate the Jews and other targeted groups. He authorized the Final Solution in 1942. When World War II began, he built an elite military SS (Waffen-SS). In 1943 Hitler made him minister of interior, and in 1944 a Reichskommissar for defense of the home-front. Captured by the British in April 1945, he committed suicide in May before coming to trial.

Paul von Hindenburg (1847–1934). Career military officer who served in the Seven Weeks' and Franco-Prussian Wars. He retired in 1911, but was recalled in 1914 to command troops on the Russian front at the beginning of World War I. His overwhelming victory at Tannenberg made him a national hero. He was appointed chief of the German General Staff (1916–1918), but retired at the end of the war. He blamed German defeat on domestic politics. In 1925 he was elected as the second president of the Weimar Republic. He defeated Hitler and was reelected to a second term in 1932. Despite his personal objections, he was persuaded to appoint Hitler as chancellor in January 1933. The Nazi seizure of power left him a figurehead until his death in August 1934.

Adolf Hitler (1889–1945). An Austrian who served honorably in the German Army during World War I, Hitler joined the small German Workers' Party in 1919, taking leadership of it the following year. He changed its orientation and name to the National Socialist Workers Party. His goals were to overturn the Versailles terms and remilitarize Germany. Arrested, tried and convicted to a five-year prison term for the Beer Hall Putsch of 1923, he used the time to write *Mein Kampf*, which spelled out his perceptions of fascism, anti-Semitism, and expansionism. He decided to use legal means to seize power, and was helped by the Depression crisis, which brought the Nazi Party to national strength in the 1930 election. In 1932 Hitler was a candidate for the presidency, losing to Hindenburg. Appointed chancellor in January 1933, he used the

Reichstag fire as the premise for the Enabling Act (1933) which vested legislative authority in the chancellor. He purged the Nazi dissidents in the Night of the Long Knives (June 1934); then added presidential powers at Hindenburg's death in August 1934. He chose to be called the Fuehrer rather than president. He began to implement his program with the anti-Semitic Nuremberg Laws (1935), rearmament (1935), and expansion through unification (*Anschluss*) with Austria (1938) and the takeover of Czechoslovakia (1938–1939). After concluding the Hitler-Stalin non-aggression pact with the Soviet Union, Germany invaded Poland in September 1939, launching World War II. Hitler's decision to invade the Soviet Union in June 1941 led to the inevitable military defeat of the Third Reich. He survived an assassination attempt in July 1944, but committed suicide on April 30, 1945, rather than surrender to the encroaching Soviet army.

Chlodwig zu Hohenlohe-Schillingsfuerst (1819–1901). German statesman who served as Bavarian minister president (1866–1870), German ambassador to France (1874), and Governor of Alsace-Lorraine (1885–1894) before becoming Prussian minister president and third chancellor (1894–1900) of the German Empire. He tried to manage William II's "personal regime" by delaying the implementation of his demands. He retired peacefully in 1900.

Erich Honecker (1912–1994). Became a Communist as a teenager and studied at the party school in Moscow in 1930. He was imprisoned by the Nazis in 1935 and remained there until the end of World War II. After the war he was a founding member of the Socialist Unity Party in East Germany and rose through the ranks to become party secretary in 1958. He headed the security forces that maintained the Berlin Wall. Succeeding Walter Ulbricht in 1973, he took advantage of the Ostpolitik to improve relations with West Germany, visiting there in 1987. He was unable to suppress or control the peaceful reform movement in 1989 and was removed from power. He went into exile in Chile. Accused of a number of crimes against humanity, he was never tried. He died of a terminal illness in 1994.

Joseph II (1741–1790). Son of Maria Theresa of Austria, Holy Roman emperor (1765–1790). He was an enlightened despot who tried to introduce religious toleration and freedom for the serfs into his holdings. These reforms were reversed at his death in Vienna in February 1790.

Helmut Kohl (1930–). Entered West German politics as a Christian Democrat member of the Landtag in Rhineland-Palatinate (1959), later serving as the state's minister president (1969–1976). As chairman of the CDU (1973), he was elected to the Bundestag (1976–1982). He became chancellor in 1982 and has served longer than any other chancellor of the Federal Republic to date. He continued Germany's participation in the European Union and advocated reunification of Germany in 1989. He was elected the first chancellor of the unified Federal Republic in 1990, and narrowly gained reelection in 1994. He was defeated in 1998.

Erich Ludendorff (1865–1937). Career military officer who was appointed to the General Staff in 1894. Served in World War I with General Hindenburg in the victory over the Russians at Tannenberg (1914). Appointed Hindenburg's quartermaster general, he became increasingly political, pushing for unlimited submarine warfare in 1917. He was dismissed after the German defeat. After the war he championed German nationalist causes. He marched beside Hitler in the Beer Hall Putsch (1923), for which he was arrested but later acquitted. He served as a National Socialist Reichstag deputy from 1924 to 1928.

Martin Luther (1483–1546). Although the son of a miner, Luther completed his master's degree at Erfurt University in 1505. He then chose to enter an Augustinian monastery, and was ordained a priest in 1507. After studying theology, he received his doctorate in 1512 and became a professor at Wittenberg University. Coming to question Catholic theology and practice, Luther published his 95 Theses in October 1517, which set off the Reformation conflict. He was excommunicated by the Church and declared an outlaw by Emperor Charles V in 1521. Given shelter at Wartburg Castle by Saxon Elector Frederick the Wise, Luther left the priesthood and began a life of writing. His translation of the Bible into German set a standard for the written language. Married Katharina von Bora in 1525. Died in February 1546.

Maria Theresa (1717–1780). As the archduchess of Austria and queen of Bohemia and Hungary (1740–1780), she was the only heir to Holy Roman Emperor Charles VI of Austria. He arranged the Pragmatic Sanction to allow the imperial succession to continue through her to her male heir.

Maximilian I (1459–1519). Hapsburg king of the Germans (1486–1519) and Holy Roman Emperor (1493–1519) who restructured the Empire. He established a court of appeals and set up ten administrative circles with diets and taxation systems. He added Burgundy and the Flemish cities to the realm and married his son Phillip to Joanna the Mad of Spain to extend Hapsburg power to the Iberian peninsula.

Otto I, The Great (912–973). Duke of Saxony and king of the Franks. He tried to consolidate Germans by collaborating with the Roman Catholic Church and expanding eastward to gain new fiefs to grant to loyal nobility. He formed new bishoprics in the east, including the bishopric of Magdeburg. He defeated the Huns in 955 at Lechfeld. He also had to campaign in Italy to subdue the Lombards. He was known in his day as Otto the Great.

Wilhelm Pieck (1876–1960). Together with Otto Grotewohl, he served as chairman of the SED (1946–1954). After the formation of the German Democratic Republic in October 1949, Pieck became its first president (1949–1960).

Erwin Rommel (1891–1944). German general who gained fame for brilliantly commanding the Africa Corps. He was known as the Desert Fox. Recalled to Germany in 1943, he was put in command of the German fortifications on the Atlantic coast. He was implicated in the July 1944 assassination attempt against Hitler's life, and elected for suicide rather than a trial.

Rudolf of Hapsburg (1218–1291). Prince from Switzerland who was elected Holy Roman Emperor in 1273 because of the political weakness of his family. By making careful marriage alliances, he founded the Hapsburg dynasty, which ruled the Holy Roman Empire and later Austrian empires until 1918.

Helmut Schmidt (1918–   ). Elected to the Social Democrat faction of the Bundestag in 1953, Schmidt served in the Brandt cabinet as defense minister (1969–1972) and as minister of finance (1972–1974). He became chancellor (1976–1982) when Brandt resigned. He continued the Ostpolitik and the improvement of relations with France, and took a leading role in developing the European Community.

Gerhard Schroeder (1944–   ) Elected chancellor in 1998 as candidate of the Social Democratic Party, defeating the incumbent Helmut Kohl. As a life-long socialist, Schroeder had chaired the young socialists and served in the state legislature for Lower Saxony (1980–1986) and was that state's minister president (1990–1998). He formed a coalition with the Greens to achieve a majority for his cabinet.

Kurt Schumacher (1895–1952). A veteran of World War I, he joined the radical workers' movement in 1918. From 1920 to 1924 he edited the Social Democrat *Schwaebischen Tagwacht* of Berlin. He was elected a member of the SPD faction in the Wuerttemberg Landtag (1924–1931) and the Reichstag (1930). The Nazis put him in a concentration camp in 1933, and he remained there throughout the war. He led the postwar Social Democrat Party, resisting consolidation with the Communist Party. In 1949 he led the SPD as the opposition party in the Adenauer Bundestag. Unlike Adenauer, he supported a conciliatory policy toward East Germany.

Claus Schenk von Stauffenberg (1907–1944). Army colonel and member of the General Staff who agreed to join an army conspiracy to assassinate Hitler. Crippled by war wounds, he planted a bomb in the "wolf's lair" staff headquarters where Hitler attended a planning meeting on July 20, 1944. Unaware that the explosion failed to kill Hitler, Stauffenberg issued a proclamation explaining the act. He and his fellow conspirators were captured and executed.

Gustav Stresemann (1878–1929). German statesman who was the youngest member of the imperial Reichstag when he was first elected as a National Liberal deputy (1907–1912, 1914–1918). After the war he became a member and leader of the German People's Party in the Reichstag (1919–1929). He served briefly as chancellor in 1923 and ended the Ruhr crisis of that year. Thereafter he served as foreign minister in every successive cabinet until his death in 1929, earning the respect of the victor nations. Determined to overturn the Versailles settlement, Stresemann devised the conciliatory policy of fulfillment to demonstrate that the treaty's terms were too drastic to implement. He signed the Locarno Treaties in 1925, for which he earned the 1926 Nobel Peace Prize. He also signed the Kellogg-Briand Peace Pact (1928) and the Young plan to restructure reparations. He died in office in October 1929.

Theodoric (453–526). Ostrogoth of the Amali tribe, raised as a hostage in Constantinople from age 7 to 18. Crowned king in 471, he was sent by Byzantine Emperor Zeno to Italy in 488 to battle Odoacer, who had deposed the last western Roman emperor, Romulus Augustulus, in 476. He defeated Odoacer in 493 and thereafter ruled Italy in the name of the emperor. He sought good relations with other Germanic tribes and married the sister of Clovis, the king of the Franks.

Alfred von Tirpitz (1849–1930). German secretary of the navy (1865–1897) who presided over the building of the modern imperial navy. He advocated the unrestricted submarine warfare that eventually provoked the United States to declare war on Germany in 1916. He served as a member of the Reichstag (1924–1928) in the Weimar Republic.

Walter Ulbricht (1893–1973). Joined the Communist Party in 1919 and served as KPD delegate in the Reichstag (1928–1933). He went into exile during the Nazi regime and World War II, returning under Soviet auspices in 1945. He helped found the Socialist Unity Party of East Germany in 1946 and served in the important position of party secretary. In the Democratic Republic he held office as deputy premier (1949–1950) and chairman of the Council of State (1960–1973). He ordered the construction of the wall between the two German states.

Richard von Weizsaecker (1920–   ). First elected to the Bundestag CDU faction in 1969, he continued his political career in West Berlin. He served in the West Berlin legislature in 1979 and was elected mayor of Berlin in 1981. In 1984 he was elected president of the Federal Republic.

William I (1797–1888). King of Prussia (1861–1888) who presided over the first unification of Germany. He appointed Otto von Bismarck as Prussian minister president in 1862. Following the wars of unification, he headed the North German Confederation (1867–1870) and was elected German emperor in January 1871, during the Franco-Prussian War (1870–1871). He deferred to Bismarck in most matters of policy. He died in March 1888.

William II (1859–1941). King of Prussia and third and final ruler of the German Empire (1888–1918). He was unprepared in government affairs when he succeeded his father, Frederick III, in 1888. Bright but headstrong, he soon clashed with Bismarck and engineered his resignation in 1890. Thereafter he established his "personal regime" based on his belief in his divine right to rule and his quest to make Germany a dominant world power. His rule was characterized by abrupt changes in policy and tensions with his chancellors and government ministers. Germany industrialized and expanded its military capability under his regime, notably building a modern navy. His adventurous and aggressive foreign policy, which discarded most of Bismarck's careful alliance system, alienated the other European powers and made Germany increasingly dependent on Austrian support. When the heir to the Austrian throne was assassinated in 1914, William's assurance that Germany would back Austrian actions led to World War I. He abdicated on November 9, 1918, at the urgings of his generals and ministers and retired in exile to Doorn, Holland, where he died in 1941.

Annotated Bibliography

The purpose of this bibliography is to introduce the reader to sources available in the English language that expand the basic narrative provided in this text. The items listed are, for the most part, the work of historians and scholars, both German and non-German. Although detailed and sometimes rather scholarly in tone, these books should be useful for students and general readers interested in specific topics. Most of these works also have excellent bibliographies to guide readers further in more focused study. The listings recommend the latest editions; where many editions are available, such as for *Beowulf*, the choice is left up to the reader.

CHAPTER 2: GERMANS IN ANTIQUITY AND THE EARLY MIDDLE AGES

Thanks to the literacy promoted by the Roman Empire and the Roman Catholic Church, there are some very readable and lively early eyewitness accounts of the Germans. Tacitus's first-century essay, *The Germans*, provides an excellent introduction to the military and tribal structure so characteristic of German society. *Beowulf* depicts the Germanic *comitatus* of the age of migrations. This epic is Germanic in origin; its designation as English literature reflects the migration of the oral tradition, with the Saxons, to England. The earliest extant English manuscript dates to the eleventh century, and has added a veneer of Christian piety to the originally pagan epic. Gregory of Tours's *History of the Franks*, translated by Lewis Thorpe (London: Viking Press, 1983) is devoutly Christian, and focuses on Clovis as a Christian hero. *The Song of Roland* shows how this combination of *comitatus* and heroic Christian leadership formed the basis for chivalry and the national epic of the Franks. Both Einhard the Frank's *Life of Charlemagne* and Notker the Stammerer's *Charlemagne*, in *Two Lives of Charlemagne*, translated by Lewis Thorpe (London: Penguin Books, 1969) carry through these themes. All of these accounts are voices directly from the past. They help us understand how the early Germans viewed their world.

On a more scholarly level, Malcolm Todd, *The Early Germans* (Oxford: Blackwell Publishers, 1992), analyzes the German migrations. Edward James, *The Franks* (Oxford: Basil Blackwell, 1988), and Thomas Burns, *A History of the Ostro-Goths* (Bloomington, IN: Indiana University Press, 1984), examine the two major tribal societies that comprised the early German societies. Anthony King, *Roman Gaul and Germany* (Berkeley: University of California Press, 1990), details their interaction with the Roman Empire. Walter Goffart, *Barbarians and Romans, A.D. 418–584: The Techniques of Accommodation* (Princeton: Princeton University Press, 1980), explores the distinctive vitality of the Germanic tribes. These works combine historical narrative with discussion and photographs based on archaelogical evidence.

CHAPTER 3: THE GERMAN DYNASTIES

Often called the "dark ages," the Middle Ages were dynamic years of experimentation that stabilized the social structure as well as the state and religious institutions of Europe. To appreciate them, a comprehensive overview is very helpful. One of the best is *Medieval Europe: A Short History*, by C. Warren Hollister (8th ed., New York: McGraw-Hill, 1998), lively, very readable, and well illustrated by pictures and maps. *The Penguin Guide to Medieval Europe*, by Richard Barber (London: Penguin Books, 1984), goes into depth discussing the medieval church, the empires, the aristocracy, and the emergence of the universities, providing excellent maps and contemporary photographs of important sites. More standard scholarly surveys include Robert Fossier, ed., *The Cambridge Illustrated History of the Middle Ages* (Cambridge: Cambridge University Press, 1996), and George Holmes, *The Oxford History of Medieval Europe*

(Oxford: Oxford University Press, 1992). Geoffrey Barraclough, *The Origins of Modern Germany* (New York: Capricorn Books, 1963), is a classic discussion of the political nature of early medieval Europe.

Heinrich Fichtenau's *The Carolingian Empire* (Toronto: University of Toronto Press, 1979) draws heavily on medieval sources for a penetrating analysis of the disorderly Frankish state and its leader. Donald A. Bullough's *The Age of Charlemagne* (New York: Putnam, 1966) is a standard. William Stubbs, *Germany in the Later Middle Ages, 1200–1500* (New York: H. Fertig, 1969), is an early specialized study, dated in style, but lively and informative as well as analytical. Friedrich Heer, *The Holy Roman Empire* (New York: Praeger, 1968) is a sweeping study of the German dynasties from Charlemagne and the Carolingians through the Austrian Hapsburgs, Maria Theresa, and Joseph II.

Three works present the best modern scholarship on the German Middle Ages. Alfred Haverkamp's *Medieval Germany 1056–1273* (Oxford: Oxford University Press, 1988) provides a close analysis of religious and social elements. Written by a German expert, it is very detailed on specific aspects of German feudal society. Timothy Reuter, *Germany in the Early Middle Ages, 800–1056* (London: Longman, 1991), is an excellent recent reexamination of the period. Reuter also translated *Germany in the High Middle Ages*, by Horst Fuhrmann (Cambridge: Cambridge University Press, 1986).

The literature on the religious conflicts in Germany is voluminous, so the emphasis here is on focus. An accessible introduction is Geoffrey R. Elton, *Reformation Europe 1517–1559* (Cleveland: Meridian Books, 1964). A classic study of Germany in the Reformation is Hajo Holborn, *A History of Modern Germany: The Reformation* (Princeton: Princeton University Press, 1982). Detailed, scholarly, and comprehensive, this important work examines the Reformation from its prehistory through the Treaties of Westphalia in 1648. It is the first of three volumes of German history, through 1945, by one of the most eminent modern German historians. The standard biography of Martin Luther is that by Roland H. Bainton, *Here I Stand: A Life of Martin Luther* (New York: New American Library, 1950). His chief adversary, Emperor Charles V, has been carefully examined by Karl Brandi, *The Emperor Charles V: The Growth and Destiny of a Man and a World Empire* (New York: Knopf, 1939).

CHAPTER 4: THE RISE AND IMPACT OF PRUSSIA

As the core state of the future German Empire, historians have examined Prussian history and impact from the very beginning. The rise of the Hohenzollern monarchy, with its Junker aristocracy and militaristic bureaucracy, begins the discussion. H. W. Koch, *A History of Prussia* (London; New York: Longman, 1978), is a good introduction. Francis Carsten, *The Origins of Prussia* (Oxford: Clarendon Press, 1982), offers a more scholarly approach. Hajo Holborn's *A History of Modern Germany 1648–1840* (Princeton: Princeton University Press, 1982), the second volume in his major work, is a comprehensive study of the rise of Brandenburg-Prussia, its competition with Austria, and its collapse and recovery from the French Revolution. Hans Rosenberg's classic *Bureaucracy, Aristocracy and Autocracy: The Prussian Experience 1660–1815* (Boston: Beacon Press, 1966) and Robert M. Berdahl's more recent work, *The Politics of the Prussian Nobility: The Development of a Conservative Ideology, 1770–1848* (Princeton: Princeton University Press, 1988), both focus on the deep strain of conservatism that influenced Prussian political, social, and economic structure well into the modern era.

There are a number of biographies of Frederick II, the Great. That by G. P. Gooch, *Frederick the Great* (New York: Knopf, 1947), is readable, balanced, and analytical. Christopher Duffy's *The Military Life of Frederick the Great* (New York: Atheneum, 1986) depicts the soldier-king. Thomas M. Barker, ed., *Frederick the Great and the Making of Prussia* (New York: Holt, Rinehart and Winston, 1972), provides a selection of essays by a number of historians who assess Frederick and his achievements.

The influence of the French Revolution on Prussia has also given rise to an extensive discussion of the dimensions of political reform in nineteenth-century Prussia prior to German unification. John L. Snell, *The Democratic Movement in Germany, 1789–1914* (Chapel Hill, NC: University of North Carolina Press, 1976), is an important scholarly overview of the period. Friedrich Meinecke, *The Age of German Liberation 1795–1815*, edited and translated by Peter Paret (Berkeley: University of California Press, 1957), offers the interpretation of this period by one of Germany's most revered historians. W. O. Henderson, *The Rise of German Industrial Power 1834–1914* (Berkeley: University of California Press, 1975), focuses on economic development. Theodore S. Hamerow, *Restoration, Revolution, Reaction: Economics and Politics in Germany, 1815–1871* (Princeton: Princeton University Press, 1958), is enjoyable to read and a classic bestseller. It analyses the impact of change on society at all levels.

German unification under Prussian leadership has long fascinated the historians. Michael Gorman, *The Unification of Germany* (Cambridge: Cambridge University Press, 1989), offers a brief introduction and excerpts from some of the relevant documents. Otto Pflanze, *The Unification of Germany 1848–1871* (Malabar, FL: Robert E. Krieger, 1979) offers a similar treatment by one of the most respected contemporary historians. Modern surveys of German history tend to begin with this period. Three of the best are Gordon A. Craig, *Germany 1866–1945* (New York: Oxford University Press, 1978); Hajo Holborn, *A History of Modern Germany 1840–1945* (Princeton: Princeton University Press, 1982); and Koppel S. Pinson, *Modern Germany, Its History and Civilization* (2nd edition, Prospect Heights, IL: Waveland Press, 1989). Theodore S. Hamerow's two-volume study, *The Social Foundations of German Unification 1858–1871: Ideas and Institutions* (Princeton: Princeton University Press, 1969), and *Struggles and Accomplishments* (Princeton: Princeton University Press, 1972), gives considerable detail about the social history of unification. Otto Pflanze's analytical three-volume study, *Bismarck and the Development of Germany* (Princeton: Princeton University Press, 1990), begins with 1815 and carries through to the chancellor's death in 1898. Erich Eyck, *Bismarck and the German Empire* (New York: Norton, 1958), critiques the period from a liberal perspective. Elmar M. Hucko, ed., *The Democratic Tradition: Four German Constitutions* (Leamington Spa, UK: Berg, 1987), introduces the Constitutions of 1849, 1871, 1919, and 1949, with English translations of each, allowing the reader to assess the depth of democratic traditions in each era.

CHAPTER 5: THE SECOND GERMAN EMPIRE, 1871–1914

With the Second Empire, and especially the reign of Emperor William II, the historians begin the ongoing debate about the true nature of modern German history. Some espy in the Empire the roots of the later Nazi state; others deny the continuity. It is important to review the period before examining the controversy. In addition to the surveys already mentioned, Dietrich Orlow, *A History of Modern Germany: 1871 to Present* (3rd edition, Englewood Cliffs, NJ: Prentice Hall, 1995), and Hans Ulrich Wehler, et al., *The German Empire 1871–1918*, translated by Kim Traynor (Dover, NH: Berg, 1985), offer modern German overviews focused on this period. Arthur Rosenberg's *Imperial Germany: The Birth of the German Republic*, translated by Ian F. D. Marner (Boston: Beacon Press, 1966), is a classic analysis by a contemporary socialist struggling with the conservatism of the Wilhelmian era. Fritz Fischer, *Germany's Aims in the First World War* (New York: Norton, 1967), claims that the Kaiser's government deliberately organized for war in order to make Germany a world power, thus setting a model for the Hitler government. This is the landmark work that launched the controversy over German historiography.

There are many works on Emperor William II. Michael Balfour, *The Kaiser and His Times* (New York: W. W. Norton, 1972), has long been the standard scholarly work. Alan Palmer, *The Kaiser: Warlord of the Second Reich* (New York: Charles Scribner's Sons, 1978), is a more general biography, clearly influenced by the Fischer viewpoint. Lamar Cecil's *William II* (Chapel Hill, NC: University of North Carolina Press, 1989), consolidates the latest scholarship on this most problematic emperor. Theo Aronson's *The Kaisers* (London: Bobbs-Merrill, 1971) offers a readable collective biography of the three emperors. J. Alden Nichols's *The Year of the Three Kaisers: Bismarck and the German Succession, 1887–88* (Urbana: University of Illinois Press, 1987) exposes the tensions within the imperial Constitution and among the major political figures in the Empire. John C. G. Rohl, *The Kaiser and His Court: Wilhelm II and the Government of Germany*, translated by Terence F. Cole (Cambridge: Cambridge University Press, 1994), and James Retallack, *Germany in the Age of Kaiser Wilhelm II* (New York: St. Martin's Press, 1996), expand the discussion of Kaiser and his leadership.

The analysis of the government of the Empire has resulted in many excellent focused monographs. None of the other imperial chancellors has been so discussed as Bismarck, but there is good information on them available, including J. Alden Nichols, *Germany after Bismarck: The Caprivi Era 1890–1894* (Cambridge, MA: Harvard University Press, 1958); J. C. G. Rohl, *Germany without Bismarck* (Berkeley: University of California Press, 1967); *Memoirs of Prince Chlodwig of Hohenlohe Schillingsfuerst,* two volumes (New York: Macmillan, 1906); *Memoirs of Prince von Buelow,* four volumes (Boston: Little, Brown, 1931–1932); and Konrad Jarausch, *The Enigmatic Chancellor: Bethmann Hollweg and the Hubris of Imperial Germany* (New Haven, CT: Yale University Press, 1973). Carl E. Schorske, *German Social Democracy 1905–1917: Development of the Great Schism* (Cambridge, MA: Harvard University Press, 1955), discusses the dilemma of the most popular party, preaching revolution while accepting the benefits of the Empire's economic development. Richard Evans, *Society and Politics in Wilhelmine Germany* (London: Croom Helm, 1978), offers insight into the most pertinent political controversies of the period. Heinrich Mann's novel, *Man of Straw* (Harmondsworth: Penguin Books, 1984), provides satirical insight into the social structure of the Empire.

CHAPTER 6: THE FIRST WORLD WAR AND THE WEIMAR REPUBLIC

Europe controlled 84 percent of the world's territory before World War I, and still seems to long for that lost glory. Barbara Tuchman, *The Proud Tower: A Portrait of the World before the War 1890–1914* (New York: Macmillan, 1966), sketches the society that the war destroyed. Holger Herwig, *The Outbreak of World War I* (5th ed., Lexington, MA: D.C. Heath, 1991), compiles a chronology and selections from a number of major historians into a very useful and slim introduction to the war. David Child's *Germany in the Twentieth Century* (New York: HarperCollins Publishers, 1991) gives a good overview.

The German Empire's responsibility for World War I is discussed in Volker Rolf Berghahn, *Germany and the Approach of War in 1914* (New York: St. Martin's Press, 1973). Martin Kitchin, *The German Officer Corps, 1890–1914* (Oxford: Oxford University Press, 1968), and Ivo N. Lambi, *The Navy and German Power Politics* (London: Allen & Unwin, 1984), analyze the growth of the military establishment. Gary E. Weir, *Building the Kaiser's Navy: The Imperial Navy Office and German Industry in the Tirpitz Era, 1890–1919* (Annapolis, MD: Naval Institute Press, 1992), underscores the important role played by Alfred von Tirpitz. Holger Herwig, *The First World War: Germany and Austria-Hungary, 1914–1918* (London: Arnold, 1997), destroys the myth of Germanic military invincibility.

On the war itself, Barbara Tuchman's prize-winning *The Guns of August* (New York: Macmillan, 1962), together with Erich Maria Remarque's *All Quiet on the Western Front*, translated by A. W. Wheen (Boston: Little, Brown, 1996), capture the anguish and horror of the first modern war fought by industrialized societies. Alistair Horne, *The Price of Glory: Verdun 1916* (New York: St. Martin's Press, 1961), underscores that theme in its depiction of one of the war's most futile yet costly battles. Juergen Kocka, *Facing Total War: German Society, 1914–1918*, translated by Barbara Weinberger (Cambridge, MA: Harvard University Press, 1985), catalogues the inexorable destruction of the German home front. C. Paul Vincent, *The Politics of Hunger: The Allied Blockade of Germany, 1915–1919* (Athens, OH: Ohio University Press, 1985), outlines the completeness of the German collapse.

Postwar diplomacy and the Treaty of Versailles have been thoroughly analyzed. Harold Nicholson, *Peacemaking 1919* (New York: Grosset and Dunlap, 1965), and Arno J. Mayer, *Politics and Diplomacy of Peacemaking:*

Containment and Counterrevolution at Versailles 1918–1919 (New York: Knopf, 1967), are two of the classics that offer penetrating critiques of the process. William R. Keylor, *The Legacy of the Great War, Peacemaking, 1919* (Boston: Houghton Mifflin, 1998) provides a very accessible introduction to the many schools of thought regarding the peacemaking, together with a chronology, a list of the principle proper names, and suggestions for further reading.

The formation and troubled history of the Weimar Republic have long fascinated historians. Although dated, still one of the best overviews is S. William Halperin's *Germany Tried Democracy* (New York: Norton, 1946). Erich Eyck's *History of the Weimar Republic* in two volumes (New York: Atheneum, 1970) offers the interpretation of a liberal democrat who lived through the period. Richard Bessel's *Germany after the First World War* (Oxford: Clarendon Press, 1993) offers both original research and the insights of more recent scholarship in an analysis of the social impact of the war on the efforts to found a new, democratic state. Martin Kitchen's *Europe between the Wars: A Political History* (London: Longman, 1988) helps explain the negative impact of the war on the other European countries.

The Weimar Republic struggled to find a political identity. Francis L. Carsten, *Revolution in Central Europe, 1918–1919* (Berkeley: University of California Press, 1972), analyzes the competing factions. James Diehl, *Paramilitary Politics in Weimar Germany* (Bloomington: Indiana University Press, 1977), shows the strong influence of the army and veterans in the Republic. Richard Hunt's *German Social Democracy 1918–1933* (New Haven, CT: Yale University Press, 1964) analyzes the successes and failures of the Left; Herman E. Lebovics' *Social Conservatism and the Middle Classes in Germany* (Princeton: Princeton University Press, 1969) discusses the opposition; and Dietrich Orlow's *The History of the Nazi Party 1919–1933* (Pittsburgh: University of Pittsburgh Press, 1969) charts the rise of the radical fascism that finally usurped the political process and power. Peter Gay's *Weimar Culture: The Outsider as Insider* (New York: Harper & Row, 1968) studies the attitudes and fleeting brilliance of the 1920s.

John Maynard Keynes's *The Economic Consequences of the Peace* (New York: Harcourt, Brace and Howe, 1920) correctly predicted that draconic economic punishment of the Central Powers would spell disaster for Europe. The Weimar Republic was unable to cope successfully with the economic crises of the 1920s. The collection of essays edited by Fritz K. Ringer, *The German Inflation of 1923* (New York: Oxford University Press, 1969), thoroughly explains the crisis that devastated the middle class and discredited the Social Democrat party. James Harold, *The German Slump: Politics and Economics, 1924–1936* (Oxford: Clarendon Press, 1986), and Juergen von Krudener, *Economic Crisis and Political Collapse: The Weimar Republic* (Princeton: Princeton University Press, 1989), link these crises to the collapse of democracy. The essays in Richard J. Evans and Dick Geary, eds., *The German Unemployed, 1918–1936* (New York: St. Martin, 1987), further amplify this perspective. Stephen A. Schuker's *The Financial Crisis of 1924 and the Adoption of the Dawes Plan* (Chapel Hill, NC: University of North Carolina Press, 1976) questions whether the Versailles Treaty was really as draconic as the Germans claimed. Charles P. Kindleberger, *The World in Depression, 1929–1939* (Berkeley: University of California Press, 1973), puts the great economic crisis in world perspective.

Weimar diplomacy is also intriguing, especially the question of whether its goal was actually fulfillment or only revision of the Versailles settlement. Robert P. Gratwohl assesses this dilemma in *Stresemann and the DNVP: Reconciliation or Revenge in German Foreign Policy, 1924–1928* (Lawrence: University of Kansas Press, 1980). John Jacobson, *Locarno Diplomacy: Germany and the West, 1922–1929* (Princeton: Princeton University Press, 1972), discusses Germany's dramatic reentry into the diplomatic arena after its postwar isolation. H. W. Gatzke's *Stresemann and the Rearmament of Germany* (Baltimore: Johns Hopkins University Press, 1954) draws contrasts in the contradictory profile of Weimar's greatest diplomat. John W. Wheeler-Bennett, *Nemesis of Power: The German Army in Politics 1918–1945* (New York: St. Martin's Press, 1964), depicts the powerful influence of the military in national politics. Gustav Hilger and Alfred G. Meyer, *The Incompatible Allies—A Memoir-History of German-Soviet Relations, 1918–1941* (New York: Macmillan, 1953), discusses the curious interdependency that these two normally antagonistic nations developed to deal with the diplomatic hostility of the victorious World War I powers.

The rise of Hitler and the Nazi Party have been the subject of numerous works for decades. Martin Broszat, *Hitler and the Collapse of Weimar Germany* (Leamington Spa, UK: Berg, 1987), and A. J. Nicholls, *Weimar and the Rise of Hitler* (3rd ed., New York: St. Martin's Press, 1991), offer synopses of recent scholarship.

There are a number of excellent biographies that give insight into the Weimar era. They include Henry A. Turner, *Stresemann and the Politics of the Weimar Republic* (Princeton: Princeton University Press, 1963); Klaus Epstein, *Matthias Erzberger and the Dilemma of German Democracy* (Princeton: Princeton University Press, 1959); Andreas Dorpalen, *Hindenburg and the Politics of the Weimar Republic* (Princeton: Princeton University Press, 1964); John W. Wheeler-Bennett, *The Wooden Titan* (New York: St. Martin's Press, 1967); Harry von Kessler, *Walter Rathenau, His Life and Work*, rev., translated by W. D. Robson-Scott and Lawrence Hyde (New York: H. Fertig, 1969); David Felix, *Walter Rathenau and the Weimar Republic; the Politics of Reparations* (Baltimore: Johns Hopkins University Press, 1971); Paul Froehlich, *Rosa Luxemburg: Her Life and Work*, translated by Johanna Hoornweg (New York: Monthly Review Press, 1972); Allan Bullock, *Hitler: A Study in Tyranny* (London: Odhams Press, 1952); and Joachim C. Fest, *Hitler* (New York: Harcourt Brace Jovanovich, 1973).

CHAPTER 7: HITLER AND THE SECOND WORLD WAR

The classic study that describes the strategy and tactics used by the Nazis is William S. Allen, *The Nazi Seizure of Power: The Experience of a Single German Town, 1922–1945* (rev. ed., New York: Franklin Watts, 1984). Karl Dietrich Bracher's *The German Dictatorship: The Origin, Structure, and Effect of National Socialism*, translated by Jean Steinberg (New York: Praeger, 1970) is scholarly in nature, but still acknowledged as the best work on the subject. Klaus Hildebrand's *The Third Reich*, trans. by P. S. Falla (London: Allen & Unwin, 1984) offers a good overview and a discussion of the historical interpretations of the era. Richard Bessell, ed., *Life in the Third Reich* (New York: Oxford University Press, 1987), and David Schoenbaurm's *Hitler's Social Revolution* (New York: Doubleday, 1966) provide insight into life under the dictatorship. Thomas. L. Jarman's *The Rise and Fall of Nazi Germany* (New York: New York University Press, 1964) offers a short overview of the Third Reich. Alan Mitchell, ed., *The Nazi Revolution* (Lexington, MA: D. C. Heath, 1990), collects essays and excerpts from noted historians to explain the period. Jeremy Noakes, ed., *Documents on Nazism, 1919–1945* (Atlantic Highlands, NJ: Humanities Press, 1974), translates basic documents into English. George Mosse's *Nazi Culture* (New York: Schocken, 1981) discusses the intellectual constraints imposed by Nazi ideology.

Edward Crankshaw, *Gestapo: Instrument of Tyranny* (New York: Viking Press, 1956), gives details of the enforcement branch of the dictatorship. Edward N. Peterson, *The Limits of Hitler's Power* (Princeton: Princeton University Press, 1969), and Ian Kershaw, *The "Hitler Myth": Image and Reality in the Third Reich* (Oxford: Oxford University Press, 1989), both suggest that Hitler's power was not absolute.

Although A. J. P. Taylor, *The Origins of the Second World War* (2nd ed., New York: Atheneum, 1961), argues that Hitler blundered into the conflict, most historians assert that he was determined to use war as the means for achieving German control of the continent. Joachim Remak, *The Origins of the Second World War* (Englewood Cliffs, NJ: Prentice Hall, 1976), offers both essays and excerpts of documents to outline Hitler's deliberate steps toward the conflict. Andreas Hillgruber, *Germany and the Two World Wars*, translated by William C. Kirby (Cambridge, MA: Harvard University Press, 1981), compares the levels of responsibility of the German leadership for the two European conflicts. Peter Calvocoressi and Guy Wint, *Total War: Causes and Courses of the Second World War* (New York: Penguin, 1972), offers an excellent analysis. Norman Rich, *Hitler's War Aims: Ideology, the Nazi State, and the Course of Expansion* (New York: Norton, 1973), analyzes the motivations for conquest. Edward W. Bennett, *The German Rearmament and the West, 1932–1933* (Princeton: Princeton University Press, 1979), reveals how the economy and government planning pointed toward eventual war. Klaus Hildebrand, *The Foreign Policy of the Third Reich*, translated by Anthony Fothergill (London: Batsford, 1973), shows how diplomacy worked to the same end.

Gerhard L. Weinberg's *Germany, Hitler and World War II: Essays in Modern German and World History* (Cambridge: Cambridge University Press, 1995) offers the insights of the premier historian of twentieth-century Germany. Weinberg's *The Foreign Policy of Hitler's Germany* (Chicago: University of Chicago Press, 1983) and *A World at Arms: A Global History of World War II* (Cambridge: Cambridge University Press, 1994) also provide well-focused detail and analysis of the period. William L. Shirer's *The Rise and Fall of the Third Reich* (New York: Fawcett Crest, 1990) is a journalist's eyewitness description of the period. Earl R. Beck, *Under the Bombs: The German Home Front, 1942–1945* (Lexington: University Press of Kentucky, 1986), shows the devastating impact on civilians of modern air warfare. Hugh R. Trevor-Roper, *The Last Days of Hitler* (3rd ed., New York: Collier Books, 1962), discusses the collapse of the Reich. Sebastian Haffner, *The Meaning of Hitler*, translated by Ewald Osers (Cambridge, MA: Harvard University Press, 1983), is the work of a well-read German journalist who tries to put the Third Reich in historical perspective.

The brutality of the Third Reich was notorious. Alexander Dallin, *German Rule in Russia 1941–1945* (Boulder, CO: Westview, 1981), reveals the chilling side of conquest. The Holocaust, the genocide of European Jews imposed during the conquest, has been chronicled in many works. Raul Hilberg's *The Destruction of the European Jews* (New York: Holmes

& Meier, 1985) is the best one-volume collection of essays and documents to detail how historical religious anti-Semitism was transformed into political racism by the Nazi government. It exposes the design and implementation of genocide, which used industrial models. Gerald Fleming, *Hitler and the Final Solution* (Berkeley: University of California Press, 1984), shows Hitler's direct responsibility for the policy. Christopher Browning, *The Path to Genocide: Essays on Launching the Final Solution* (New York: Cambridge University Press, 1992), explores a number of aspects. Daniel J. Goldhagen, *Hitler's Willing Executioners: Ordinary Germans and the Holocaust* (New York: Knopf, 1996), is a controversial new analysis that claims broad support for the genocide within Germany. Elie Wiesel's *Night*, translated by Stella Rodway (New York: Bantam, 1982), is the haunting account of the life of a Jewish teenager in a death camp. Charles S. Maier's *The Unmasterable Past: History, Holocaust, and German National Identity* (Cambridge, MA: Harvard University Press, 1988) grapples with the legacy of the Holocaust.

The potential of resistance to Hitler has been examined by a number of authors. Henri Michel, *The Shadow War: European Resistance, 1939–1945* (New York: Harper & Row, 1972); Kenneth J. Macksey, *The Partisans of World War II* (New York: Stein & Day, 1975); Jan M. Ciechanowski, *The Warsaw Rising of 1944* (New York: Cambridge University Press, 1974); and Fitzroy Maclean, *Eastern Approaches* (New York: Time, 1964), show efforts abroad to resist German military might. Within Germany, some efforts were made, as indicated by Peter Hoffman, *German Resistance to Hitler* (Cambridge, MA: Harvard University Press, 1988); Gerhard Ritter, *The German Resistance: Carl Goerdeler's Struggle against Tyranny* (New York: 1958); John H. Backer and Julian Frisby, *Helmuth von Moltke: A Leader against Hitler* (Freeport, NY: Books for Libraries, 1970); and Theodore S. Hamerow, *On the Road to the Wolf's Lair: German Resistance to Hitler* (Cambridge, MA: Belknap Press of Harvard University Press, 1997). Inge Scholl, *The White Rose: Munich 1942–1943*, translated by Arthur R. Schultz (Middletown, CT: Wesleyan University Press, 1983), is the true story of a tragic student-led resistance movement, told by the surviving sister of Hans and Sophie Scholl, who were executed for their activities.

For information on Hitler's collaborators during this period, see John A. Leopold, *Alfred Hugenberg: The Radical Nationalist Campaign against the Weimar Republic* (New Haven, CT: Yale University Press, 1977), on the media mogul who promoted Hitler; Peter D. Stachura, *Gregor Strasser and the Rise of Nazism* (London: Allen & Unwin, 1983), on one of the important founders of the Nazi Party; and Peter R. Black, *Ernst Kalten-brunner* (Princeton: Princeton University Press, 1984), on the individual most instrumental in carrying out the Holocaust. Albert Speer, *Inside the Third Reich*, translated by Richard and Clara Winston (New York: Macmillan, 1970), and *Spandau: The Secret Diaries*, translated by Richard and Clara Winston (New York: Macmillan, 1976), give autobiographical interpretations of his responsibility for Germany's war preparations and his sentencing by the Nuremberg war crimes tribunal. David J. Irving's *Goering: A Biography* (New York: Morrow, 1989) examines the former World War I ace who became the Nazi president of the Reichstag and a leading figure in Germany's World War II air force, the Luftwaffe. Geoffrey J. Giles, *Stunde Null: The End and the Beginning Fifty Years Ago* (Washington, DC: German Historical Institute, 1997), includes eight thoughtful essays by contemporary historians about the total defeat of the Germans.

CHAPTER 8: FROM OCCUPATION TO SOVEREIGNTY, 1945–1949

The controversial diplomatic background of the occupation is examined by John H. Backer, *The Decision to Divide Germany* (Durham, NC: Duke University Press, 1978); Herbert Feis, *Between War and Peace: The Potsdam Conference* (Princeton: Princeton University Press, 1960); and Diane Clemens Shaver, *Yalta* (New York: Oxford University Press, 1971).

Michael Balfour's *Four Power Control of Germany and Austria 1945–46* (London: Oxford University Press, 1956) provides an introduction to the occupation. James K. Pollock and James H. Meisel, *Germany under Occupation, Illustrative Materials and Documents* (Ann Arbor, MI: George Wahr, 1947), documents the policies of the occupying forces. For information on the individual zones, see John P. Nettl, *The Eastern Zone and Soviet Policy in Germany 1945–50* (New York: Oxford, 1951), indicating the integration of East Germany into the Soviet orbit; Lucius Clay, *Decision in Germany* (Garden City, NY: Doubleday, 1950), by the general who commanded the American Military Government; and Harold Zink, *The United States in Germany 1944–55* (Princeton: Van Nostrand, 1957), for an analytical overview of the transition in American policy toward Germany. F. Roy Willis, *The French in Germany 1945–49* (Stanford, CA: Stanford University Press, 1962), and Arthur Hearnden, ed., *The British in Germany* (London: Hamilton, 1978), detail how the the two smaller occupying powers governed their zones before the unification of the western zones.

Hermann Glaser, *The Rubble Years: Cultural Roots of Postwar Germany* (New York: Paragon House, 1986), and Edward N. Peterson, *The Many Faces of Defeat: The German People's Experience in 1945* (New York: Peter Lang, 1990), discuss the immediate postwar circumstances in Germany. Gregory W. Sanford, *Hitler to Ulbricht: The Communist Reconstruction of East Germany, 1945–1946* (Princeton, NJ: Princeton University Press, 1983), and David Pike, *The Politics of Culture in Soviet-Occupied Germany, 1945–1949* (Stanford, CA: Stanford University Press, 1992), address the Russian efforts to sovietize East Germany. Charles Maier, with Gunter Bischof, ed., *The Marshall Plan and Germany* (Providence, RI: Berg, 1991), explores the impact of foreign aid on German economic and diplomatic rehabilitation. Alan S. Milward, *The Reconstruction of Western Europe, 1945–1951* (Berkeley: University of California Press, 1984), suggests that the importance of the Marshall Plan has been exaggerated.

The Nuremberg war crimes trials were precedent setting and an important aspect of the de-Nazification policy agreed upon by all four occupying powers. Adalbert Rueckerl, ed., *The Investigation of Nazi Crimes, 1945–1978*, translated by Derek Rutter (Heidelberg: C. F. Mueller, 1979), provides necessary documentation to understand the process. Eugene Davidson, *The Trial of the Germans* (New York: Macmillan, 1966), analyzes the trial of the major Nazi leaders.

The Cold War began during the occupation period. Anton W. DePorte, *The Enduring Balance between the Super Powers* (New Haven, CT: Yale University Press, 1979); Gerald Freund, *Germany between Two Worlds* (New York: Harcourt, Brace, 1961); and Daniel Yergin, *The Shattered Peace: The Origins of the Cold War and the National Security State* (Boston: Houghton Mifflin, 1977), introduce the problems and the transition of Germany from defeated foe to potential ally. Mary Fulbrook, *The Two Germanies, 1945–1990: Problems of Interpretation* (Atlantic Highlands, NJ: Humanities Press International, 1992), is a brief, thoughtful introduction with an excellent bibliography.

CHAPTER 9: THE GERMAN FEDERAL REPUBLIC, 1949–1990

Alfred Grosser, *Germany in Our Time*, translated by Paul Stephenson (New York: Praeger, 1971), and Michael Balfour, *West Germany: A Contemporary History* (New York: St. Martin's Press, 1982), are solid introductions to the preunification period.

Works dealing with recovery of the major political parties include

Tony Burkett, *Parties and Elections in West Germany: The Search for Stability* (New York: St. Martin's Press, 1975); Kendall L. Baker, Russell J. Dalton, and Kai Hildebrandt, *Germany Transformed: Political Culture and the New Politics* (Cambridge, MA: Harvard University Press, 1981); Eva Kolinsky, *Parties, Opposition, and Society in West Germany* (New York: St. Martin's Press, 1984); Geoffrey Pridham, *Christian Democracy in Western Germany: The CDU/CSU in Government and Opposition, 1945–1976* (New York: St. Martin's Press, 1977); Gerald Braunthal, *The West German Social Democrats, 1969–1982* (Boulder, CO: Westview Press, 1983); John D. Nagle, *The National Democratic Party: Right-Radicalism in the Federal Republic of Germany* (Berkeley: University of California Press, 1970); and Elim Papadakis, *The Green Movement in West Germany* (New York: St. Martin's Press, 1970). Julian Becker, *Hitler's Children: The Story of the Baader-Meinhof Terrorist Gang* (Philadelphia: Lippincott, 1977), discusses the radical student movement.

For discussion of the diplomacy and international posture of the Federal Republic, see Simon Bulmer and William Paterson, *The Federal Republic of Germany and the European Community* (London: Allen & Unwin, 1987); Michael Freund, *From Cold War to Ostpolitik* (London: Oswald Wolff, 1972); Helga Haftendorn, *Security and Detente: Conflicting Priorities in German Foreign Policy* (New York: Praeger, 1985), and N. Edwina Moreton, ed., *Germany between East and West* (Cambridge: Cambridge University Press, 1987). Ann Tusa's *The Last Division: A History of Berlin, 1945–1989* (Reading, MA: Addison-Wesley, 1997) gives a concise history of the European Cold War and its influence on Berlin.

A number of works illuminate the economic and social issues in West Germany. E. Owen Smith, *The West German Economy* (Beckenham, UK: Croom Helm, 1983); Volker Berghahn, *The Americanisation of West German Industry, 1945–1973* (Leamington Spa, UK: Berg, 1986); and Herbert Giersch Karl-Heine Paque, and Holger Schmieding, *The Fading Miracle: Four Decades of Market Economy in Germany* (New York: Cambridge University Press, 1992), portray the flow and ebb of the West German economy. Ray C. Rist, *Guestworkers in Germany: The Prospects for Pluralism* (New York: Praeger, 1978), and Eva Kolinsky, *Women in West Germany* (Oxford: Berg, 1989), give insight into social change.

There are some very interesting studies about the West German chancellors. Terence Prittie, *The Velvet Chancellors: A History of Postwar Germany* (New York: Holmes & Meier, 1979), gives a good overview. Konrad Adenauer, *Memoirs*, translated by Beate Ruhm von Oppen (Chicago: Henry Regnery, 1966); Ludwig Erhard, *Germany's Comeback in the World*

Market (New York: Macmillan, 1954); and Helmut Schmidt, *Men and Powers: A Political Retrospective*, translated by Ruth Hein (New York: Random House, 1989), let these men speak for themselves. Terrence Prittie, *Willy Brandt: Portrait of a Statesman* (New York: Schocken Books, 1974), introduces the leading Social Democrat and author of the Ostpolitik.

CHAPTER 10: THE GERMAN DEMOCRATIC REPUBLIC, 1949–1990

Stephen R. Burant, ed., *East Germany: A Country Study* (3rd ed., Washington, DC: Department of the Army, 1988), is factual and clear, and offers much basic information about the Constitution, political parties, history, and government policies. Mike Dennis, *German Democratic Republic* (London: Pinter, 1988), is very readable. H. Heitzer, *GDR: An Historical Outline* (Dresden: Verlag Zeit im Bild, 1981), is the government's official history, but it is very difficult to find.

Arthur W. McCardle and A. Bruch Boenau, *East Germany: A New German Nation under Socialism?* (Lanham, MD: University Press of America, 1984), offers essays by a number of East Germans on a variety of issues. Ian Jeffries and Manfred Melzer, *The East German Economy* (London: Croom Helm, 1987), analyzes the strengths and weaknesses of the former Soviet bloc's strongest economy. David Childs, *The GDR: Moscow's German Ally* (London: Allen & Unwin, 1983), discusses the links to Eastern Europe. A. James McAdams, *East Germany and Detente: Building Authority after the Wall* (New York: Cambridge University Press, 1985), discusses the political problems created by building the wall. Gert Lipton and Manfred Melzer, *Economic Reform in East German Industry* (London: Oxford University Press, 1978), reveals the problems of the reforms attempted after 1963.

Because of the controlling influence of the Soviet Union, East German political leadership was relatively stable. Peter Christian Ludz, *The German Democratic Republic from the Sixties to the Seventies: A Socio-Political Analysis* (Cambridge, MA: Center for International Affairs, 1970), provides some insight into this stability. John Sandford, *The Sword and the Ploughshare: Autonomous Peace Initiatives in East Germany* (London: Merlin Press/END, 1983), discusses East German diplomacy.

The East German government always struggled with internal resistance. Arnulf M. Baring, *Uprising in East Germany: June 17, 1953* (Ithaca, NY: Cornell University Press, 1972), describes the first major episode of resistance to the Communist government. W. Leonhard, *Child of the Rev-*

olution, translated by C. M. Woodhouse (Chicago: H. Regnery, 1967), and Robert Havemann, *An Alienated Man* (London: Davis-Poynter, 1973), are first-person accounts of dissenters. Robert M. Slusser, *The Berlin Crisis of 1961* (Baltimore: Johns Hopkins University Press, 1973), examines East Germany's most audacious domestic and diplomatic action. R. Woods, *Opposition in the GDR under Honecker, 1971–85* (London: Macmillan, 1989), gives an overview.

Studies of individual leaders of the Democratic Republic still need to be written. Walter Ulbricht, *Whither Germany? Speeches and Essays on the National Question* (Dresden: Zeit im Bild Publishing House, 1966), and Erich Honecker, *The German Democratic Republic: Pillar of Peace and Socialism* (New York: International Publishers, 1979) offer the statements of its two political leaders. Carola Stern, *Ulbricht: A Political Biography* (New York: Praeger, 1965), is a useful biography. Honecker's *From My Life* (New York: Pergamon, 1981) needs to be corroborated by an objective biography.

CHAPTER 11: THE GERMAN FEDERAL REPUBLIC AFTER 1990

Walter Hanel, Susan Stern, and James G. Neuger, *Off the Wall—a Wacky History of Germany since 1989* (Frankfurt: Frankfurter Allgemeine Zeitung GmbH Informationsdienste, 1993), uses political cartoons in a humorous introduction to unification. Pekka Kalevi Hamalainen, *Uniting Germany: Actions and Reaction* (Boulder, CO: Westview, 1994), and James Harold and Marla Stone, eds., *When the Wall Came Down: Reactions to German Unification* (New York: Routledge, 1992), set the scene in a more scholarly manner. Dieter Grosser, ed., *Uniting Germany: The Unexpected Challenge* (Providence, RI: Berg, 1992), collects essays on aspects of reunification. Problems that emerged are discussed in Konrad H. Jarausch, *The Rush to German Unity* (New York: Oxford University Press, 1994). Arnulf Baring, ed., *Germany's New Position in Europe: Problems and Perspectives* (Oxford: Berg, 1994), offers a collection of essays by leading historians.

To keep current with German affairs, the annual government publication, *Facts about Germany*, is available from German consulates and is extremely informative. Users of the Internet can obtain current government press releases in the English language at http://www.government.de, and from the German Information Center at http://www.germany-info.org/.

Index

Adenauer, Konrad, 138, 142, 146–55, 164, 171, 191
African Campaign (World War II), 129, 131
Agricultural cooperatives, 137
Agriculture, forestry and fishing, 13
Alaric, 22
Alcuin of York, 30
Alexander (Czar), 82
All Quiet on the Western Front (Remarque), 96
Alliance for Germany, 178–79
Alliance 90, 10, 179, 182, 187
Allied Control Council, 138, 141, 150
Alsace-Lorraine, 82, 85, 88, 93, 97, 100
Anglo-German Naval Agreement (1935), 121
Anschluss (1938), 122–23
Antiquity, 19–26
Anti-Semitism, 108–9, 115, 118–20, 126, 129, 147, 186
Anti-Socialist Law, 79, 84–85
Appeasement, 122–25
Arianism, 23

Armistice (1918), 100, 108
Article 48 (Emergency Clause), 103
The Arts, 17
Asylum seekers, 185–86
Augsburg Confession, 49
Augsburg, Peace of (1555), 49, 51
Augustus Caesar, 19–20
Auschwitz, 130
Austrasia, 26
Austria, 46–47, 52, 55, 59–64, 66–72, 82, 89–91, 120, 122–23
Austrian Empire, 63
Austrian Republic, 99
Austrian Succession, War of Austro-Hungarian Empire, 73, 94
Axis Powers, 121, 125, 127, 129

Bach, Johann Sebastian, 60
Baden, 62–64, 68–69, 73
Baden, Max von, 99
Balkan Wars, 89–90
Barbarossa, Frederick, 44
Basic Law, 5–8, 142, 178–80, 185–86

Basic Treaty (1972), 158, 165, 172

Battle of Britain (1940), 128

Bavaria, 34, 36, 43–44, 46–48, 50, 56, 58–59, 62–64, 66–69, 73, 104

Bavarian Succession, War of (1778–1779), 60

Bebel, August, 78

Beowulf, 21

Berlin, 9; blockade and airlift, 141–42; Four-Power Agreement (1971), 158; occupation, 134, 145, 150–51, 155, 158, 162, 164; Wall, 154, 168–69, 174, 176–77

Berlin Conference (1884–1885), 83

Berlin, Congress of (1878), 82

Berlin Decree (1807), 64

Berlin Ultimatum (1958), 153

Bernstein, Eduard, 88

Bethmann-Hollweg, Theobald von, 89, 91, 98, 191–92

"Big Three," 131–32, 134

Bismarck, Otto von, 72–85, 87, 110

Bizonia, 139–40

Black Death, 46

"Blank Check," 91

Blitzkrieg, 126, 128

Bohemia, 36, 39, 46–47, 50, 58, 60, 72–73, 124

Bonaparte, Jerome, 66, 68

Bonaparte, Napoleon, 62–69

Boniface (Bishop), 29

Bonn, 9, 147, 173, 182

Bonn Treaty (1950), 150–51

Brandenburg, 44, 47–48, 52, 56

Brandt, Willi, 154, 157–59, 171, 192

Brest-Litovsk, Treaty of (1918), 98, 100

British naval blockade (1917), 97, 101–2, 110

Bruening, Heinrich, 107

Buelow, Bernhard von, 86, 88, 193

Buelow Bloc, 88

Burgfrieden, 37

Burgundy, 26, 35, 37–39, 47–48

"Cabinet of Barons," 108–9, 113

Calvinism, 51–52

Canossa, 40, 43

Canute the Great, 38

Capital, 9

Caprivi, George Leo von, 85, 193

Carinthia, 36

Carolingian dynasty, 26–27, 29–30, 32, 34

Casablanca Conference (1943), 131

Catholic League, 57

Catholicism, 3, 16–17, 24, 28, 32, 36, 41, 50, 55, 60, 78–79, 115, 138

Center Party (Zentrum), 78–80, 102, 107, 138

Central Powers, 94, 98, 100

Chamberlain, Neville, 123–24, 126

Charlemagne (771–814), 27, 29–31, 33–34, 193

Charles the Bald (875–877), 32, 34

Charles the Fat (876–887), 34

Charles V, Holy Roman Emperor (1519–1556), 47–50, 193–94

Childeric (d. 481), 24

Christian Democratic Union, 10, 136, 138, 142, 146, 151, 153–55, 157, 159–61, 177–78, 182, 187–88

Christian Social Union, 10, 138, 146, 153–54, 157, 159–61, 177–78, 182, 187–88

Churchill, Winston, 128, 131, 135, 138

Clay, Lucius (General), 137

Climate, 4

Clovis (481–511), 24–26, 194

Cold War, 140, 145, 163

Collectivization of agriculture, 168

Colonies, 83, 85, 87, 97, 101

COMECON, 152, 166, 168

Comitatus, 20, 25

Common Market, 168, 187, 189

Communications, 14

Communist Party, 102–4, 107–9, 114, 136, 138, 140, 145, 163–64, 174, 181, 184

Concentration camps, 118, 130, 134

Concordat of Worms (1122), 42

Confederation of the Rhine, 64

Congress of Vienna (1814–1815), 68

Conrad (Duke of Franconia), 34

Conrad II (1024–1039), 37

Conrad III (1138–1152), 43
Conservative Party, 77, 88, 108
Constantine (Emperor), 22, 24
Council of Europe, 149
Counter Reformation, 50
Crusades, 41–42, 44
Customs Union (*Zollverein*), 70, 72
Czechoslovakia, 106, 122–25

Daily Telegraph Affair (1908), 88
Danes, 76, 88
Danish War (1864), 72
Danzig, 101, 125
Dawes Plan, 105, 110
Declaration of Pillnitz (1791), 62
de Gaulle, Charles, 147, 151, 155
de Mazicre, Lothar, 178–179
Demilitarization, 101, 131, 135
Democracy Now Party, 176–77
Democratic Awakening Party, 177
Democratic Bloc, 143
Democratic Peoples' Party, 138
Democratic Women's League, 166,
   172
Democrats, 102
De-Nazification, 131, 139, 165, 185
Depression, 103, 106, 109–10, 117,
   122
Detente, 171
Dictatorship, 114–18
Diet of Worms (1521), 48
Diocletian (Emperor), 21–22
Diplomatic recognition, 149, 151–52,
   176
Disarmament, 105, 108, 120–21, 131,
   135
Doentiz, Karl, 132, 134
Dual Alliance (1879), 82, 84

East Berlin Uprising (1953), 170
East German Zone, 131, 134, 136–40;
   defections from, 154, 161, 168, 174,
   176; Evangelical Church, 166, 175
Ebert, Friedrich, 102, 104, 106, 194
"Economic Miracle," 149
Economy, 11–12, 80–81, 85, 88, 104–5,
   107, 110, 117–18, 133–38, 140–41,

147–53, 155–57, 160–62, 164–69, 172,
   174, 177, 183–84, 186, 188
Edict of Restitution (1628), 51
Education, 15
Einhard, 29
Eisenhower, Dwight, 129, 131–32
Elections, 7, 107–9, 113–16, 118, 136–
   39, 151, 153–54, 157, 159–61, 168,
   178–79, 182, 187–88
Elysee, Treaty of (1963), 154–55
Emigration, 88
Employment, 12
Enabling Act (1933), 114, 146
Entente Cordiale, 86–87
Erhard, Ludwig, 138, 148, 155, 171,
   194
European Coal and Steel Community,
   150, 153
European Defense Community, 150–
   51
European Recovery Plan. *See* Marshall
   Plan
European Union, 141, 153, 187
Evangelical Church, 16, 115
Expellees, 134

Fascism, 110, 118, 121–22, 125, 163
Federal States, 5–6
Ferdinand I (1558–1564), 50
Ferdinand II (1619–1637), 50–51,
   194
Feudalism, 28, 33, 35, 38
Final Solution, 130
Five Percent Law, 148
Five-Year Plan, 166–69
Foederati, 23–24
Four-Power Agreement on Berlin
   (1971), 171
Four-Year Plan (1934), 117
Fourteen Points, 99, 101
Francis II (1792–1806), 60, 62
Franconia, 34, 37, 44, 47
Franco-Prussian War (1870–1871), 74,
   76, 82; Treaty of Frankfurt (1871),
   74, 76–77
Frankfurt Accords (1949), 151
Frankfurt Parliament (1848), 71, 75

Franks, 24–32
Franks, Kingdom of, 24, 27
Franz Ferdinand (Archduke), 90, 101
Franz Josef (Emperor) (1848–1916), 71, 82, 90
Frederick I (1688–1713), 56, 195
Frederick II, the Great (1740–1786), 57–59, 195
Frederick II, *Stupor Mundi* (1212–1250), 44–45
Frederick III (1440–1493), 47
Frederick III (1888), 84
Frederick of Palatinate, the "Winter King" (1616–1623), 51
Frederick William, the Great Elector (1640–1680), 56, 195
Frederick William I (1713–1740), 57
Frederick William II (1786–1797), 62
Frederick William III (1797–1840), 63–68, 196
Frederick William IV (1840–1861), 71–72, 196
Free Conservative Party (*Reichspartei*), 78
Free Democratic Party, 10, 139, 142, 154–55, 157, 182, 187–88
Free German Trade Union Federation, 165, 172
Free German Youth, 165–66, 172
Freikorps, 102–3
French Revolution, 61–67; Declaration of Pillnitz, 62; humiliation of Prussia, 64–67; Peace of Paris (1814), 68; reorganization of German Empire through *Reichsdeputationshauptschluss*, 63–64, 68; War of First Coalition (1792–1797), 62; War of Liberation (1813–1814), 67–68; War of Second Coalition (1788–1801), 62–63; War of Third Coalition (1805–1807), 63–64. *See also* Congress of Vienna
Fugger family, 48
Fulfillment policy, 105, 110

Gastarbeiter (Guest Workers), 160
Geography, 1, 3–4

German Confederation, 67, 69–70, 72–73, 77
German Confessional Church, 115
German Democratic Party, 146
German Democratic Republic (1949–1990), 142–43, 151–53, 160–80; constitutions, 163–64, 168, 171–72; economy, 166–69, 173, 174; foreign policy, 164, 171–72, 174; police and security forces, 170, 176, 177–78, 185; political parties, 164–66, 168, 172, 177–78; population, 165; protest movements, 170–71, 174–78; relations with German Federal Republic, 173–74, 176–80; relations with the Soviet Union, 169, 175
German Empire (800–1152), 31–44
German Empire (1871–1918), 75–102; colonial empire, 83–84; constitution, 75–77; diplomacy, 81–83, 86–87, 89–91, 94, 96; economy, 80–81; political parties, 77–81, 88; population, 87; Reichstag, 76–78. *See also* Bismarck, Otto von
German Federal Republic (1949–1990), 142, 145–12; Basic Law, 142; economy, 148–49, 160; foreign policy, 149–51, 154–55, 157–59, 161–62; political parties, 148, 153, 156–57; refugees, 147–48; relations with the German Democratic Republic, 151–54, 157–58; student revolt, 156
German Federal Republic (1990–), 1–17, 181–89; climate, 4; cultural affairs, 15–17; economy, 11–14; elections, 182, 187; geography, 1–4; government, 5–9; political parties, 9–10, 185; population, 1, 3; relations with Soviet Union/Russia, 184–85; STASI legacy, 185; state and local government, 10, 182–83; *Volksdeutsche* and asylum seekers, 185
German princes (*Princeps*), 42
German Progressive Party, 77
German Republic (1920–1933). *See* Weimar Republic
German-Soviet Non-Aggression Pact (1939), 125–26

Germania (Tacitus), 20
Germanic tribes, 19–26
Gestapo (secret police), 118
Gleichschalltung, 114, 118
Goebbels, Joseph, 113, 115–16, 132, 139, 196
Goering, Hermann, 110, 113–14, 116–17, 139, 196–97
Goethe, Johann Wolfgang von, 60
Golden Bull (1352), 47
Gorbachev, Mikhail, 161–62, 175–79
Government, 5
Grand Coalition, 155–57
Green Party, 10, 157, 161, 182, 187–88
Gregory (Bishop of Tours), 24–25
Gregory, Pope (1073–1085), 40–41
Gross domestic product, 11
Grotewohl, Otto, 136, 143, 163–64, 168, 197

Hallstein Doctrine, 152, 155, 158, 164, 171
Hambach Festival (1832), 70
Hanover, 63, 73
Hapsburg dynasty (1273–1918), 34, 46–47, 50, 52, 55, 57–58, 60–61, 98–99
Hardenberg, Karl, 66
Hayden, Joseph, 60
Heinlein, Konrad, 123
Helsinki Agreements (1975), 159, 174
Henry (Duke of Saxony), 34–35
Henry II (1002–1024), 37
Henry III (1039–1056), 39
Henry IV (1056–1106), 39–43, 197
Henry V (1106–1125), 42–43
Henry VI (1190–1197), 47
Henry the Lion, 43–44
Hermann (Arminius), 20, 197
Heuss, Theodor, 138, 142, 146, 197–98
Himmler, Heinrich, 116, 139, 198
Hindenburg, Paul von, 74, 106–11, 113–14, 120, 198
History of the Franks (Gregory), 24
Hitler, Adolf, 103–4, 107–10, 113–32, 139, 163; diplomacy, 120–26; goals,

117, 120; *Mein Kampf*, 108, 117; subordinates, 116–17, 198–99
Hohenlohe-Schillingsfuerst, Chlodwig zu, 85–86, 199
Hohenstaufen dynasty (1138–1254), 34, 43–46
Hohenzollern dynasty, Prussia (1417–1918), 56
Holocaust, 126, 129–30, 133, 156, 158, 163
Holy Alliance, 69
Holy Roman Empire (1155–1806), 44–47, 52, 55–57, 63–64, 71
Honecker, Erich, 160–61, 173–74, 176, 177, 199
Hugenberg, Alfred, 109
Huguenots, 50
Human rights, 174
Hungary, 37, 39, 42, 58

Imperial Civil Code, 85
Independent Socialist Party, 102
Industrial League, 87
Industry and technology, 13–14
International Military Tribunal. *See* Nuremberg Trials
"Iron Curtain," 138
Islam, 26–27, 32, 38
Italy, 37–42, 44, 46, 48, 83–84, 131

Joseph I (1780–1790), 59–61
Judiciary, 8
Junkers, 56, 59, 64, 77, 80–81, 85, 87, 137
Jutland, Battle of (1916), 96

Kapp Putsch (1920), 103–4
Karlsbad Decrees (1819), 70
Kellogg-Briand Pact (1928), 106
Khrushchev, Nikita, 153, 170
Kiel Canal, 86
Kiesinger, Kurt Georg, 155
Kohl, Helmut, 8, 159–62, 177–79, 182–84, 188–89, 200
Korean War, 149–50
Krenz, Egon, 176–77
Krueger telegram, 86
Kulturkampf, 79

Labor front, 115
Land reform, 166, 168
Landlords' League, 87
Lay investiture controversy, 40, 42
League of Nations, 100–102, 106, 120, 127
Lebensraum, 119, 125
Legislature, 6–7
Leningrad, 131
Leo III (Pope), 31
Leopold I (1658–1805), 57
Leopold II (1790–1792), 60–61
Liberal Democratic Party, 138–39, 177
Liberal Party, 78, 136
Liebknecht, Karl, 99, 102
Liebknecht, Wilhelm, 78
Liebniz, Gottfried, 60
The Life of Charlemagne (Einhard), 29
Locarno Treaties (1925), 106, 121
Lombardy, 35
Lothair (840–855), 32, 34
Lothair of Saxony, 43
Louis the Child, 34
Louis the German (843–876), 32, 34
Louis the Pious (814–840), 31–32
Louis Napoleon, 73–74
Ludendorff, Erich, 94, 200
Ludwig IV (1314–1347), 46, 104, 108
Luther, Martin, 48–49, 200
Lutheranism, 16, 48–49, 52
Luxemburg, Rosa, 102

Majority Socialist Party, 102, 107
Malanchthon, Philip, 49
Maria Theresa (1740–1780), 58, 60, 200
Marshall Plan, 140, 148–49, 152, 166–67
Martel, Charles ("Charles the Hammer"), 26–27, 29
Maximilian I (1493–1519), 47, 200–201
Maximilian II (1564–1546), 50
Medieval synthesis, 33, 49
Mein Kampf (Hitler), 108, 117
Merovingian dynasty, 25–26, 29
Metternich, Klemens von, 68–71, 110
Michaelis, George, 98

Middle Ages, 33–47
Ministeriales, 38–39, 42–43
Minorities, 3
Missi dominici, 30
Modrow, Hans, 177–78
Monarchists, 103
Moravia, 124
Morocco crises (1906, 1911), 87
Moscow Treaty (1970), 157–58, 171
Mozart, Wolfgang Amadeus, 60
Munich Agreement (1938), 124–25
Munich "Beer Hall" Putsch (1923), 108
Munich Olympic Games (1972), 159
Mussolini, Benito, 110, 118, 121, 124, 127–28

National Assembly, 99, 102
National Association, 77
National Liberal Party, 78, 80, 88
National Party, 155
National Socialist German Workers' Party (NAZI), 107–9, 113–16, 119, 122–23, 130, 134–35, 137–39, 146–47; Hitler's bodyguard (SS), 116, 118, 130; security service (SD), 118; Storm Troopers (SA), 107, 109, 113–16, 118
NATO, 151–53, 155, 162, 170, 178–79, 187
Navy, 86–88, 94, 96–97, 99, 101
Navy League, 87
Neo-Nazis, 186
Neustria, 36
New Economic System (1963), 169
New Forum Party, 177, 176
Nicholas II (Czar), 86, 98
Niebelungenlied, 35
Niemoeller, Martin, 115
Night of Broken Glass (1938), 119
Night of the Long Knives (1934), 116
Normandy Invasion (1944), 131
North German Confederation (1867–1871), 73–74, 77
Northern War (1655–1660), 56
Nuclear missiles, 161–62
Nuremberg Laws (1935), 119–20
Nuremberg Trials, 134, 139

Occupation, 105–6, 131, 134, 137, 139–42, 145, 150, 153, 165; Berlin blockade and airlift, 141–42; transition to sovereignty, 142–43; zones, 134, 136–40
Odoacer, 23
Office of Military Government (OMGUS), 137
Operation Barbarossa, 128
Ostmark, 36, 44
Ostpolitik, 157–58, 171
Ottonian dynasty (914–1002), 34–37
Otto I (936–973), 35–36, 201
Otto II (973–983), 36
Otto III (983–1002), 36–37

Pan-Slavism, 82, 89–90
Papacy, 36, 39–43, 48, 50
Papen, Franz von, 108–9, 113, 115–16, 139
Paris Peace Conference (1919), 100
Party of Democratic Socialism, 10, 177, 179, 182, 184, 188
Peasant War (1524–1525), 48
"Personal Regime" (William II), 84
Pétain, Henri-Philippe, 127
"Phony War" (1939), 126–27
Pieck, Wilhelm, 136, 163–64, 168, 201
Pippin (752–759), 29
Poland, 37, 39, 42, 56, 59, 62, 68, 76, 81, 88, 95, 97–98, 106, 109–10, 120, 124–26, 132–33, 136, 158, 162
Polish Corridor, 100
Political parties, 7, 9–10, 77–81, 103, 114, 118, 137–38, 142
Pomerania, 44, 56, 68
Population, 1, 3, 134
Potsdam, 58
Potsdam Conference (1945), 134–39, 141, 143
Pragmatic Sanction, 57–58
Prague, Peace of (1635), 51
Press, 79, 96, 109, 115–16, 139, 154–55
Progressive (Freisinnige) Party, 78
Progressive Peoples' Party (Fortschrittliche Volkspartei), 78

Progressive Union (Freisinnige Vereinigung), 78
Protestant League, 50
Protestants, 3, 16, 51, 56, 115, 138
Prussia, 48, 51, 55, 74, 76–77, 79, 85, 88, 100, 115; absolutism, 56–57, 76–77; army, 64; constitution, 72; Landtag, 71–72, 77; three-class voting system, 77
Prussian Union Plan, 72
Publicly Owned Enterprises (VEB), 167–69

Quadruple Alliance, 69
Quisling, Vidkun, 127

Rapallo, Treaty of (1922), 105–6
Rearmament, 106, 116–17, 120–21, 126, 151–53, 170
Reconstruction, 135
Red Front, 107, 115
Reform Association, 77
Reformation, 47–52
Refugees, 134, 136–37, 147–48
Reichsbanner, 107, 115
Reichstag Fire (1933), 113
Reinsurance Treaty (1881), 83, 86
Rentenmark, 104, 117
Reparations, 101, 104–5, 110, 135–36, 147, 166–67
Resistance movements, 130
Reunification (1990), 143, 146, 151–53, 158, 162, 177–80, 182–84, 189; Ten-Point Plan, 177; Two-Plus-Four-Agreement (1990), 162, 178–80; Unification Treaty (1990), 162, 179, 182
Reuter, Ernst, 142
Revolution of 1848, 71
Rhineland, 100–101, 121
Right-wing parties, 156
Roman Empire, 19–22, 16
Rommel, Erwin, 129, 201
Roosevelt, Franklin D., 129, 131, 135
Rudolf of Hapsburg (1273–1291), 46, 201
Rudolf II (1576–1612), 50
Ruhr uprising, 103–4, 109–10

Saar region, 100, 120, 137, 151–52
Salian dynasty (1002–1125), 34–43
Salic Law, 25
Saxony, 34–35, 40, 43–44, 47–48, 56, 58–60, 66–68, 136
Scandinavia, 127
Schacht, Hjalmar, 117, 139
Scheidemann, Philip, 99, 102
Schleicher, Kurt von, 109
Schleswig, 48
Schleswig-Holstein, 71, 73, 76
Schlieffen Plan, 94, 97
Schmalkaldic War (1546–1547), 49
Schmidt, Helmut, 8, 159, 173, 201
Schroeder, Gerhard, 188, 201–2
Schumacher, Kurt, 138, 150–51, 202
Schuman Plan, 149–50
Schussnigg, Kurt von, 122
Seven Weeks' War (1866), 72
Seven Years' War (1756–1763), 58
Seyss-Inquart, Arthur, 122
Sicily, 44–46
Silesia, 57–60, 66, 77, 79
Slavs, 44
Social Democratic Party, 10, 77–81, 85, 88, 96, 99, 113–15, 136, 138, 142, 148, 151, 155, 157, 159–61, 163, 179, 187–89
"Social market economy," 12, 138, 148
Social welfare insurance, 81, 87, 105, 107, 148, 181, 183–84
Socialist Unity Party, 136, 138–39, 143, 164–68, 170, 172, 176–77
Solidarity Pact (1992), 184
Song of Roland, 30–31
Soviet Military Administration in Germany (SMAD), 136–37, 163
Soviet Union, 120, 124–31, 133–34, 136, 140, 145, 152–53, 161, 172–73, 184
Spanish Civil War, 121
Spartacist Rebellion (1919), 102
Der Spiegel Affair, 154–55
Stahlhelm, 107, 115
Stalin, Joseph, 125, 131, 135, 153, 169–70
Stalingrad, Battle of (1942), 131
STASI, 178, 185

State and local government, 10–11
Stauffenberg, Claus Schenck von, 130, 202
Stolpe, Manfred, 185
Strasser, Gregor, 109, 116
Strauss, Franz Josef, 154–55, 159, 173
Stresemann, Gustav, 104–6, 110, 117, 120, 202
Student rebellion (1968), 156–57
Stunde Null, 133
Submarine warfare, 97
Sudetenland, 122–24
Swabia, 34, 42–44, 47
Switzerland, 46–48
Synod of Worms (1076), 40

Tacitus, 20
Tannenberg, Battle of (1914), 95
Teutoberg Forest, Battle of (9 C.E.), 20
Teutonic Knights, 45, 52
Theodoric, 23, 202–3
Third Reich, 114–32; anti-Semitism, 118–20; 129–30; dictatorship, 114; fascism, 118; foreign policy, 120–26; Holocaust, 129–30; Nuremberg Laws, 119–20; resistance, 130–31
Thirty Years' War (1618–1648), 50
Three Emperors' League, 82, 87
Thuringia, 34
Tilly (General), 51
Tilsit, Treaty of (1807), 66
Total war, 96
Tours, 24, 27
Transportation, 13–14
Tribal duchies, 33–35, 38, 40, 42–43, 52
Triple Alliance, 83–84, 87, 89–91, 94, 97
Triple Entente, 87, 89, 90–91, 93, 95–100
Trizonia, 140
Truman Doctrine, 140
Truman, Harry, 135
Trust Agency (Treuhandanstalt), 183

Ulbricht Doctrine, 170
Ulbricht, Walter, 143, 157–58, 164, 168–72, 203

Unconditional surrender, 131–32
Unification (1871), 75. *See* Reunification (1990)
United Left Party, 178
United Nations, 153, 158, 172–73, 187
United States, 97–98, 129

Valentinian III, 23
Valvassores, 38
Verdun, Battle of (1916), 95
Verdun, Treaty of (843), 34
Versailles, Treaty of (1919), 100–103, 105–16, 108, 110, 113, 120–21; Article 231 ("war guilt" clause), 101, 110; reparations, 101, 104–5, 110
Vikings, 32, 34, 38
Volksdeutsche, 185–86

Waiblinger (Ghibellines), 43–44
Wallenstein (General), 51
Wannsee Conference (1942), 130
War guilt, 101, 110
Warsaw, Grand Duchy of, 66
Warsaw Pact (1955), 152, 155, 157, 170–71, 178
Warsaw Treaty (1970), 158, 171
Wartburg Castle, 48
Weimar Republic (1920–1933), 102–14, 120, 146, 163; Article 48 (Emergency Clause), 103; collapse, 107–11; constitution, 102–3; crises, 103–5; the Depression, 106–7; rehabilitation, 105–6

Welfs (Guelphs), 43–45
Die Wende (Turning Point), 176, 181
Western European Union, 151
Westphalia, 47
Westphalia, Kingdom of, 66
Westphalia, Treaty of (1648), 52
White Rose, 130
William I (1861–1888), 72–74, 76, 80, 82, 84–85, 91, 203
William II (1888–1918), 84–86, 94 99, 108, 203–4
Wilson, Woodrow, 99
Wittelsbach dynasty (Bavaria), 46, 56
Workers' Codetermination, 148
World War I (1914–1918), 86, 90–91, 93–100; diplomacy, 96; technology 96; two front war, 94, 98–99. *See also* Versailles, Treaty of
World War II (1939–1945), 126–32; Africa Campaign, 128, 131; attack on Poland, 126; Balkan Campaigns, 128; Battle of Britain, 128; defeat, 131–32; fall of France, 127; Holocaust, 129–30; "Phony War," 126–27; Russian front, 128; Scandinavia, 127
Wuerttemberg, 62–64, 68, 73

Yalta Conference (1945), 135
Yeltsin, Boris, 184
Young Plan, 106

Zhukov, Georgi, 131, 136

About the Author

ELEANOR L. TURK is Professor of History at Indiana University East. She has written widely on German history. She has published a number of articles on the history of civil liberty, on the political press and pressure groups in Wilhelmian Germany, and on German emigration in the nineteenth century. Her current research focuses on German immigration to agricultural frontiers in the Americas and Australia.

Other Titles in the
Greenwood Histories of the Modern Nations
Frank W. Thackeray and John E. Findling, Series Editors

The History of Japan
Louis G. Perez

The History of Israel
Arnold Blumberg

The History of Spain
Peter Pierson

8/02 ⑨ 5/02

12/05 ⑱ 10/05

3/07 ⑲ 5/06